CW01033370

Tornado GR1
An Operational History

Tornado
GR1

An Operational History

Michael Napier

Pen & Sword
AVIATION

First published in 2017 by
Pen and Sword Aviation

An imprint of
Pen & Sword Books Ltd
47 Church Street
Barnsley
South Yorkshire
S70 2AS

ISBN 978 1 47387 302 5

Editor: Jasper Spencer-Smith
Design and artwork by Nigel Pell

Printed and bound in India
by Replika Press Pvt. Ltd.

Pen & Sword Books Ltd incorporates the Imprints of
Pen & Sword Aviation, Pen & Sword Family History, Pen & Sword Maritime,
Pen & Sword Military, Pen & Sword Discovery, Pen and Sword Fiction,
Pen and Sword History, Wharncliffe Local History, Wharncliffe True Crime,
Wharncliffe Transport, Pen & Sword Select, Pen & Sword Military Classics,
Leo Cooper, The Praetorian Press, Seaforth Publishing and Frontline Publishing

For a complete list of Pen & Sword titles please contact
PEN & SWORD BOOKS LIMITED
47 Church Street, Barnsley, South Yorkshire, S70 2AS, England
E-mail: enquiries@pen-and-sword.co.uk
Website: www.pen-and-sword.co.uk

Contents

Foreword

By
Air Chief Marshal
Sir Stuart Peach GBE, KCB, ADC, DL
Chief of the Defence Staff

As we approach the centenary of the Royal Air Force – the world's first independent air force – few aircraft can match the Tornado in operational service for span of years, continuous development of capability, range of roles and missions and, for me, the most important – battle honours for crews and squadrons.

Throughout military history the truism is that men and women win wars not machines, but when the machine is as capable and flexible as the Tornado has proven to be, it is true that the machine played a part.

Conceived at the height of the Cold War, the Tornado has been the mainstay of the RAF's ground-attack capability during the last four decades. In the twenty-first century, the Tornado provides the RAF with a uniquely precise tool with which to strike small targets with deadly accuracy from medium level; yet these are the same aircraft that, as the Tornado GR1, held the frontline of the Cold War in the 1980s as a low-level nuclear bomber. When the Tornado GR1 was introduced to front-line service in 1982 it gave the RAF, for the first time, a true all weather low-level strike capability, by both day and night; I know – I was on that first squadron. This capability also brought with it an inherent operational flexibility, the benefits of which could hardly have been foreseen. Indeed, the staff officers who wrote, in the Concept of Operations for the Tornado in 1977, that 'no separate provision will be made to operate the aircraft in a non–NATO role' could not have imagined that just fourteen years later the Tornado GR1 force would be fighting a 'hot' war over Iraq, largely at medium level and armed with laser-guided weapons. Nor could they have foreseen that the aircraft would subsequently be involved in continuous air operations over Iraq for the next nine years, nor even that when Tornado GR1 eventually flew on NATO combat operations – long after the Cold War – they would consist of six-hour long-range missions over the Balkans, returning night after night to their base in Germany in remarkable parallel to the crews of RAF Bomber Command in the Second World War.

The ability of the Tornado GR1 force to carry out, so effectively, all of its wide-ranging and vastly differing tasks over the decades is testament not only to the aircraft, but also to the aircrew who flew it and to the ground crew whose hard work kept the aircraft flying. This book tells the story of the many achievements of Tornado GR1 crews in the twenty years of the aircraft's service, from its spectacular debut performance in the USAF Strategic Air Command Bombing Competition in 1984, through the tense routine of the Cold War in the late 1980s as the Warsaw Pact imploded, the intense air campaign over Iraq during the Gulf War of 1991 and the sustained operations over north and south Iraq that followed in the 1990s (often downplayed for their local intensity), to the short but decisive campaign over Kosovo in 1999. Of course even this remarkable tale told by Mike Napier is only Part I of the true story.

As an ex-Tornado GR1 pilot with nearly ten years' worth of experience flying the aircraft, Mike Napier is well placed to write with authority about the exploits of his former colleagues. Apart from researching contemporary records, he has canvassed many former Tornado crew and ground crew, and recorded their stories. All of this work has enabled him to pull together, for the first time, a truly comprehensive account of the Tornado GR1 in operational service with the RAF.

Since the advent of the GR4 version of Tornado continuous combat operations have mounted: Iraq from 2003 to 2009; then in Afghanistan from 2009 to 2014; again over Iraq from 2014 and, at the time of writing, over Syria. It is a record of a remarkable aeroplane flown and maintained by remarkable people.

So there is a Part II to come. As the Royal Air Force celebrates its 100th birthday, Tornado will still be the old warhorse of the air. In those 100 years, I would argue no other machine and the men and women who flew, maintained and supported the type can match this span of operations. This book is a tribute to them all.

Introduction & Acknowledgements

This book is not a technical description of the Tornado and nor does it include the experiences of the German, Italian or Saudi Arabian operators of the aircraft. It is, rather, a history of the Tornado GR1 in front-line RAF service, from its introduction to squadron service in 1982 up until it was withdrawn and replaced by the Tornado GR4 in 2001. As such, it represents the first serious attempt to pull together all the various strands of the operational experience of the Tornado GR1 force: apart from recording the peacetime routine of the Tornado GR1 squadrons, it is the first comprehensive account of Tornado GR1 operations during the Gulf War and in subsequent operations over Iraq and the conflict over Kosovo. More than anything, though, it is a record of the fine accomplishments of the extraordinarily talented and dedicated people who flew and serviced the Tornado GR1 throughout its service life.

The official records relating to the activities of Tornado squadrons from 1984 onwards have not yet been released into the public domain, so I have relied instead on unclassified documents and on the reminiscences, diaries, photograph albums and logbooks of a large number of Tornado personnel who have been kind enough to share their stories (and photographs) with me. I am very grateful indeed for the generosity, assistance and patience by the following 'Tornado folk' who have helped me greatly in researching this book: Dave Armstrong, Steve Barnes, Pete Batson, Chris Bearblock, Steve (Bamber) Beardmore, David Bellamy, Darren Berris, Tom Boyle, Gordon Buckley, Trevor Burbidge, Bernie Burnell, Ricci Cobelli, Steve Cockram, Marcus Cook, Nige Cookson,

Chris Coulls, Mal Craghill, Jim Crowley, Ian Dugmore, Pete Dunlop, Andy Glover, Wally Grout, Simon Hadley, David (Buster) Hales, Ian Hall, Rod Hawkins, Andy Heard, Nick Heard, Les Hendry, Simon (Gilbert) Hulme, Nigel King, Steve Kinnaird, Jim Klein, Darren Legg, Paul Lenihan, Ian Long, Robbie Low, Mike Lumb, Kev Noble, Gordon Niven, Bob McAlpine, Paul McDonald, Paul McKernan, Tim Marsh, Dick Middleton, Douglas Moule, Nigel Nickles, Kev Noble, Mark Paisey, Jeremy Payne, Chris Peace, Al Pease, Mitch Preston, Chris Purkiss, Bill Ramsey, Dirk Reid, Nige Risdale, Andy Robins, Dougie Roxburgh, Mark Royce, Dave Sandys, 'AJ' Smith, Lars Smith, Martin Spanswick, Jerry Spencer, Doug Steer, Chris Stradling, Greig Thomson, Pete Ward, Gavin Wells, Larry Williams, Carl Wilson, Martin Wintermeyer, Jerry Witts, and Andy Youngs. This list covers the whole range of the Tornado experience, from squadron commander to first-tourist aircrew and from senior engineering officer to junior technician; it also covers all of the roles in which the aircraft flew and all of the stations and units which operated the aircraft. I personally know all of those named above and I have to say that I regard it as having been an honour and a privilege to have served with each one of them during my ten years as a Tornado GR1 pilot.

Thanks, too to Nikki Thomas (OC 12 Squadron), Paul (Zig) Froome (OC XV Squadron), James Freeborough (OC 31 Squadron), and Bill Gibson ('Uncle' of II Squadron) for giving me access to their 'crew-room diaries' and to Andy Renwick and Ian Alder at the RAF Museum for their help in getting copies of photographs. I am also very grateful indeed to Kate Yates at BAe Heritage for her help in sourcing photographs from the company's archives, to Geoffrey Lee for his generosity in allowing me to use some of his excellent air-to-air images and also to Rick Brewell, a former comrade from my Brüggen days, who has also let me use some of the fantastic photographs he took when a PR photographer for the RAF. Thank you, also, to Adrian Walker who kindly allowed me to use some of his wonderful photographs taken while walking in the Lake District. Finally to Chris Sandham-Bailey for the superb colour profiles which illustrate Appendix 1.

I am very grateful to Air Marshal Sir Stuart Peach, now Chief of the Defence Staff, but once a contemporary of mine on 31 Squadron, for writing the foreword to the book: it would be difficult to find someone more qualified or more appropriate to do so. Thank you also to my editor Jasper Spencer-Smith for his continued enthusiasm and support. Finally I am grateful beyond words to my wife Shani who has had to share me with the family computer as I have researched and written the book.

1

1982-1984
Early Days

The End of an Era

The disbandment of IX (Bomber) Squadron, on 29 April 1982, marked the end of an era. The squadron had spent twenty years operating the Avro Vulcan, those iconic delta winged V-bombers that seemed to epitomize the RAF itself: now, surplus to the needs of the RAF, the aircraft sat forlornly around the perimeter at RAF Waddington (near Lincoln), plainly visible to any passer-by on the A15 main road as they were reduced to scrap. Just a month later, a handful of remaining Vulcans would carry out the longest-range bombing raids in the history of the RAF by flying some 7,800 miles from Ascension Island to the Falklands and back. However, despite this impressive achievement the days of the V-bomber were over, but the days of IX Squadron were not: a new IX Squadron was poised to take the place of its predecessor on the frontline of the Cold War using a very different aeroplane – the Panavia Tornado GR1.

The Vulcan, which had first flown in the early 1950s, was designed to operate at high altitude: in the early days the Vulcans, Vickers Valiants, Handley-Page Victors and English Electric Canberras of RAF Bomber Command would typically fly at altitudes up to 50,000ft. Wings and engines optimized for the rarefied air at high altitude gave the bombers a long range and their electronic equipment enabled crews to locate their targets, both by day and by night. However, by the early 1960s the Soviet military had made advances in surface-to-air missile (SAM) and radar technology which forced the bombers down to lower levels in an attempt to get below the cover of radars and under the engagement envelope of the missiles. The RAF officially adopted a low-level policy from late 1963, but the tactic brought its own problems. Firstly, wings designed for high flight were not really suited to the low-level regime, where the turbulence and the stresses of low-level manoeuvring caused metal fatigue. The first

The prototype MRCA P01 first flew from Manching, Bavaria on 14 August 1974 with Paul Millet (BAe) and Niels Meister (MBB) at the controls. (Bae Heritage)

The second prototype MRCA P02, which was built at Warton, with the wings fully swept at 67°. (Bae Heritage)

A Tornado GR1 with wings swept to 67°– this view demonstrates how the under-wing pylons swivelled to keep the stores parallel to the direction of flight. In fact, this wing-sweep setting was rarely used on the frontline, since 45° offered better manoeuvrability. (Geoffrey Lee/Plane Focus)

casualty of this phenomenon was the Valiant, which had to be hastily withdrawn from service in December 1964 when cracks were found in the wing spars of most of the fleet. Secondly, the thicker air at low level reduced performance: for example the high-level tactical radius of the Vulcan was 2,300 miles when cruising at 0.86 Mach (M) (equating to a groundspeed of approximately 480kt) was reduced at low level to 1,700 miles at a speed of just 250kt. Thirdly, target acquisition and weapon delivery became more difficult: crews could not see targets until they were much closer to them – and they also had to avoid being damaged by debris thrown up by their own weapons. Lastly, low flying could only be achieved safely in daytime and in good weather, which limited an offensive capability to much less than half the time that it might be needed.

The first two of these problems were solved in the late 1960s with the introduction of aircraft such as the Blackburn Buccaneer, McDonnell-Douglas F-4 Phantom, and the Hawker-Siddeley (later BAe) Harrier and, later, the SEPECAT Jaguar: All of which were more suited to low-level flying. Low-level tactics developed as RAF crews gained experience, and as improvements were made to radars and Inertial Navigation Systems (INS). Specialized weapons, such as retarded bombs, and specialized attack profiles, such as toss deliveries, also enabled crews to attack targets successfully from low level. However, even in the late 1970s, the RAF still lacked an offensive low-level capability at night or in adverse weather.

The Multi-Role Combat Aircraft (MRCA)

This was not for want of trying: the British Aircraft Corporation (BAC) TSR-2, which would have provided an all-weather capability, was cancelled in 1965 and the order for its successor,

A wing sweep of 25° was used for flight below 300kt: it gave the Tornado a good turning performance, which could be further improved by the 'manoeuvre' setting of the full-span leading-edge slats and trailing-edge flaps. (Nigel Nickles)

the General Dynamics F-111K, was placed in 1967 then cancelled in 1968. But while the RAF might have lost the F-111K in 1968, that same year was the genesis for the MRCA, a multi-national project to provide a successor to the Vulcan, Buccaneer and the Lockheed F-104 Starfighter. Although a number of countries showed an early interest in MRCA, the programme stabilized with just three partners: UK, Germany and Italy. The heart of MRCA was a fully-integrated Terrain Following Radar (TFR) and autopilot as well as a complex Ground Mapping Radar (GMR). These systems gave the MRCA the ability to fly automatically at low level and to attack targets accurately by day or night in all weather conditions. The prototype made its maiden flight on 14 August 1974 from Manching, near Ingolstadt, Germany and the following year the MRCA was officially christened 'Tornado'.

Similar in size to the Phantom, the Tornado appeared to be a surprisingly large aeroplane when approached for the first time. Its angular shape was dominated by a tall tailfin, from which the aircraft derived its aircrew nickname 'The Fin.' The other immediately obvious feature was the 'variable geometry' of the wings, which could be swept from a forward position of 25°, optimized for low-speed flight, back to 67° for high speeds. In fact the fully-swept position was rarely used and it was usual to use 45° sweep for most low flying. The Command Stability Augmentation System (CSAS) in the aircraft ensured that handling characteristics remained almost constant regardless of speed or wing sweep. The aircraft was, by the standards of the day, very straightforward to fly. Two pylons on each wing rotated to remain pointing forward when the wings were swept: the inner pylons were typically used to carry external fuel tanks, while the outer pylons were used for Electronic Counter Measures (ECM) pods. 'Shoulder' pylons under the fuselage could be used for weapons or further fuel tanks.

The Tornado cockpits were roomy, comfortable and well-designed ergonomically. The front seat was dominated by the Head–Up Display (HUD), which projected information from the main flying instruments onto the pilot's forward view. Below the HUD was a moving map display, on either side of which were (left) the main flying instruments and (right) the engine instruments. The throttles on the left console selected reheat if pushed through a 'gate' or reverse thrust (on the ground) if rocked outboard. The wings were swept by means of a lever just inboard of the throttles. The major feature of the rear cockpit was the Combined Radar and Projected Map Display (CRPMD) flanked by two TV tabulators, through which the navigator communicated with the main navigation and

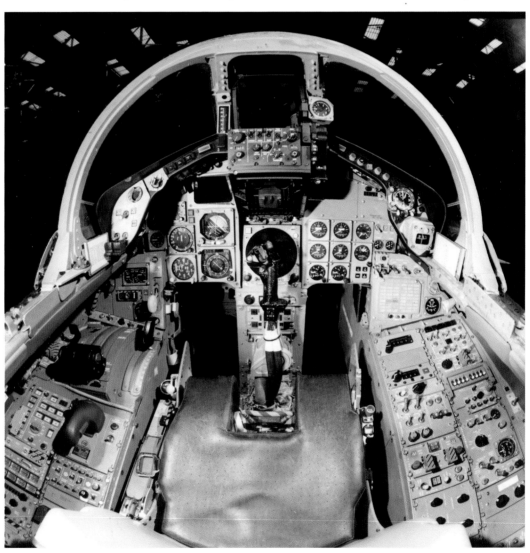

The front cockpit of the Tornado GR1 was well laid out, dominated by the Head-Up Display (HUD) in the centre of the windscreen with the Projected Map Display (PMD) just below. Wing sweep was selected manually by a lever inboard of the throttles on the left console.(Bae Heritage)

Wilbur Wilson sits at readiness in a Hardened Aircraft Shelter (HAS). Aircrew safety equipment included a life jacket with sleeves onto which arm restraints were attached: these were designed to prevent injuring flailing limbs during ejection. (Simon Hadley)

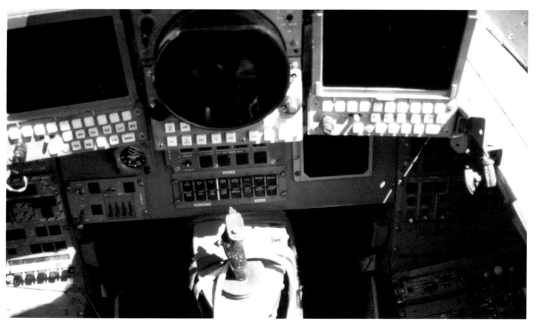

The Tornado GR1 rear cockpit was dominated by the Combined Radar and Projected Map Display (CRPMD) in the centre, flanked by two TV tabulators which were used for navigation displays and for programming the main computer. The hand controller in the centre is for guiding the radar cursor.

Three Tornado GR1s (British, German and Italian) from the Tri-National Tornado Training Establishment (TTTE), based at RAF Cottesmore. Each nation provided aircraft and instructional staff to the unit, which trained all RAF, GAF, German Navy and ItAF Tornado aircrew. (Geoffrey Lee/ Plane Focus)

weapon aiming computer. While the lookout from the front cockpit was good, the view from rear cockpit was limited forwards by the CRPMD and downwards by the engine intakes, which protruded forwards on either side.

Crew conversion training for the Tornado was split over two courses. The initial conversion for all pilots and navigators from the Royal Air Force, German Air Force (GAF), German Navy and Italian Air Force (ItAF) was carried out at the Tri-National Tornado Training Establishment (TTTE), which was based at RAF Cottesmore, near Oakham. Here a common course, comprising a month-long ground school followed by a 40-hour flying phase, was taught by instructors from all three nations. The syllabus introduced trainee crews to the pure flying aspects of the complex aircraft. Apart from aircraft handling, instrument flying and close formation, crews also started to use the TFR system to low fly in day and night conditions.

After graduating from TTTE, the next location for RAF crews was the Tornado Weapons Conversion Unit (TWCU) at RAF Honington. Here, the dedicated RAF course was more tactically focussed. Crews started with theoretical and practical range work, using all the various different delivery and sensor profiles before moving on to tactical formation, Simulated Attack Profile (SAP) and Air Combat Manoeuvring (ACM) sorties. Although a graduate from TWCU might have 80-hours experience on the Tornado, in operational terms he would only have the most basic capability and would still need to complete a Combat Ready (CR) work-up on a front-line squadron.

A Tornado GR1 from the Tornado Weapons Conversion Unit (TWCU) drops a 3kg practice bomb on the range at RAF Donna Nook. Based at RAF Honington, the TWCU carried out the tactical and weapons training for all RAF aircrew after they had graduated from TTTE. (Nigel Nickles)

The Engineers' Perspective

A Tornado GR1 squadron had between thirty and forty aircrew; by far the largest part of the squadron were the some 140 engineers of assorted trades. For the engineers, who might otherwise have been posted to an anonymous part of Engineering Wing (EW) to carry out routine major servicing work, being a member of a flying squadron was a source of immense pride. 'Being on a squadron was special,' recalled Chief Technician (C.Tech) M. Spanswick (who served on 14 and 31 Squadrons), 'you were part of something unique and you were very proud of that fact. Whenever you walked into Personnel Services Flight (PSF) in the station headquarters (SHQ) and the clerk asked who you were, you would get a kick and a buzz out of saying you were on "X" Squadron. Being on a squadron was not just an eight till five job. It was your life and you, and more importantly your family, adapted to live around the life of

Chief Technician Martin Spanswick grapples with a Turbo Union RB199 during an engine change at Cottesmore. The Tornado was designed to be relatively easy to service and access to most of the equipment was far better than on previous types. (Martin Spanswick)

being on a squadron. I remember my eldest daughter Leona (she was about fourteen at the time) saying to me "Dad, you are nothing in school unless your dad is on a squadron"; for me that summed up the pride that that most of us felt for being on a squadron.' That view was also shared by Corporal (Cpl) A.J. Youngs (who served on IX and 31 Squadrons) for whom tours on flying squadrons gave 'a sense of belonging: squadron life was a way of life. All in all my time on the squadrons in Germany were the best times of my adult life. I made more close friendships in that time than any other time in my life. I am immensely proud to have served at RAF Brüggen during the Cold War years.'

An RB199 is about to be raised into position during an engine change at Cottesmore. The exhaust nozzles are clearly visible: these would open outwards to increase the size of the jet-pipe when reheat was selected. Reheat on the RB199 doubled the thrust to 16,000lbs. (Martin Spanswick)

Unlike the designers of most aircraft of previous generations, the Tornado design team had put some thought into the routine servicing of the aircraft. 'From the onset the Tornado was designed with maintenance at the forefront,' explained Squadron Leader (Sqn Ldr) L.J.T. Hendry, the Senior Engineering Officer (SEngO) on 31 Squadron. 'It had a plethora of easy–open panels providing access to the numerous Line Replaceable Units (LRUs). This made the aircraft easy for the fitment of test equipment and replacement of defective units. However, the aircraft systems were highly integrated and diagnosis could at times be extremely tricky; this was particularly so in the early days of its service life. The skills and knowledge of the ground crew are crucial in keeping downtime to a minimum.'

'The biggest problem with the early Tornado GR1 was unserviceability,' confirmed C. Tech Spanswick. 'In those early days, the aircraft seemed to be permanently broken, particularly if it was left out in the rain. However, in comparison to other types, such as the Phantom, Jaguar and Lightning, the Tornado was extremely maintainable. The aircraft was obviously considered very complex, but after a couple of years you got to know the snags and how to deal with them. When the Tornado GR1 was first introduced into service, it was a whole new ball game for engineers: 'sootys' and riggers [engine and airframe technicians] suddenly became electricians, as did armourers to a certain extent; but they already did quite a bit of electrical work previously on other aircraft. Interesting diagnostics were carried out, particularly by 'sootys' on their electronically-controlled aircraft. This was much to the amusement of the "real" electrical tradesmen who would quite often have to step in and provide guidance: all done with a huge amount of banter of course. The avionics trade suddenly quadrupled in size with various areas of responsibilities such as communications, flight control, radar… et cetera.'

Although working on the Tornado was not without its frustrations, the aircraft was generally well-liked by the engineers. 'I spent thirteen years on the Tornado GR1, and it was a great aircraft to work on' agreed Cpl Youngs. 'We all had "duff gen" books that we used for every day fault diagnosis. That made the task so much easier, but would be highly illegal nowadays. Our main problem was the lack of spares, which became a real hindrance and each squadron had its own "Christmas tree" aircraft for spares or we had to rob the spare off another jet, which meant we were doing the job twice.'

IX Squadron

The RAF's first Tornado squadron, the new IX Squadron, had begun to form at RAF Honington (near Bury St Edmunds, Suffolk) in early 1982 under the command of Wing Commander (Wg Cdr) P.J. Gooding, AFC. New aircraft were delivered relatively quickly, and Wg Cdr Gooding and Flight Lieutenant (Flt Lt) C.D. Davies flew the first IX Squadron Tornado sortie on 6 April. The unit was formally re-formed on 1 June 1982, just after the disbandment of the Vulcan squadron, but it still had only a handful of Tornado crews. It was several months before the squadron reached full strength, as crews trickled through the conversion courses onto the squadron.

For IX Squadron the CR work-up for new crews was relatively straightforward, because the initial compliment was made up from experienced crews who, between them, had previously flown Buccaneer, Harrier, Phantom, Jaguar, Canberra and Vulcan. Nevertheless, it would take over a year before the squadron was declared fully operational.

Despite an initial lack of crews, IX Squadron ran a busy flying programme from the start: apart from sorties in the UK Low Flying System (UKLFS), the flying included frequent deployments to Germany to use the weapons ranges at Vliehors (Netherlands) and Helchteren (Belgium). Daily flying also included using the automatic-Terrain Following (auto-TF) system whenever possible as it was a very new experience for everyone. In the autumn, the squadron took part in Trial Daze which was designed to optimize the main computer software for 'loft' attacks using 1,000lb bombs. Although this weapon delivery profile was referred to as 'loft' in the Tornado force, it was, more correctly, a 'toss' attack: starting from an attack speed of around

Two Tornado GR1s on IX Squadron, each carrying four inert 1,000lb bombs, near the Severn Bridge during a low-level training flight. The low-level long range of the Tornado enabled crews to make the most of the UK Low Flying System (UKLFS). (via Nigel NIckles)

480kt the pilot selected reheat and pulled up at 3 to 4g approximately four miles from the target. The weapon was released by the weapon-aiming system and flew on towards the target, while the aircraft carried out an escape manoeuvre, turning away from the target and returning to low level. The loft recovery manoeuvre comprised a loaded roll to 145°, reducing to 90° as the nose passed the horizon and to wings level by 5° nose down: it was usually commenced at around 2,000ft and it was flown by the pilot entirely on the head-down instruments. The loft recovery was a manoeuvre that, if not flown rigidly 'by numbers', gave great scope for killing oneself. Largely thanks to the efforts of IX Squadron crews on Trial Daze, lofted attacks by the Tornado were surprisingly accurate.

In October 1982, the squadron also participated in Exercise *Priory*, the annual RAF Strike Command air-defence exercise, carrying out simulated attacks on the air-defence sites at RAF Boulmer and RAF Staxton Wold. An early priority for the squadron was to become proficient at Air-to-Air Refuelling (AAR): the standard range of the Tornado was much less than the Vulcan and AAR support would be needed to reach its wartime targets in Eastern Europe. The work-up started in October using Victor and Buccaneer tankers. Sortie lengths were

A Tornado GR1 from the TWCU releases four inert 1,000lb bombs from a loft pass. This delivery profile gave the aircraft a stand-off capability of 2 to 3 miles and due to the computer-controlled weapon-aiming system it was very accurate. (Nigel Nickles)

gradually increased and Flt Lt I.L. Dugmore and Sqn Ldr M. Holmes managed a nine-hour sortie in October. The following month, the same crew flew a twelve-hour sortie to carry out a simulated attack on RAF Akrotiri, Cyprus; a sortie that required six AAR brackets. 'The aim was to demonstrate that the RAF had not lost its ability to conduct long-range attacks despite the Tornado having much shorter range than the Vulcan,' explained Dugmore. 'We carried four 1,500-litre external tanks and because of the fully-open bleed valves [in the engines] we couldn't get much above fifteen thousand feet when the tanks were full after AAR. At the time nobody knew if the Tornado could fly for twelve hours, so before our trip on 8 November there were proving flights of six hours then nine hours then twelve hours round the UK. We launched from Honington with a spare Tornado and two Buccaneers (primary and spare) to meet two Victors out of RAF Marham for an AAR check. Once we had proved the aircraft could refuel, we set off with one Buccaneer and a Victor.' After flying over France and across Italy, the Tornado left the Victor near Crete and let down to low level to continue towards Cyprus, accompanied by the Buccaneer. 'We were supposed to tank from the Buccaneer before our airfield attack on Akrotiri. However it was turbulent at low level, so we missed that bracket and refuelled at low level from the Buccaneer on the way home,' continued Dugmore. 'The Buccaneer recovered to Cyprus and we climbed up to rendezvous with another Victor over Italy. We logged 9hr 25min day and 2hr 45min night. I think 12hr 10min is still a record for the Tornado and it's the only time I have ever used a pee bag.'

Meanwhile more typical flying continued apace, with aircraft deploying routinely to RAF Laarbruch, RAF Wildenrath, RAF Brüggen and the GAF base at Schleswig in Germany for

A IX Squadron Tornado refuels from the starboard wing hose of a Handley-Page Victor K2 tanker. With full internal tanks and two under-wing 1,500-litre tanks, the Tornado GR1 carried 7,400kg of fuel. (Nigel Nickles)

low-flying on the continent. Live 1,000lb bombs were dropped at Garvie Island near Cape Wrath and inert 1,000lb bombs on the Otterburn range. On 15 December, Wg Cdr Gooding and Flt Lt Davies – the same crew who had flown the first Tornado sortie – completed the 1,000th hour of Tornado GR1 flying by IX Squadron. The squadron was declared to Supreme Allied Command Europe (SACEUR) as strike combat ready in January 1983.

Concept of Operations

In 1977, the Concept of Operations (Con Ops) for the Tornado envisaged that 144 aircraft would replace the Vulcan and Buccaneer strike aircraft in 1 Group, the Buccaneer in RAF Germany (RAFG) and Canberra photo-reconnaissance (PR) aircraft. Armed with the British-built WE177 nuclear-strike weapon and fitted with three external fuel tanks, it was calculated that the Tornado could reach strike targets as far as longitude 21° East (around the longitude of Warsaw) using a 'hi-lo-hi' profile from the UK or a 'lo-lo-lo' profile from Germany. There were to be: one strike (nuclear)/attack (conventional weapons) squadron at Honington, two strike/attack squadrons each at Marham and Laarbruch, one reconnaissance squadron at Laarbruch and another at a yet to be decided location, plus two maritime strike/attack squadrons based at RAF Lossiemouth. UK-based Tornado strike/attack squadrons would have an establishment of sixteen aircraft and twenty crews, while RAFG squadrons would have eighteen aircraft and twenty-seven crews to reflect the increased requirement to maintain Quick Reaction Alert (Nuclear) (QRA[N]).

A WE177 drill round dropped by a Tornado GR1. The primary role of the Tornado GR1 was that of nuclear strike using the British-built weapon. (14 Squadron Association)

Interestingly, there was no indication at this stage that Tornado might replace the Jaguar strike/attack aircraft in Germany, although ex-Jaguar units would eventually make up nearly half of the operational Tornado squadrons. Indeed, rather than just two strike/attack Tornado squadrons in RAFG there would actually be seven. The Con Ops also stated that 'whilst Tornado GR1 will be included in national contingency plans, no separate provision will be made to operate the aircraft in a non-NATO role' – a statement which the benefit of hindsight shows to be somewhat flawed.

27 and 617 Squadrons

The next two Tornado GR1 squadrons formed at Marham during the first half of 1983. Air and ground crews had begun to join 617 Squadron during the previous autumn, so when the unit was formally re-formed under the command of Wg Cdr A.J. Harrison on 4 January, it already had ten Tornado crews and ten aircraft. In the words of Sqn Ldr A.J. Laidler, 'because of a large amount of preparatory work carried out prior to re-formation, the squadron has been able to mount a substantial flying programme from the first day.' However, despite that work, the squadron still suffered from the teething problems that might be expected with the introduction of a new aeroplane. 'Aircraft were in short supply, out of twelve we had at least six "Christmas Trees",' recalled Flt Lt W. Grout, 'the spares back-up was almost non-existent. The engineers were very frustrated at not being able to give us more jets.'

The first personnel posted to 27 Squadron, Warrant Officer (WO) Cooke and five NCOs, had arrived at Marham in December and the aircraft started to arrive three months later. The squadron commander, Wg Cdr J.B. Grogan, flew the first Tornado painted in 27 Squadron markings with Sqn Ldr Bradley on 28 March.

Meanwhile at Honington, IX Squadron continued with a full and varied flying programme. AAR was being practised daily with Victor, Vulcan and Buccaneer tankers and fourships [formation] were being flown regularly as part of the squadron's attack work-up. There was also an emphasis on auto-TF sorties at night: the aircrews were divided into an early and a late shift to extend the flying day and to make the most of the opportunities for night flying. As experience and confidence were gained with the auto-TF system, crews were authorized to fly at lower altitudes: by April 1983, crews were permitted to fly at 500ft by day and 750ft at night. Most of the night low-level flying took place in the Highlands Restricted Area (HRA) in north-west Scotland; however the relatively long transit to the HRA meant that from a 150 minutes (2½hr) sortie, only some 25 minutes would offer high-value training.

In April 1983, both IX and 617 Squadron participated in Exercise *Mallet Blow*. This exercise, which was run periodically throughout the year, comprised tasking against tactical targets on the Otterburn range, and included routing through the Electronic Warfare Training Range (EWTR) at RAF Spadeadam, Cumbria and fighter engagement zones off the east coast of England and to the west of the Pennines. Flt Lt S.W. Peach of IX Squadron wrote that the exercise provided 'excellent training value and produced some very encouraging results.' However, crews on 617 Squadron were less enthusiastic, as poor weather limited their participation to just two sorties during the week. In fact poor weather was something of a feature of Exercise *Mallet Blow* in subsequent years and it became synonymous for most Tornado crews with low cloud and driving rain. The 617 Squadron crews were not much luckier with the weather during Exercise *Priory* later in the month.

Minevals, Maxevals and Tacevals

Short of actually going to war, the prime concern of all personnel on a Tornado GR1 squadron was to pass the annual Tactical Evaluation (Taceval), which was carried out under the auspices of HQ Strike Command for UK-based units or Commander Allied Air Forces Central Europe (COMAAFCE) in the case of RAFG units. Taceval tested every aspect of

The second Tornado GR1 squadron to form was 617 Squadron, which like IX Squadron, had formerly been equipped with Avro Vulcans. The squadron was the first Tornado unit to form at RAF Marham. (RAF Museum)

The crew of a Tornado GR1 on 27 Squadron are pushed back into a HAS at Marham after a sortie. Those HAS built at UK bases were somewhat larger than those in Germany, which had originally been designed to house aircraft the size of the SEPECAT Jaguar. (BAe Heritage)

the unit's preparedness for war, including a check (Taceval Part I) that it could generate the assigned number of armed aircraft and crews without notice and within strict time limits. Each squadron was also required to demonstrate (Taceval Part II) over two or three days that it could continue to operate effectively in Nuclear, Biological and Chemical (NBC) environments and under conditions of damage to the airfield. Maintenance crews and weapon loading teams were watched closely and flying sorties were 'chased' by Taceval evaluators. Although both parts of the Taceval tended to be run as a single three-day exercise in RAFG, under the UK regime they were often carried out as two discrete exercises split perhaps by a few months.

Taceval was taken very seriously and most Tornado flying stations might expect a station-run exercise – a Mineval – each month. The next level of evaluation would be a Maxeval, run by external evaluators and designed to give the station a good workout prior to the Taceval. Regardless of other detachments and more exotic exercise commitments, the annual calendar for a Tornado squadron was dominated by the Taceval plot and was punctuated by Minevals and Maxevals.

All three Tornado squadrons, IX, 27 and 617 Squadrons would be declared operational first in the strike (nuclear) role, so the early exercises concentrated on perfecting the strike procedures. This included working out how best to operate from the newly-built hardened aircraft shelters (HAS) at both Honington and Marham. Command and control was something of a challenge in NBC conditions, when the squadrons' personnel would be scattered in concrete bunkers across a fairly large site. The first Tornado Taceval was that of IX Squadron whose Part I was passed with flying colours on 5 July 1983. Part II started on 26 September 1983, but unfortunately this phase was marred by a fatal accident, which occurred on 27 September. Tornado GR1 (ZA586), crewed by Sqn Ldr M.D. Stephens and Flt Lt N.F. Nickles suffered a total electrics failure while descending towards Honington at the end of a night sortie. Nickles described what happened: 'suddenly, CLUNK – all the lights go out. Thinks… how the hell did I do that… second thinks… if I have no electrics then the engines will go bang. BANG… I hate it when I'm right. Hang on, no engines means no hydraulics, means no flying controls, means a very expensive lead glider. This is not in the script. I don't think I'm going to like this. Send first 'Mayday' out into the cockpit voice recorder, well the buttons are next to each other and it is very dark. Take deep breath, find green aircrew torch, work out where the switches are and try again. Have an off-intercom shouting match with man [pilot] with hands on stick and throttle. "I've turned for the Wash," he replies. Guess he reckons it's properly broken then. I notice aircraft is very quiet, just a whooshing noise as the airflow sweeps back and forward across the canopy as we Dutch Roll. I really do hope that Martin Baker [ejection seat manufacturer] are as good as they say they are, but I bet it's going to hurt. We both fiddle with useless switches hoping maybe somebody will put the lights back on.

'Ninety seconds later (at least three lifetimes) my pilot commands "GO NOW"… Oh ★★★★, feet forward… visors down… head back… close eyes and pull. Boy oh boy… for 1.25 seconds it goes quite quick, just flashes from the canopy-ejection motors, mind-boggling acceleration and hey presto… two pulled neck muscles. At least my back does not hurt and I can open my eyes now.

'Start drills. Take off oxygen mask… can't. Somebody has tied my arms to the seat… that means the seat has failed. I don't believe it. In fact I do not believe it because I've just remembered about the automatics. But how do I breathe, come on 'Bloggs' do keep up… why not use some of the oxygen they put on the seat. Mmm… maybe this is not so bad after all. I suppose I should feel cold but the blood is going round so fast friction is keeping me warm. I wonder how fast I am going… I probably do not really want to know then OUCH… the parachute adds a pulled groin to the list of injuries.' Although Nickles escaped from the aircraft successfully, Stephens did not eject and was killed. The Taceval was terminated and the Tornado fleet was grounded for a week while investigations were carried out.

Routine Flying

For their routine daily flying, the Tornado squadrons based at Honington and Marham had the whole of the UK Low-Flying System (UKLFS) on their 'doorstep.' Most of mainland England, Wales and Scotland comprised a series of interlinked Low-Flying Areas (LFAs) in which aircraft could fly down to a minimum of 250ft by day and 500ft by night. Weapons ranges on the East Coast, RAF Holbeach and RAF Wainfleet in the Wash and RAF Donna Nook and RAF Cowden to the north and south, respectively of the Humber, were also nearby. Slightly further afield there were also weapons ranges at RAF Tain and RAF Rosehearty in north-east Scotland and RAF Jurby Head on the north-west coast of the Isle of Man. Additionally the Phantom and Lightning fighter squadrons from RAF Wattisham, RAF Coningsby, RAF Binbrook and RAF Leuchars were usually available for affiliation training and AAR could be arranged with the Victor tankers based at Marham. So, high-quality training sorties could

A Tornado GR1 from 27 Squadron, loaded with two inert free-fall 1,000lb bombs. Inert bombs were filled with concrete, but matched the size, weight and ballistic characteristics of the live weapon. (Benny Bentham)

easily be planned, using a combination of the UKLFS, weapons ranges, fighters and tankers. Although some singleton Simulated Strike Profile (SSP) sorties were flown, the bulk of this routine training was done in pairs or in four-ship formations. In the IX Squadron diary, Flt Lt Peach recorded that 'daily flying now consists of morning four-ship formations, afternoon singletons to practise reversionary procedures and night flying to practise auto-TF.'

There were also routine detachments abroad. Each month, Exercise *Eastern Vortex* would see at least one pair from each Tornado squadron deploy to one of the RAFG stations or GAF Tornado bases to familiarize crews with the low-flying procedures in continental Europe; it was also a chance for crews to get used to the characteristics of different radar emitters on the Radar Warning Receiver (RWR) display. Similarly there was usually at least one deployment each month to the Italian Air Force Tornado base at Ghedi, just south of Lake Garda. The squadrons also participated in exercises in Denmark and the Baltic Approaches, including Exercise *Brown Falcon* (IX Squadron from Rygge in April 1983 and 617 Squadron from Schleswig in September) and Exercise *Blue Moon* (617 Squadron in June and September). IX Squadron sent a pair of Tornados to Royal Danish Air Force (RDAF) Karup for Exercise *Botany Bay*, which involved leading a mixed formation of German Navy F-104G Starfighters against a variety of targets from NATO navies. The largest annual exercise in continental Europe was Exercise *Central Enterprise* and after four aircraft from IX Squadron took part from Laarbruch in June 1983, Flt Lt Peach commented that the 'squadron flew in the Offensive Counter Air (OCA) role, concentrating on airfield attacks. All exercise sorties were successful with all tasked targets hit on time. Additional parts of the exercise which proved to be of value were use of the Sup-Plan M routing [a system to de-conflict attack aircraft from the NATO air-defence systems], experience in communications jamming, minimum radio procedures and rapid planning to meet tasked Time over Target (ToT)... Experience gained in Exercise

Central Enterprise high-lighted the fact that Tornado needs precise target information to match the accuracy of its weapons system.'

Back in the UK, Exercise *Mallet Blow* continued to be the source of excellent training value: in July, for example, both IX and 617 Squadron fourships took part and 27 Squadron also participated for the first time with one Tornado flown by Flt Lt E.D. Smith and Flt Lt D.B. Chamberlain.

The Tornado squadrons were also called upon from time to time to help with trials work to investigate various improvements into the weapons aiming system, auto-TF techniques or electronic-warfare equipment and tactics. For IX Squadron this meant trying to auto-TF at the same time that the Skyshadow ECM pod was attempting to jam a ground-based radar; the result was that the pod also jammed the TFR, so a solution to this problem had to be found. Early in the operational life of the Tornado, the Central Tactics and Trials Organization (CTTO) had recognized that most of the operational trials lay outside the remit of not only front-line squadrons but also pure test flying units such as the Aircraft & Armaments Experimental Establishment (AAEE), so the Tornado Operational Evaluation Unit (TOEU) was set up and commanded by Wg Cdr J.G. Lumsden. Flt Lt T.V. Blackwod, one of the first navigators to join the unit, recalled that the TOEU 'was formed in July 1983. Basically, with the introduction of Tornado, CTTO wanted a method of evaluating various operational aspects of the jet which could not be accomplished by squadron aircrew or AAEE Boscombe Down aircrew. Three crews were selected and 73 ground crew. All were experienced and we operated as a lodger-unit at Boscombe… My first trip was a delivery flight from Marham to Boscombe on 16 August 1983 and first sortie over the ranges of the Royal School of Artillery (RSA) at Larkhill on 18 August. We completed several trials at Larkhill and the Ministry of Defence (MoD) site at Aberporth. The Larkhill flying was to evaluate the laser as a ranging sensor and Aberporth was part of the Skyshadow trial which ultimately led to Trial *Phasia*, the first large detachment to Eglin AFB in August 1984.'

Canada

The first deployment to Canada by a front-line Tornado squadron was Exercise *Master Stroke* on 30 August 1983. Three aircraft 617 Squadron led by Wg Cdr Harrison, with Sqn Ldr Laidler, flew non-stop from Marham to Toronto, supported by AAR, for the Canadian National Exhibition Air Show. However, in October IX Squadron deployed to Canadian Forces Base (CFB) Goose Bay for the first of a rather more typical detachment. Exercise *Western Vortex* would become one of the cornerstones in the annual calendar of a Tornado GR1 squadron.

Goose Bay at the foot of Lake Melville in Labrador had its heyday in the 1940s and 50s, firstly as an important staging post on the North Atlantic ferry route and later as a forward operating base for strategic bombers. By the 1970s, the advent of longer-range aircraft and ballistic missiles had left a large and under-used airfield in the midst of a massive area – approximately the same land area as the whole of England – of almost unpopulated terrain: in other words, ideal low-flying country. Strike Command had originally used Goose Bay as a low-level training area for the Vulcan, so when they were replaced by the Tornado, it was a natural step for the Tornado squadrons to 'inherit' the facilities at Goose Bay.

However, the isolated location of Goose Bay was a double-edged sword: on the one hand the emptiness of the training areas meant that there were virtually no restrictions on low

Four Tornado GR1s from 617 Squadron during a medium-level transit sortie. (617 Squadron)

flying which could be carried out down to 100ft throughout the area. Also with exclusive use of the training areas, Tornado crews could practice auto-TF in low cloud and fog without fear of hitting anything else – something that was not possible in Europe. However all this freedom came at a cost: there were no targets and no defences to practise against. To an extent the target problem could be solved for Instrument Meteorological Conditions (IMC) attacks using a certain ammount of imagination: eskers [linear glacial deposits] became runways, small islands became command bunkers, while larger islands became ships, but none of these were particularly realistic in good visibility.

'From an engineering point of view Goose Bay was a hard detachment,' recalled C.Tech Spanswick. 'The aircrew really made the aircraft work hard to its full capability and sometimes this took its toll on the engines and mechanical components. Also all of the avionics was required to be spot on so the 'fairies' [avionics technicians] were maxed out trying to make sure that could be achieved. We generally worked a normal shift of a week of days and a week of nights. The day shift concentrated on meeting the flying programme by turning round the jets as fast as they could and fixing snags in-between. Night shift would then concentrate on heavy rectifications and it was very rare that the shift finished before 06:00hrs in the morning. Now and again there would be a period of night flying and to achieve that the length of the day shift would be increased to accommodate the extra work load. The biggest nightmare with Goose Bay was the jets were not our own and so it took a few days to get to know them and sometimes we could inherit a complete nightmare depending on who the previous squadron was.'

Tacevals – and More Exotic Exercises

617 Squadron was declared Strike Combat Ready on 1 November 1983 and passed its Part I Taceval two weeks later. On their return from Goose Bay, IX Squadron successfully

completed their Taceval Part II over 29 and 30 November. Marham also held a Mineval on 30 November, about which Flt Lt A. Thomson from 27 Squadron wrote 'prior to this all the station exercises had been for the benefit of 617 Squadron and it was felt that 27 Squadron had suffered because of our requirement to support 617 Squadron during their aircraft generation phase.' In fact 27 Squadron now became more of a priority at Marham, as the squadron was to be declared Strike Combat ready on 1 March 1984.

However, before that date 27 Squadron would deploy to the Sultan of Oman's Air Force (SOAF) base at Thumrait, during the first week of February for Exercise *Magic Carpet*. Four Tornados left Marham in two separate pairs at 08:00hrs on 27 January. After a six-hour flight involving two AAR brackets they stopped at Akrotiri before completing the flight (which included two more AAR brackets and took over five hours) onwards to Thumrait. During the exercise the Tornados flew in pairs for low-level sorties that included weaponry at Rubkut range. However, on 2 February the SOAF held a tactical reconnaissance and bombing competition, which involved flying through three 'gates,' bombing a new target at Rubkut range and finding a tactical reconnaissance target. The 27 Squadron team won overall, having won the individual prize and taking first and third places in the team competition. On 4 February, two aircraft also visited Abu Dhabi for an air display then all four Tornados returned to Marham via the Royal Saudi Air Force (RSAF) base at Dhahran.

In January, 617 Squadron learned, too, that they would be involved in an interesting exercise later in the year: they were to represent RAF Strike Command at the USAF Strategic Air Command (SAC) Bombing Competition in the autumn. This would be known as Exercise *Prairie Vortex*. However, the immediate priority for 617 Squadron was to complete its attack work-up. A squadron tactics committee was formed and Flt Lt S.G. Tranter described how it was made up 'of aircrew experienced in both air defence and ground-attack roles. During January they presented their ideas as a basis for tactical operations in all areas of the squadron's roles.' Flt Lt Grout's view of the process was a little more cynical: 'as you would expect we had Harrier, Jaguar, Phantom and Buccaneer pilots trying to agree and Buccaneer, Phantom and Vulcan navigators playing second fiddle.'

With 27 Squadron back from Oman, both Marham squadrons were working hard towards Taceval in March. The Part I for both squadrons was held on 1 and 2 March, followed by a Mineval and Exercise *Elder Forest*, an 11 Group exercise. In 27 Squadron's diary, Flt Lt Thomson wrote that the 'UK was defended by Phantoms, Lightnings and Hawks as well as other NATO fighters and this provided crews with an ideal opportunity to try out their evasion tactics.' The exercise sorties were flown at high level to a point 100 miles off the coast; then the aircraft let down to low level and headed back towards the coast to carry out simulated attacks against air-defence sites at RAF Boulmer and RAF Buchan or the airfield at RAF Lossiemouth. The sorties usually also involved a First Run Attack (FRA) at Tain range and a run through the EW-training range at Spadeadam. But Taceval work was never far away and during March, 617 Squadron reported that of twenty-two working days, twelve were occupied directly by Taceval, Mineval or pre-Taceval training. The preparation paid off and both squadrons were successful in the Part II Taceval, which took place in the last week of the month.

Typical Goose Bay scenery (1), as seen through the HUD. The training areas in Labrador comprised miles of rolling forests, rivers and lakes – most of which was uninhabited. (Lars Smith)

Typical Goose Bay scenery (2). The HUD readouts show that this Tornado is flying at 585kt and 150ft above the impressively steep-sided Harp Lake in northern Labrador. (Lars Smith)

Typical Goose Bay scenery (3) – the view from the rear cockpit as the aircraft enters Harp Lake, a narrow, steep-sided 25-mile stretch of water. Unfortunately, the forward view from the rear seat was limited by the CRPMD and the back of pilot's seat. (Wally Grout)

XV, 16, 20 and 45 Squadrons

Closely following the plan outlined in the Con Ops, the next two squadrons to be re-equipped were XV and 16 Squadrons, the two Buccaneer units at Laarbruch. However, unlike the squadrons in UK, which remained under direct national control, the RAFG squadrons fell under the operational command of SACEUR; as such they were required to maintain the declared number of combat-ready strike aircraft, so both Buccaneer squadrons had to remain at full strength until they could be replaced by combat ready Tornado squadrons. For this reason, parallel 'Designate' squadrons were formed to work up with the Tornado and eventually to replace the Buccaneer squadrons of the same number.

XV (Designate) Squadron was formally formed under the command of Wg Cdr B. Dove at Laarbruch on 1 September 1983 and 16 (Designate) Squadron (commanded by Wg Cdr R.H.

The first RAF Germany (RAFG) unit to convert to the Tornado GR1 was XV Squadron at RAF Laarbruch, which had previously operated the Hawker Siddeley Buccaneer S2. (Geoffrey Lee/Plane Focus)

Goodall) followed four months later. Also, in a departure from the original Con Ops, a third Tornado squadron formed at Laarbruch in May 1984: 20 (Designate) Squadron, under Wg Cdr J.B. Hill, would replace 20 Squadron, which operated the Jaguar from Brüggen. In each case a small cadre of engineers arrived a few months earlier to carry out the initial setting up, before the aircraft and the aircrew arrived.

Another 'extra' squadron to appear in 1984 was 45 (Reserve [R]) Squadron: TWCU adopted the guise of 45 (Reserve) Squadron at the beginning of January. However the new identity caused more confusion than anything else, not least amongst personnel in the unit, since it continued to be referred to as 'TWCU.'

Exercise *Prairie Vortex* 1984

In April, 617 Squadron started its work-up for Exercise *Prairie Vortex* in earnest. 'The scenario for *Prairie Vortex*,' explained Flt Lt Tranter, 'involved a hi-lo-hi profile, attacking Radar Bomb Scoring Unit (RBSU) targets in a hostile EW environment.' Initial work-up sorties were flown by singletons, each involving two to three hours auto-TF and including short AAR brackets, timed FRAs on various ranges and runs through Spadeadam to use the RBSU and practise against the EW threats. Six crews then deployed to Ellsworth AFB, near Rapid City, North Dakota, on 9 May where they spent a fortnight gaining experience operating under competition conditions. Each day three Tornado sorties were flown, supported by a Victor tanker. They were planned to give crews the opportunity to use auto-TF in mountainous terrain of a much grander scale than that in the UK and to get used to working with American RBSUs. Additionally the detachment provided the opportunity to develop and perfect Victor to Tornado AAR techniques. The crews recovered to Marham on 24 May.

While the aircrew concentrated on preparing for the flying aspects of the exercise, there was much behind the scenes work preparing the aircraft, including software upgrades. A new operational flight programme was introduced, which amongst other improvements presented groundspeed in the HUD (it normally displayed only airspeed) and increased the maximum distance for radar offsets from 10 to 20 miles. By now eight aircraft had been selected for the detachment and six crews had been nominated as potential competitors. For these crews the flying continued with 'half route simulations' of the expected competition profile. The sortie started with a transit to Spadeadam at 16,000ft for a medium-level RBSU run, followed by an AAR bracket over northern Scotland. The crews then let down to low level for an auto-TF run through the highlands and down to Dumfries and Galloway for a low-level RBSU run at Luce Bay, followed by another at Spadeadam and then a final AAR bracket before returning to Marham. By now the best technique for the tanker rendezvous had been finalized: the two aircraft would approach head-on and at a pre-determined range, the Victor would make a 180° turn, while the Tornado continued 20° offset from its original heading. If this technique was flown correctly, the two aircraft would meet exactly as the Victor rolled wings level. Throughout the summer the crews flew the 4hr 45min sortie profile four times a week.

Loaded with eight inert 1,000lb bombs, a Tornado GR1 carries the markings of 16 Squadron, the second of the Buccaneer units at Laarbruch to convert to the Tornado. (Nigel Nickles)

Another area of preparation was to ensure that there was sufficiently accurate map coverage of the target areas so that the weapon aiming system had the precise information it needed. In early August, a survey team visited the United States and found that the fix-point library supplied by the USAF was incomplete and inaccurate; as were the local maps. The team therefore decided to produce its own fix-point catalogue and selected a number of suitable radar-significant offsets (for example oil tanks or grain silos) for each potential target. 'I had spent a lot of the summer since we did the reconnaissance in May,' recalled Flt Lt R.H. Middleton, 'going through the radar film with Dermot [Dolan] to try and find good offsets. We gave a list of what we thought would be the best ones to the survey team. They confirmed some but found others.' Having found the offsets, the survey team then ensured that the co-ordinates were measured and positioned exactly.

'We were fairly confident that we would find the low-level offsets,' continued Middleton, 'but the radar was not optimized for medium level and so finding medium-level offsets was tricky and it was always a relief when one showed up. Because it was difficult to see small objects from medium level, we had to use larger objects and find the right place to aim; I think we went for the middle of the leading edge – we were pretty good at defining the middle of something – and we believed that the effect of pixel size was less there. In the run up we spent long hours discussing map projections; working out spherical trigonometry problems to make sure the distances used by the aircraft were the same as the ones on the map; and familiarizing ourselves with the aircraft main computer's hexadecimal counting system.'

A neat four-ship box formation flypast over the dispersal pan at RAF Honington by aircraft from TWCU, which also had the identity of 45 (Reserve) Squadron. (Nigel Nickles)

A pair of Tornado GR1s from 617 Squadron at medium level. Squadron crews spent much of the year practising the USAF Strategic Air Command bombing competition profile, which involved both medium- and low-level tactical flying. (617 Squadron)

On 29 August, six Tornados and three Victors deployed to Ellsworth AFB, via Goose Bay. By now the competition crews had been finalized as: Team 'A' comprising Sqn Ldr P. Dunlop with Flt Lt R.H. Middleton, Flt Lts I. Hunter and D. Dolan and Team 'B' consisting of Flt Lt J. MacDonald with Sqn Ldr A.H.C. Dyer-Perry and Flt Lt S. Legg with Sqn Ldr V. Bussereau. The crews spent most of September training in theatre. Apart from getting used to the restrictive USAF procedures, the crews were able to familiarize themselves with the terrain, both visually and on radar, and to verify the offsets which the survey team had chosen. The flights also presented an opportunity to ascertain the best operating programme for the Skyshadow ECM pod. In order to ensure that no sorties were lost because of unserviceability, three aircraft were manned for each sortie, of which two taxied and one then actually flew the mission. Simulated attacks were flown against the RBSU sites at Powell (to the east of the Yellowstone Park, Wyoming), Gillette (north of Caspar, Wyoming), Wibaux (eastern Montana) and Scobey (also in Montana, close to the Canadian border), as well as practise weapon releases on the ranges at Nellis AFB near Las Vegas.

The first competition sortie, which was flown on 1 October, comprised a high-level transit to Nellis, with AAR prior to descending into the ranges to transit through a Combat Air Patrol (CAP) mounted by CAF CF-101 Voodoos. The aircraft were also engaged by EW threats as they dropped practice bombs on two separate no-show targets (the first drop of which was at a pre-assigned ToT). Unfortunately McDonald and Dyer-Perry suffered a weapons hang-up during a drop at Nellis, which cost them dearly in points, but the rest of the Tornado sorties went well. The next phase started ten days later.

On 10 October, the weather conditions were very poor with thick fog covering Ellsworth. When Sqn Ldr Dunlop and Flt Lt Middleton lined on the runway early that morning, Dunlop

A 617 Squadron Tornado turns towards Ellsworth Air Force Base, near Rapid City South Dakota, at the end of a sortie during the USAF Strategic Air Command bombing competition. (Dick Middleton)

could only just see a few of the runway lights ahead of him. It also took some high-level coaxing to persuade the Victor to take off in weather that was well below peacetime limits. This time the Tornados flew at high altitude to the RBSU at Powell for a high-level 'tone drop' before rendezvousing with the Victor over central Montana. 'I remember the long periods of transit with not much to do between bomb runs and refuelling brackets,' wrote Middleton later. 'Pete [Dunlop] was keen on Annie Lennox at the time so we had her tapes playing on the Cockpit Voice Recorder (CVR) endlessly... There was always a sense of relief when the first offset showed up; we used the system of going from large objects for the initial aiming through something smaller but still significant and on to the final small aiming offset. We tried to get an aiming offset beyond the target so we could continue aiming right up to release.' After refuelling, the aircraft descended to join a low-level route for a low-level 'tone drop' at Powell followed by another at Gillette RBSU. After climbing up for a second AAR bracket, they continued at low level for two more simulated attacks at the RBSUs at Wiboux and Scobey. Dunlop and Middleton returned to Ellsworth after a 5hr 50min sortie. They were pleased that their sortie had gone well: all the offsets, which had been so carefully measured previously, showed up well on the radar and they had hit all four targets exactly on their allotted ToT. Also the other Tornado crews felt that their sorties had been successful.

The third (night) phase of the competition was flown on 15 and 16 October. The route was the same as that on the day phase, but this time the route was reversed. Once again, all of the Tornado crews were pleased with their performance, although GMR on Hunter and Dolan's aircraft failed as they descended to low level, so they had to carry out the final two bomb runs without being able to update the navigation system.

Tornados from 617 Squadron prepare to launch at dusk for a night sortie at Ellsworth AFB.
(Dick Middleton)

The detachment from 617 Squadron returned to Marham over 22 and 23 October, before flying out to Barksdale AFB, Louisiana, by VC10 of RAF Transport Command for the results and prize giving ceremony on 31 October. When the results were announced, the Tornado crews' confidence was completely vindicated: in the words of Wg Cdr Harrison 'for all those concerned with our participation in the 1984 SAC Bombing Competition, the results obtained were nothing short of a triumph.' Having scored a total of 2,616 points out of a possible 2,650, Dunlop and Middleton were the outright winners of the Curtis LeMay Bombing Trophy for the crew gaining the highest total score. Closely behind in second place were Legg and Bussereau with 2,612 points, thus putting the Tornado crews in the top two positions out of 42 competitors. The Tornado crews were also highly successful in the other trophies, which were competed for in teams of two crews each: the 617 Squadron teams took first and third places out of eight in the John C. Meyer Trophy for the best F-111 or Tornado team, and second and sixth out of the 21 teams competing for the Mathis Trophy to be the best overall team.

Summer Exercises

While 617 Squadron had been busy with Exercise *Prairie Vortex*, the other Tornado squadrons had continued the established routine. Both IX and 27 Squadrons continued with monthly Exercise *Eastern Vortex* deployments to Germany, while the Laarbruch squadrons continued their work up towards combat readiness. In April 1984, Exercise *Mallet Blow* was undertaken by IX, 27 and XV Squadrons and all three units also took part in Exercises *Brown Falcon* in May and *Central Enterprise* in June. Of the latter, Flt Lt K. Delve of IX Squadron reported that 'excellent

The winning 617 Squadron team, left to right: Pete Dunlop and Dick Middleton with the Curtiss LeMay Trophy, Tony Harrison (OC 617 Squadron), Dermot Dolan and Iain Hunter with the John C. Meyer Trophy. Pete Dunlop later went on to command 31 Squadron at Brüggen. (Dick Middleton)

tasking provided opportunity for squadron crews to operate as elements of large attack packages and thus gain valuable experience,' while the 27 Squadron diarist noted that 'the complex sorties and bad weather meant that crews had to use their skill and experience and the aircraft's avionics suite to the full.' Exercise *Central Enterprise* was also the first major commitment for the crews of 16 Squadron, but they also found that the weather limited their flying.

On 1 July 1984, XV Squadron was declared Strike CR. The immediate effect of this on the squadron was that crews and aircraft had to start taking their place in QRA(N). Although one of the squadrons at Laarbruch was now operational in the strike role, the attack work up continued for all three squadrons on the Wing. During September, Laarbruch ran a station exercise to coincide with Exercise *Lionheart* which, as Flt Lt H.W. Price described in 16 Squadron's operations diary, was 'an army exercise run every four years and designed to exercise British Army Of the Rhine (BAOR) and its reinforcements in their war role… unfortunately throughout this period, the weather was very poor and the mission success rate, in spite of a high sortie rate, was not very good.' 16 Squadron had instituted twenty-four hour manning for the exercise, but the nightshift found itself somewhat under-tasked.

Apart from flying in Germany, the Laarbruch Wing also participated in exercises such as *Mallet Blow* and *Priory*. The Exercise *Mallet Blow* operations in mid-October were flown as hi-lo-hi sorties from Laarbruch, but on Exercise *Priory*, flown towards the end of the month, the

A Tornado GR1 of 20 Squadron, one of the three GR1 squadrons at Laarbruch, carries three live 1,000lb bombs towards the range at Garvie Island, near Cape Wrath. The unit had previously flown SEPECAT Jaguars from Brüggen. (Lars Smith)

squadron landed at Kinloss to refuel between sorties. The Initial Taceval for 16 Squadron took place on 17 and 18 October. The squadron was declared Strike CR shortly afterwards and Wg Cdr Goodall and Sqn Ldr J. Broadbent stood the squadron's first QRA(N) on 28 October. The focus of intensive station exercise then fell on 20 Squadron, with three two-day Minevals in the month of November.

For IX Squadron, Exercises *Mallet Blow* and *Priory* in October 1984 (in which the squadron had tested its evasion tactics against the defending Phantoms, Lightnings and Hawks) had been an ideal start to the work up for Exercise *Green Flag 85/3*, which would take place at Nellis AFB in March 1985. The following months included range slots at Garvie Island, near Cape Wrath, to drop live 1,000lb bombs and more evasion training against the Lightning squadrons from RAF Binbrook.

The Goose versus Parallel Track Debate

In July, 27 Squadron was deployed to Goose Bay. On 4 and 5 July, eight aircraft were flown in two waves of four directly to Canada with Victor AAR support. At Goose Bay the squadron was able to carry out some evasion training against CAF CF-101 Voodoos and GAF F-4 Phantoms, but the emphasis was on practising auto-TF. In particular, the squadron looked into the point of contention which vexed all Tornado operators at the time, namely how to produce a sortie plan which was suitable for all weathers – i.e. both visual flying and auto-TF, and that could also be switched from visual to auto-TF (and back) as weather conditions varied. The main problem was that of 'de-confliction:' in visual flying formation members could see and avoid each other, whereas in auto-TF aircraft in the same formation, would have to be procedurally de-conflicted because

A navigator's view of low flying at Goose Bay. To the north of the training area, the forest gave way to bare rocks. (Simon Hadley)

A Tornado GR1 from XV Squadron at low level over the typical landscape of Goose Bay. Quite often there was snow on the ground even in the summer months. (XV Squadron)

they could not see each other. Two schools of thought prevailed on how to achieve this: parallel track and single track/Goose.

In a parallel track plan, two separate routes were planned, each parallel to the other separated by two miles; a timing split would be designed so that aircraft were de-conflicted in time wherever the routes intersected, for example over the target during an attack. The routes could then be flown by a pair in standard 'battle formation' (i.e. line abreast two miles apart) in visual conditions, but if the weather – or daylight – was no longer good enough for visual flying, each aircraft could then simply fly its own route completely independently, but still be in formation should the conditions improved sufficiently to resume visual flying. The only requirement was to make the correct ToT at the target. If the formation was a fourship, the parallel track route lent itself ideally to a card formation – two pairs separated by 15 to 20sec in visual conditions, or 40sec in auto-TF. Again, provided each crew adhered to their ToT 'contract' everyone was safely de-conflicted from everyone else. IX Squadron had experimented with this technique earlier in the year and Flt Lt Peach commented that 'although this tactic is time-consuming and complex to plan, it allows several aircraft through a narrow time window at the target in all-weather conditions.' Indeed the only real drawback with parallel track planning was the length of time it took to plan properly – although, providing the Computer Planning Ground Station (CPGS) map table was working, this was still well within the proscribed NATO standards.

On the other hand, a single-track plan was simpler and could be planned much more quickly. The premise for this technique was that both aircraft carried the same route. In visual conditions the leader flew the route and the wingman positioned his aircraft to fly a visual battle formation. If conditions deteriorated the wingman turned behind the leader and engaged the auto-TF to fly the same route 40sec behind the leader. In a pair this was probably relatively simple to achieve, but a fourship offered more of a challenge: in this case a 'Goose' formation was flown consisting of the front pair flying in trail, followed by the rear pair flying abreast in battle formation. In order to compress the formation so that it was suitable for visual conditions, the leader would fly 20sec late, so that the Number 2 was on time and the Number 3 would fly 20sec early. In the event of needing to switch to auto TF, the leader would accelerate to make his 'time-line,' the Number 2 would stay where he was so that he was forty seconds behind the leader and Number 3 would drop back to be 40sec behind Number 2; the challenge was for Number 4 who now had to lose 60sec worth of time before he could join the route 40sec behind Number 3 at the end of the trail.

Wg Cdr Grogan was less than impressed with the Goose technique: 'as sorties progressed during the detachment,' he wrote, 'and as more problems were encountered, it became clear that the Goose concept has many severe limitations… certainly Goose formation should not be accepted as the Tornado Standard Operating Procedure (SOP).' On 23 and 24 July, the squadron returned to Marham, unfortunately less one aircraft, which had crashed on recovery to Goose Bay due to a control malfunction.

By the end of 1984, the RAF had three combat ready strike/attack Tornado squadrons in the UK. At Laarbruch there was one Tornado squadron, which would be declared strike/ attack CR on 1 January 1985, and two further Tornado squadrons which were well into their CR work-up. Three further Tornado squadrons were about to form at Brüggen.

2
1985-1989
Cold War

RAF Germany

During the first few years of the Tornado's introduction to RAF service, the emphasis had been on the UK, and in particular on Strike Command, but in 1984 the epicentre of the Tornado GR1 force had started to move emphatically towards RAF Germany (RAFG). At the end of 1983 the RAF had three Tornado GR1 squadrons, based at Honington and Marham; by the end of 1989 it would have just two squadrons in the UK and eight in Germany, based at Laarbruch and Brüggen.

Unlike the UK-based units, which remained under British military control during peacetime, Tornado squadrons in RAFG were permanently under the operational control of SACEUR and the first priority was to meet their requirements for nuclear strike assets, known as the Force Generation Level (FGL). There were various FGLs ranging from Basic Readiness (BR), which covered only the highest priority targets and could be sustained indefinitely, to Maximum Readiness (MR), at which all the targets on the SACEUR target list were covered. MR could only be sustained for a short time, but the BR lines were held permanently – even in peacetime – at 15min readiness, which constituted QRA(N). Because of this requirement to meet the latter commitment, RAFG Tornado squadrons were larger in numbers of both aircraft and crews, than the Strike Command units.

At Brüggen and Laarbruch the QRA site comprised a small number of Hardened Aircraft Shelters (HASs) in a securely guarded compound, which had independent access to the runway. Inside each 'live' HAS there was a Tornado loaded with the WE177 nuclear free-fall bomb; its air and ground crews waited at 'crew room readiness' in a hardened shelter nearby. Aircraft that were tasked against the more distant targets (for example in eastern *Deutsche Demokratische Republik* [DDR] –East Germany or in western Poland) were typically loaded

Framed between the wingtip and engine of a VC10 tanker, a Tornado GR1 from 27 Squadron awaits its turn on the refuelling drogue. (Geoffrey Lee/ Plane Focus)

with one WE177 on the left shoulder pylon and a third fuel tank on the right shoulder; shorter-range targets might be covered by a single aircraft armed with two WE177s.

'After checking into QRA in the morning,' wrote one pilot, 'the first duty was to take over responsibility for the weapon system from the off-going crew. Although we had practised the drills many times, there was still a moment of awe when you stepped into the HAS and saw the 'Real Bomb' roosting malevolently under the aircraft.'

The enormity of the duty was not lost on the ground crew, either. 'I was fortunate to have done several nuclear QRA duties at Brüggen while I was on 31 Squadron,' recounted C.Tech Spanswick. 'To this day I will never forget when I first walked into a QRA HAS, with the aircrew, to do the daily flight servicing on the Tornado. I opened the door and just stood totally in awe looking at the nuclear weapon fitted. I remember thinking about that old statement about Brüggen being the "Sharp End" of the Royal Air Force and thinking "well it doesn't get any sharper than this." The duty itself was generally boring with a twenty-four hour on, followed by twenty-four hours off shift system. But we had a huge variety of board games to play and videos to watch. We also had our own cook who made us the most amazing meals and cakes. Now and again, and always unexpectedly, the hooter would sound and all hell would break out. Cards or chess pieces would go flying, video films would be left running unwatched and meals and cups of tea would go cold. You just ran like hell to get those HAS doors open and the crew strapped in. Neither you nor the crew knew it was for real or an exercise and without fail you reacted as if it was real. The APU would be running and you always knew that if the pilot started the right-hand engine it was real. In a perverse way it was

A Tornado GR1, painted in an early version of 20 Squadron's markings, is loaded with three inert 1,000lb Laser-Guided Bombs (LGB). The squadron spent much of summer and autumn of 1985 working up for its unusual wartime role, known as 'Option Lima'. (Chris Coulls)

Two live 1,000lb LGBs loaded under a Tornado GR1 of 20 Squadron, before a sortie to Garvie Island during the squadron's LGB operational work up in October 1985. (Chris Coulls)

This is a rare print from a Pave Spike video recording of the first live LGB drop by 20 Squadron at Garvie Island. (Chris Coulls)

always an a disappointment and anticlimax when the crew found out it was an exercise and shut the APU down and you just put the jet back to bed, ready for the next time.'

In the event of MR being declared, all strike aircraft would be included in the Coordinated Launch Sequence Plan (CLSP), which was for the mass employment of all tactical nuclear assets held by SACEUR. The CLSP was planned centrally at Supreme Headquarters Allied Powers Europe (SHAPE) each year to ensure that in the event of a mass strike all the weapon systems were de-conflicted from each other so that, in theory at least, aircraft would not be affected by the detonation of weapons from other aircraft. After being released, the crew effectively became an independent entity and would take off on time, using silent procedures, to make good their tasked Time of Detonation (ToD).

Aircraft that were not required for strike operations under the prevailing FGL were released for conventional attack operations. In peacetime, of course, this meant training sorties, but in wartime it meant initially flying pre-planned missions and, once those had been completed, responding to 'on call tasking' from the Air Tasking Operations Centre (ATOC) at Maastricht. The main pre-planned task for RAFG Tornado units was 'Option Alpha,' designed to neutralise the main Warsaw Pact airfields in the DDR such as Zerbst, Jüterbog, Merseburg, Neuruppin and Kothen and also long-range SAM-5 sites at Altengrabow and Rostock. All the Option Alpha missions were planned as TFR routes and it was expected that night-capable aircraft such as Tornado (and F-111) would probably execute their missions at night or in poor weather. The missions were planned as twelve-ship formations, with the lead squadron providing two fourships and one other squadron providing the back four-ship formation.

Broadly, the plan was to use the JP233 runway denial weapon against the airfields and 1,000lb bombs against the SAM-5 sites. The UK-based Tornado squadrons were also included in the overall Option Alpha plan, but they would require AAR support in order to reach their targets.

However, the pre-planned 'Option' for 20 Squadron was slightly different: 'Option Lima' involved using Laser Guided Bombs (LGB) to destroy key bridges, principally over the Elbe and Weser, to deny them to advancing Warsaw Pact forces. The laser designation for these targets depended on their geographical position and might be by Special Forces on the ground, or by a supporting Buccaneer aircraft equipped with a AN/AVQ-23E Pave Spike laser designator pod. In the latter case, the aircraft and crews were provided by 237 OCU, the Buccaneer conversion unit. In order to carry the LGB, the Tornados were fitted with modified shoulder pylons and also a centreline under-fuselage pylon, enabling three weapons to be carried; these extra pylons were only fitted to the aircraft of 16 and 20 Squadrons which were nominated as 'specialist' LGB squadrons.

'The primary tactic,' explained Flt Lt C.J. Coulls, a QWI navigator on 20 Squadron, 'was to attack each target with six aircraft, four Tornados and two Buccaneers equipped with Pave Spike, split into two, three-aircraft elements. Typically, the plan would involve attacking two points on each bridge... usually the bridge buttresses. Thus, each buttress would be struck by up to six weapons, almost simultaneously. Key planning considerations were line of attack and wind direction, as it was vital to choose a direction that would optimize the amount of reflected laser energy, and to strike the downwind impact point first to avoid smoke and debris obscuring the subsequent impact point.'

The squadron carried out a comprehensive work up in June 1985. Early in the month, Exercise *Central Enterprise* provided an opportunity to experience the entire end-to-end process from initial tasking all the way to executing the Option Lima profile. In the second half of the month, 237 OCU deployed to Laarbruch in order to practise various attack profiles and to develop the tactics further. 'Much work was done during 1985,' wrote Flt Lt N. Risdale, a 20 Squadron pilot, 'to develop joint Standard Operating Procedures (SOPs) for the LGB delivery from low-level loft and included teaching the Buccaneers about our TF capability – they became happy to formate on our wing while we TF-ed to the target area.' Another 20 Squadron pilot, Flt Lt W. Ramsey, recalled that 'we flew a card formation with a Buccaneer between and behind each pair. If it was a bit iffy he would formate on a Tornado using TF. Unsurprisingly they didn't like auto-TF, so manual it was unless we were feeling mischievous. The preferred attack profile was pairs loft to a single [target]. The Tornados did a one-eighty degree turn off the loft recovery and the Buccaneer did a lazy one-eighty degree turn during the designation phase, but still at a healthy distance away from the target.'

Although valuable work was done during June 1985, Flt Lt Coulls concluded that 'the defining exercise in terms of tactical development was a deployment to Lossiemouth from 7 to 15 October 1985, when we dropped inert and live LGBs at Garvie Island, with the Buccaneers designating for us. This was the first time that an operational Tornado squadron had dropped a live LGB.'

Exercises

In Germany, Minevals, Maxevals and Tacevals inevitably followed a similar scenario and were called at no notice, most often in the early hours of the morning. QRA crews were immediately

A Tornado GR1 of 17 Squadron at low-level over Germany. During 1985, the Jaguar squadrons which had formed the Brüggen Wing were re-equipped with the Tornado. (via Dick Middleton)

called to cockpit readiness, before being stood down once they had called 'on state' within the NATO-approved minimum time. Meanwhile the rest of the station rushed to work as quickly as possible. The aircraft were live-loaded for Option Alpha and crews briefed for their wartime target. Once everything was ready to go, there was an artificial pause while the aircraft were re-loaded with practice weapons and aircrews re-briefed an 'equivalent' practice mission, which was then flown. As the exercise progressed the FGL was incrementally raised and the procedures for the Selective Use (Seluse) of nuclear weapons were also practised. Seluse was a demonstration, of small scale and controlled use of nuclear weapons by NATO to confirm its resolve to escalate to general nuclear war if necessary.

Traditionally MR would be declared during the penultimate day of the exercise, and the rest of that day would be taken up with the loading (by the hard-worked weapons teams) and acceptance (by aircrew) of the aircraft. Early the following morning, when all aircraft had been generated in the strike role, all the crews would be sent to cockpit readiness in the HAS to await the release procedure. Eventually, and usually after long and tedious hours of cockpit readiness, the aircraft would be released on 'equivalent' routes around either north or south Germany. All the equivalent routes would feed into a two-minute stream through the range at Nordhorn for a FRA. Air-Traffic Control (ATC) procedures were silent for the CLSP and up to forty-eight aircraft would launch and recover independently. The mass run through Nordhorn for the FRAs lent itself to inter-squadron rivalry on each Wing and became a *de facto* Wing bombing competition, with great interest taken in the scores.

Tornado crews of XV and 16 Squadrons celebrate the end of a station no-notice exercise in early 1986. These exercises were very much part of everyday life in RAFG during the Cold War years. (Andy Heard)

From the engineers' perspective, C. Tech Spanswick thought that exercises 'were hard work but mainly good fun. The hooter would go off at stupid o'clock in the morning for generation exercises and no matter what, you would react and get up to the squadron as fast as you could. The majority of ground crew took it extremely seriously and on arrival at the engineer's office the atmosphere would be buzzing. In my opinion it was to my advantage to get to the squadron as quick as possible to get the best exercise jobs rather than be clobbered for guard duties. My favorite jobs were in the Hit Team Landrovers, where you would be running around fixing faults during crew inspections… et cetera. But I also enjoyed being on the line as part of a HAS team. Fully dressed up in NBC 'goon gear' and sometimes chemical contamination wash suits, doing engine running winch backs and OTR [Operational Turn Around] servicing was exhausting work particularly in the summer, but again the adrenalin rush, the excitement and the desire to achieve the task in the fastest time was immensely satisfying. I also remember the first mass launch at Brüggen of the entire fleet. I was on the end of the runway in a Hit Team Landrover and witnessed fifty-two Tornados, one after another, take off. It looked like pure chaos as jets were lined up everywhere from all four corners of Brüggen and they all seemed to be battling with each other to be able to take off first. It was truly an amazing sight.'

Apart from the almost continuous sequence of station exercises, all crews also were subject to an annual check by the Weapon Standardization Team (WST). The team, based at RAF Wittering, visited each strike unit (including the UK-based Tornado squadrons) to ensure their proficiency in all nuclear weapons procedures. The WST check included practical and oral tests to check that all crews had a good knowledge of all the regulations and procedures pertinent to nuclear weapons. WST was taken extremely seriously and a failure of the WST check would mean an instant posting away to a non-strike station.

A Tornado GR1 of 14 squadron, the last Jaguar unit at Brüggen to re-equip with the Tornado, at low-level during Exercise Blue Moon *in early 1986.*

Flying in Germany

By early 1985 all three Tornado squadrons at Laarbruch were at full strength and had been declared Strike CR. XV Squadron was also declared operational in the attack role and 16 and 20 Squadrons were well on the way to following suit. Although the RAFG squadrons took part in periodic UK exercises such as *Mallet Blow, Elder Forest* and *Priory*, most of the routine flying was in Germany. Low flying down to 500ft was permitted over the whole of the Federal Republic of [West] Germany (FRG), except over major the conurbations, and there were eight LFAs where flying down to 250ft was allowed. Since the RAFG stations were in the northern half of the country (which coincided with the Second Allied Tactical Air Force's [2 ATAF] area of responsibility) and so were six of the eight LFAs, the preference of Tornado crews was naturally to fly in northern Germany. The whole region was full of military targets such as the SAM sites of the Nike and HAWK missile belts, numerous barracks and military facilities, as well as troops and armour deployed on exercise, also bridges, both permanent and temporary. The airspace was also full of 2 ATAF aircraft, from RAFG and from the air forces of the Netherlands, Belgium and Germany as well as the USAF. Additionally there were weapons ranges at Nordhorn, Vliehors (Netherlands) and Helchteren (Belgium) and the EW range at Borgholzhausen (Germany). Low-level 'link routes' across the Netherlands joined the FRG low-flying system to the range at Vliehors and the Belgian Ardennes was also a 250ft LFA. All in all, it was not difficult to put together a challenging 1hr 45min low-level training sortie which typically included two simulated attacks against realistic targets, a run through the EW range, fighter affiliation and a range detail. If the weather precluded the 2 ATAF areas, then Tornado crews might venture south into the 4 ATAF area, although the only 250ft LFA was a relatively small one just to the southwest of Nuremburg. Also weapons range options were

A Tornado GR1 of 31 Squadron over the Irish Sea; 31 Squadron had been the first squadron at Brüggen to receive the Tornado in late 1984. This photograph was taken a few years later at a Missile Practice Camp (MPC) and the aircraft is carrying an AIM-9G Sidewinder on the wing inner stub pylon.

A formation of three Tornado GR1s from 31 Squadron flying over the Aegean Sea on the way to a detachment in Cyprus.

limited, and generally restricted to Siegenburg. Although singleton sorties were not unusual, Tornado GR1 sorties tended to be flown as pairs for routine training and as fourships for exercise tasks.

Night flying on the continent was less useful for Tornado crews, because there was no scope for tactical flying using the TFR. The night flying comprised a small number of fixed routes, which were flown under radar control at around 1,500ft as they had been designed for previous generations of aircraft that were not capable of low flying at night. The 'Night Bene' route followed a clockwise flow around Belgium and the Netherlands to the range at Vliehors and back, while the 'Night Charlie' was anti-clockwise around the north German plain with a run through Nordhorn. Far better quality training could be achieved at night using the UK LFS, which allowed free routing and TFR flying. Such sorties were often flown as a hi-lo-hi profile with a third fuel tank carried on the shoulder pylon. Even with this extra fuel load, however, a 2hr sortie might only provide 20min of low-level flying; a more efficient profile was to fly an afternoon sortie to land away at a UK station and then return via a lo-hi sortie with perhaps an 60min of useful night low flying. Also the UK LFS was used from time to time for daytime flying: German bank holidays tended to be on Thursdays, so it was usual for the RAFG squadrons to deploy at least some aircraft to the UK to ensure that the flying task did not suffer.

Each RAFG squadron also had a quota of Exercise *Lone Ranger* flights, weekend land-aways to more distant destinations such as Gibraltar or Cyprus (and later to military airfields in Spain, Italy, France and Norway). Apart from familiarizing crews with deploying to and operating from unusual airfields, the *Lone Ranger* flights also exercised the procedural instrument rating, which had to be held by all RAFG pilots because of the airspace structure on the continent. Land-aways were also practised as part of the cross-servicing Exercise *Ample Gain*, which was intended to familiarize ground crew at other NATO bases with refuelling and, if necessary, re-arming the Tornado. Exercise *Ample Gain* sorties would usually be integrated into routine low-level training on the continent.

Tornado Weaponry

One detachment undertaken by XV Squadron in the autumn of 1984 was to Decimomannu, in southern Sardinia. Nominally an Italian Air Force base, 'Deci,' as it became known affectionately by generations of RAF personnel, was run quadri-nationally by the Italians, Americans, Germans and British. All four nations used the air-to-ground range at Capo Frasca on the western side of the island as well as the air-to-air ranges further off the western coast. After the visit by XV Squadron, all RAFG Tornado squadrons could expect to spend at least 14 days each year at Deci for their Armament Practice Camp (APC). Although Tornado crews visited air weapons ranges on most sorties, the weaponry was generally restricted to laydown (i.e. over-flying the target), shallow dive or loft passes using the main computer for weapon aiming and was sometimes limited by the weather conditions. At Capo Frasca an excellent weather factor, combined with a lack of distraction from anything other than weaponry and a particularly flexible range, provided the ideal opportunity for intensive weaponry practice, including some of the more esoteric events such as 'reversionary' techniques.

The Tornado was designed to attack small targets accurately by night or in bad weather. The heart of its weapon aiming system was the main computer, which was updated by the

Three Tornado GR1s from 14 Squadron carry out a flat turn onto base leg during recovery to Decimomannu, Sicily at the end of an Armament Practice Camp (APC) sortie. All aircraft carry two Carrier Bomb Light Stores (CBLS) practice bomb carriers on the shoulder pylons. (Mike Lumb)

navigator using the GMR. The prime method of attack was for the navigator to locate the target on his radar and for the aircraft to then follow the main computer commands to achieve an accurate weapon drop. This was a Phase 1 attack; in a Phase 2 or Phase 3 attack, the weapon aiming was by the pilot through the HUD. However, these attacks were prone to errors because of the low sighting angles during a low-level attack and the more practical solution was 'Phase 1½' whereby the pilot corrected any cross-track error by flying the 'bomb fall line' in the HUD visually through the target rather than blindly flying through the centre of the Phase 1 mark. Phase 2/3 was better suited to dive attacks. Attack profiles, using the main computer to carry out all the calculations, were known to crews as a 'full kit' attacks. In this case, the Weapon Release Buttons (WRB) on the top of the stick and in the rear cockpit were 'commit' buttons – that is they allowed the main computer to send a release pulse to the weapon pylon when it had computed the correct release.

In the event of failures in part by the main computer or the stores management system, it was still possible to drop weapons in a reversionary mode. Radar attacks could be carried out using a fixed-range cursor and there was a stand-by bombing sight in the HUD. In reversionary attacks the WRB became a 'pickle' button – that is it sent a release pulse directly to the weapon pylon. With many of the range details at Deci mixing kit and reversionary bombing in the same detail it was not unusual for a crew to forget this small matter and commit during a reversionary attack, only to score a very short bomb. The accuracy of these attacks were very vulnerable to any errors in timing or delivery parameters such as speed, height and dive angle, but even so, experienced crews could, with practice, achieve consistently good results.

The flying at Deci was frenetic: fourships from all four nations using the air-to-ground and air-to-air ranges were taking off and recovering almost continuously throughout each day. The 20min range slots at Frasca ran back-to-back, with a fourship arriving to start its detail as soon as the previous one left the range. Range sorties lasted just 45min or so and usually involved eight bombing passes (using 3kg practice bombs for laydown and shallow dive and 28lb practice bombs for loft, mini-loft and high-angle dive) as well as strafe using the 27mm Mauser cannons. Crews could expect to fly twice a day, and each sortie would be followed by a comprehensive debrief by the squadron's Qualified Weapons Instructors (QWIs) viewing the films of each weapons pass. After a long day it was not unusual for debriefs to continue over a can of beer in the 'Pig & Tapeworm' bar in the accommodation block.

Both aircrew and ground crew enjoyed the detachments to Deci: for Cpl Youngs 'Deci memories are of appalling red wine, awful hangovers and six-man rooms with no air-conditioning, but we loved the place. We worked twenty-four hour shifts from noon 'til noon, which enabled us to get to the beach every other day in the summer: we worked hard and played hard.' C. Tech Spanswick agreed with those sentiments, writing later that 'it honestly felt like a second home. But it was a great detachment. Working conditions were fantastic. We had the famous Deci shifts of twenty-four hours on and twenty-four off. Working on a proper line was also great fun. Eating ice-creams while seeing jets off; joining in the bombing and shooting competitions and "bidding" on aircrew was all part of the fun. We also had

The 'Pig & Tapeworm' bar at Decimomannu – the site of many a post-APC sortie debrief. Each unit left its mark for posterity. (Simon Hadley)

Garvie Island; seen through the HUD during the last seconds of a lay-down bombing pass. The island was one of the very few ranges in Europe where live 1,000lb bombs could be dropped. (JJ Burrows)

A four-ship formation of Tornado GR1s from 31 Squadron. (BAe Heritage)

A Tornado GR1 from 14 Squadron at low-level over Germany: Most of the Federal Republic of Germany was a 500ft low-flying area (LFA), with smaller areas, mainly in the northern half, where flying down to 250ft could be practised. (RAF Museum)

the famous Deci wall and amazing squadron artwork painted in both the APC engineering building and smaller ACMI hut.'

At the opposite end of the spectrum from Deci, both in terms of weather and location, was Garvie Island near Cape Wrath. Flt Lt Delve of IX Squadron described how 'the island some 800ft by 140ft sits off the northwest tip of Scotland like a granite version of the QE2 and is the only range available for live 1,000lb bombing.' In fact Garvie Island was the only European range where live 1,000lb high-explosive bombs could be dropped. Normally each squadron had a small annual allocation of live bombs and corresponding range slots at Garvie. Often the limiting factor in weapons usage was the weather over Cape Wrath. Typically aircraft would stage from their respective base into Lossiemouth or RAF Machrihanish, where they would be loaded with live weapons and then fly directly to Garvie before returning home at medium level.

The Brüggen Wing

While the Laarbruch Wing settled into the RAFG routine, the Brüggen Wing was beginning to form. The first unit, 31 (Designate) Squadron, commanded by Wg Cdr R. Bogg, started to form in September 1984, and even managed a 'guest appearance' in Exercise *Lionheart* that month, albeit rather untactically with unarmed 'clean wing' aircraft. Three months later 17 (Designate) Squadron, commanded by Wg Cdr G. McLeod, was formed, and was followed by 14 (Designate) Squadron in the middle of 1985. The rapid expansion of the Tornado force meant that there was a dearth of experience on the aeroplane, so the more experienced crews

Two Tornado GR1s from IX Squadron in close formation in the traffic pattern at Nellis AFB, Las Vegas, Nevada, during the squadron's deployment for the first participation by Tornado GR1s in Exercise Green Flag. *(Nigel Nickles)*

from the UK-based squadrons were posted into the new RAFG units to bolster them. Wg Cdr Bogg reported that 'an initial batch of NCOs and airmen, many with previous Tornado experience, was able to complete the initial work-up programme before the aircrew arrived. 31 (Designate) Squadron was particularly fortunate to have two pilots and one navigator with a full Tornado tour under their belt.' By late 1985, 14 (Designate) Squadron had also received an injection of Tornado experience in the shape of Flt Lt Hunter, Flt Lt Dolan and Flt Lt Middleton, who had made up the bulk of 617 Squadron's victorious Exercise *Prairie Vortex* team the year before, along with Flt Lt Dugmore, an ex-IX Squadron pilot and Flt Lt D.G. Steer, an ex-27 Squadron navigator. Having been through the motions of starting up a new Tornado squadron before, Flt Lt Steer found it frustrating that in the early days at Brüggen 'there was still a large Jaguar/Hunter mentality which meant, unlike the UK squadrons, the Tornado was not being used to its full potential.' Eventually, as experience was gained on type and there was more input from the UK units, the RAFG squadrons would learn to make full use of the Tornado's formidable capabilities. Initial Tacevals (IT) punctuated the year at Brüggen, as each squadron in turn was declared to SACEUR first in the strike role and then in the attack role. The last unit to be declared strike CR was 14 Squadron, commanded by Wg Cdr J.J. Whitfield, in February 1986.

Training in North America

While RAFG had been busy building up its Tornado squadrons, the Tornado units of Strike Command had also been industrious. At Marham, 27 Squadron learnt that it would be participating in *Prairie Vortex* later in the year, and started to make preparations; meanwhile

A IX Squadron Tornado turning through initials for runway 04 at Nellis AFB on recovery from an Exercise Green Flag *sortie.* (Nigel Nickles)

at Honington, IX Squadron spent the early part of 1985 working up for Exercise *Green Flag.* The work up comprised qualifying all crews in Operational Low Flying (OLF), or low flying down to a minimum height of 100ft, as well as fighter affiliation sorties using RAF Phantoms, Lightnings and Hawks.

Exercise *Green Flag* was a variation on Exercise *Red Flag*, which in turn had been started in the mid-1970s as a result of investigations into losses suffered by the USAF during the Vietnam War. The analysis identified an abnormally high loss rate amongst crews within their first ten sorties. The premise of the Exercise *Red Flag* was that survival prospects for new crews would be dramatically improved if those first few sorties could be flown in a relatively safe environment. Realistic targets such as life-size replicas of Warsaw Pact airfields, industrial sites, SAM sites and armoured columns were built on the large area of the Nellis Ranges in northern Nevada; these target areas were defended by a Soviet-style integrated air-defence system including ground-based missile and gun systems as well as fighters which operated using Warsaw Pact tactics. Perhaps the most important part of the *Flag* exercises was that they also incorporated a comprehensive debriefing system (which later included use of telemetry pods mounted on aircraft) to ensure that everyone was able to learn from the experience. On top of this, Exercise *Green Flag* overlaid an EW campaign onto the scenario; although this detail made little difference to the flying from the aircrew perspective, it did provide EW staff with valuable data to fine tune the most effective programmes for the Skyshadow pod and the radar-warning equipment.

'In terms of engineering requirements,' recalled C. Tech Spanswick, 'Exercise *Red Flag*… or *Green Flag* was somewhere in between the fast but light-hearted Deci detachment and the full on total work of the Goose Bay detachment. Again the jets were not our own but were the same ones used at Goose Bay, so sometimes this could be a problem in engineering terms. Sometimes we would operate Deci shifts at Nellis and most of the time it would work well, but on the odd occasion, because of the work load, we would have to adapt the shift, as working a full twenty-four hours was just no good. Nellis was also unique in the way we had to operate because everything was strictly to the book and more sometimes, to accommodate the American rules, especially when refuelling/defuelling was involved. As long as you had your wits about you it was fine but now and again an engineering incident would upset the Yanks. The other thing of course on the flight line was the dreaded "Red Line." You did not cross the red line to enter the flight line or you would be on the floor with a fully-loaded rifle against your head.'

IX Squadron ferried their aircraft to Nellis AFB via Goose Bay over 19 and 21 February. 'The exercise proper didn't commence until 4 March,' wrote Flt Lt N. Nickles, 'so the opportunity was taken to fly various familiarization sorties, the Grand Canyon being one of the major attractions. During the first week, Sqn Ldr Bruce Chapple gave the assembled crews a Tornado GR1 capability brief. He was accompanied by a large brass alarm clock and he frequently mentioned the importance of timing to the Tornado tactics. A small ripple of applause followed when at the exact moment he finished the brief the alarm clock rang. More was to follow as next day, with Chapple leading the squadron for an attack on one of the TV-scored targets with inert 1,000lb bombs from a loft profile. During the mass debrief, the *Green Flag* leader did his normal introduction and mentioned Chapple's brief and the importance of timing. They then scrolled to TV scored target and lo and behold the first bomb impacted as the last timing digit rolled to zero. I think the Americans were duly impressed… fortunately nobody noticed my bombs were two seconds late. The squadron also took the opportunity to try out some of the TF tactics developed in UK. We soon found out that trying to TF over mountains that were nearly 9,000ft was a bit of a test for the engines, and using reheat in TF was a new experience. The TF liked it but it was bit of a rollercoaster when you got to the top and fell off the other side of a big hill. You had to pay to do that at Disney Land and we got it for free.'

Continuing as the 'lead' Tornado squadrons in Germany, XV and 16 Squadrons also took part in a *Flag* exercise in April 1985. Hosted by the Canadian Armed Forces in the Cold Lake Air Weapons Ranges, Exercise *Maple Flag* replicated the format of the *Red Flag* exercises by borrowing much of the USAF's expertise and equipment Although *Maple Flag* could not quite match the depth of realism in terms of targets and threat simulation, the forested plains of Alberta and Saskatchewan did at least offer a more realistic simulation of Central European terrain than did the mountains and desert of Nevada. XV and 16 Squadron carried out their OLF work-up at Goose Bay in March before crossing Canada to Cold Lake (near Edmonton) for the exercise.

One point of detail about the use of Goose Bay and Cold Lake by Laarbruch squadrons was that the RAFG squadrons were not qualified in AAR. There was no operational need for AAR in the Central Region, so crews were not trained in that discipline. This in turn meant

A pair of Tornado GR1s from IX Squadron overfly the Grand Canyon. (Nigel Nickles)

A Tornado GR1 from 16 Squadron at medium level. (Nigel Nickles)

The burden of flying the 'American training' aircraft across the Atlantic at the start and end of each season fell to UK-based Tornado squadrons. A Tornado GR1 of 27 Squadron accompanies a Victor K2 tanker of 55 Squadron. (Geoffrey Lee/ Plane Focus)

that any ferrying of aircraft across the Atlantic would have to be carried out by UK-based crews. In any case, each squadron flying its own aircraft across to North America would have been a wasteful use of AAR resources; instead eight aircraft, taken from across the Tornado force, were ferried across to Goose Bay early each year by AAR-qualified UK crews for the start of the 'North American Training Season.' The aircraft would then spend the best part of the year in Goose Bay for each squadron to use in turn for their two-week Exercise *Western Vortex* and also to be staged across the USA to Nellis AFB for the '*Flag*' seasons in spring and autumn. Later, when there were seven Tornado squadrons in Germany and only two in the UK, the task of ferrying the aircraft across the Atlantic became a heavy burden for the Marham squadrons to bear; so in 1988 a small number of RAFG crews (normally those with previous AAR experience) were selected for AAR training to let RAFG take its fair share of the ferrying task.

Exercise *Prairie Vortex*

The work-up for 27 Squadron's participation in the 1985 SAC Strategic Bombing Competition closely matched that of the 617 Squadron crews a year earlier. Once again, equivalent 'half missions' were flown in the UK, and this routine continued through the summer for the crews who had been chosen to represent the RAF. The four crews selected were: Sqn Ldr D. Walmesley with Sqn Ldr J. Stone and Sqn Ldr M. Prissick with Sqn Ldr T. Cook as one team and Sqn Ldr B. Holding with Flt Lt J. Plumb and Flt Lt D. Beveridge with Flt Lt A. Bentham

The Devil's Tower in Wyoming makes an impressive backdrop to this 27 Squadron Tornado GR1 during the USAF Strategic Air Command bombing competition in October 1985. (via Benny Bentham)

as the other. Both squadrons at Marham worked together to ensure that the Wing would perform at its very best in the forthcoming competition: in May a party from 617 Squadron visited the US to verify that the details of radar offsets were still accurate and to check on other competition details. In late summer, the Exercise *Prairie Vortex* crews moved to Ellsworth AFB to practise flying the competition profile in theatre.

All the preparation and practice proved invaluable, so that, as Flt Lt Bentham later commented: 'there was no particular excitement to the competition sorties, because by the time we flew them, the whole profile was routine.' Even so, the competition sortie profiles were complex and demanding and it would require a great deal of skill – and a little luck, too, perhaps – to perform well. The Strategic Bombing Competition was held over three weeks in October and each crew flew three missions. The first two 6hr sorties (one by day and one by night) involved both medium- and low-level RBSU bombing in an ECM environment as well as air-to-air refuelling. As in the previous year, timing accuracy was also scored. On the third sortie, which also lasted 6hr, each crew dropped practice weapons against two targets on the Nellis range complex in Nevada. Flt Lt Beveridge and Flt Lt Bentham flew their three competition sorties on 8, 14 and 22 October.

When the competition results were announced at Barkesdale AFB on 14 November, the scores achieved by the 27 Squadron teams were even better than the excellent scores by RAF crews in the previous year. Tornado crews took the first two places in the Curtiss LeMay

Trophy, with the winning crew, Flt Lt Beveridge and Flt Lt Bentham, surpassing Sqn Ldr Dunlop and Flt Lt Middleton's near-perfect 1984 result, with an very impressive 98.8 percent. Apart from bombing extremely accurately, the crew had also achieved an average timing error of just 0.02sec over their sorties. The Tornado teams also took second place in the Mathis Trophy (matching the placing in the previous year) and came first and second in the Meyer Trophy (which marked an improvement on the first and third places in the previous year). Once again the Tornado GR1 had proven itself, in a hard-fought competition, to be an impressively capable ground-attack platform.

Improvements

The beginning of 1986 saw a Tornado GR1 force comprising nine squadrons: three in the UK, three at Laarbruch and three at Brüggen. The six RAFG squadrons all mounted QRA(N) from their respective bases; if one squadron was out of theatre, for example at Deci or Goose Bay, that unit's 'strike line' would be covered by another squadron. The year also saw the completion of a modification programme for the Tornado GR1. Firstly, Laser Ranger and Marked Target Receiver (LRMTS) equipment was fitted into a chisel-shaped fairing under the nose. This equipment gave the aircraft an extremely accurate ranging sensor for normal attacks and, separately, it also gave the aircraft the capability to lock

Dave Beveridge and Benny Bentham improved on the almost perfect score achieved the previous year by Pete Dunlop and Dick Middleton to become the outright winners of the Curtiss LeMay Trophy in 1985. (Benny Bentham)

An AIM-9G Sidewinder missile is fired from a Tornado GR1 of 20 Squadron on the range at RAE Aberporth. The Sidewinder was a heat-seeking missile, and was fired at a flare towed behind a Jindivik target drone. (Geoffrey Lee/ Plane Focus)

onto targets that were being illuminated by a ground-based laser designator. Secondly, the BOZ107 chaff and flare dispenser became available. Previously the aircraft had been flown either with no EW equipment, or with a 'live' Skyshadow pod on one wing and a dummy pod on the other. The arrival of the BOZ107 pod gave the aircraft a more robust EW capability and it became the standard fit to carry a Skyshadow pod on the port outer wing pylon and a BOZ107 pod on the starboard. Later in 1986, stub pylons were fitted on the inboard sides of the inner wing pylons, to carry AIM-9 Sidewinder air-to-air missiles.

In Germany, the aircraft were also re-engined with the Turbo-Union RB199-103, which gave slightly more thrust than the previous RB199-101 engines (which remained in the UK-based aircraft); additionally, a Marconi-manufactured Radar Homing and Warning Receiver (RHWR) was fitted in RAFG aircraft. The UK Tornados were fitted with an Electronica manufactured Radar Warning Receiver (RWR), which required considerable interpretation from the crew. In the RHWR, the interpretation was largely done by computer software: the screen indicated the direction of emitters and identified them, while an audio alarm alerted the crew to the presence of threats.

Information collected from nine Tornado squadrons also meant that there was now enough data on the performance of the TFR system to expand the flight envelope and crews were authorized to fly auto-TF in peacetime down to 400ft by day and 500ft by night. With a comprehensive EW self-protection suite and a credible air-to-air capability, the Tornado GR1 had, four years after its entry into front-line service, finally reached operational maturity.

A Tornado GR1 flown by a 16 Squadron crew on the range complex at Nellis AFB during an Exercise Red Flag *sortie. One of the problems of flying at ultra-low level over the desert was that the position of the aircraft was given away by its shadow. (Andy Heard)*

The arrival of IX Squadron in October 1986 completed the Brüggen Wing, which now comprised IX, 14, 17 and 31 Squadrons, each of which is represented in this photograph. (Rick Brewell)

Cold War Routine

Throughout 1986 the Tornado GR.1 squadrons settled into the Cold War routine. All were cycled through Goose Bay for auto-TF flying and, for those units earmarked to take part in *Flag* exercises, there was OLF. In fact OLF was not routinely permitted and was tightly controlled by RAFG or Strike Command: authorization was only granted specifically for *Flag* exercises and the work up period. During the year Goose Bay saw 17 Squadron in May, IX Squadron in early June, 617 Squadron in late June/early July, 27 Squadron later in July, 16 Squadron in August, and 20 Squadron in September. There was another visit from 17 Squadron in October for their work-up for *Red Flag* the following month. Both 20 and 31 Squadrons from RAFG and 617 Squadron from the UK had participated in *Green Flag* earlier in the spring. Although these squadrons carried out the bulk of the OLF qualification at Goose Bay, they had also detached to Leuchars to use the Tactical Training Area (TTA) in the Scottish borders, as well as the EW range at Spadeadam; also the fighters based at Leuchars ensured that they had practised the complexity of the missions that they might expect to encounter on the Nellis ranges.

The rear engine of a Lockheed TriStar tanker looks very close in this view from the back seat of a Tornado GR1 from 617 Squadron as it refuels.
(617 Squadron)

Deci saw a succession of the RAFG squadrons pass through: XV Squadron held its APC in February, 17 Squadron in March, 16 Squadron in April, 14 Squadron in May, 20 Squadron in June, and 31 Squadron in September. Tornados from all squadrons also took a full part, often flying four-ship formations in the various UK exercises, such as *Mallet Blow* (17, 20 and 617 Squadrons in April, 14, XV, 17, 20, 31 and 617 Squadrons in August and 16 and 617 Squadrons in October), and *Elder Forest* (14 and 20 Squadrons in April). Although some of these missions by RAFG squadrons were flown as hi-lo-hi sorties, most were flown as hi-lo sorties into UK airfields, to turn around and fly a second lo-hi sortie on the return home. Not all squadrons participated in all such exercises because there were always squadrons out of theatre in places like Goose Bay and Deci. In Europe, Exercise *Central Enterprise* took place, as it did annually, in June, with participation from most of the RAFG units as well as both squadrons from Marham. From the aircrew perspective, this exercise did not offer quite the same exciting 250ft flying as the UK exercises, but it did provide valuable experience in planning and flying as part of large 'packages' of aircraft.

The End of QRA

One of the most important developments of the Cold War took place in October 1986 when, as a result of the US-Soviet talks in Reykjavik, it was announced that QRA(N) would be suspended from the end of the month. For the RAFG Tornado personnel, this was bittersweet news: for while QRA was undoubtedly an extremely tedious and very unpopular duty, it was also one of great responsibility and importance, and it gave a real sense of perspective to the frontline of the Cold War.

Perhaps the next most important development at Brüggen in October 1986 was the arrival of IX Squadron from Honington to become the fourth squadron in the Brüggen Wing. The previous experience at Brüggen had been of new squadrons forming, but the arrival of the longest-formed and most experienced Tornado squadron was an entirely different prospect and Wg Cdr A. Ferguson, OC IX Squadron decided that his unit would make its mark right from the start. The squadron formally arrived at Brüggen on 1 October in an immaculate Diamond Nine formation. Wg Cdr Ferguson also decided that IX Squadron would 'gate-crash' the annual RAFG inter-squadron competition, the Salmond Trophy. 'The squadron was initially not allowed to take part,' recalled Flt Lt P.J.D. Lenihan a IX Squadron navigator, 'but Alfie Ferguson (the Boss) made such a fuss with Senior Air Staff Officer (SASO) at HQ RAFG that we were allowed to take part; he then bet every squadron commander that IX Squadron would win it and promised case of champagne to each if he lost. Afterwards he came to us and said "right you b*****s, this is what I've done and it's going to cost me a bloody fortune if we lose." We wiped the floor with RAFG squadrons and made a huge thing about it.' IX Squadron certainly made its mark – the only consolation to the other squadrons at Brüggen was that the victorious newcomers hastily printed T-shirts claimed that they had won the 'Salmon Trophy.'

Meanwhile in November, 617 Squadron deployed to Oman for Exercise *Saif Sareea* (Swift Sword) – the largest combined exercise staged by Britain since the Falklands conflict. The aim was to practise the ability to respond rapidly to a crisis outside the NATO area and the UK participation involved some 5,000 personnel, elements of 5 Airborne Brigade, 3 Commando Brigade and a Royal Navy task group. The Tornados flew directly to Masirah, refuelling

An AIM-9G Sidewinder missile leaves the wing of a Tornado GR1 from XV Squadron. (Geoffrey Lee/ Plane Focus)

Another Tornado GR1 from XV Squadron firing an AIM-9G Sidewinder missile. Operationally the aircraft would be equipped with the more modern AIM-9L version, which had a head-on capability. (Geoffrey Lee/ Plane Focus)

A Tornado GR1 of 14 Squadron airborne from Deci for a sortie on the ACMI range. The aircraft is being flown without under-wing fuel tanks or ECM pods to provide a more agile performance. (Andy Jeremy)

A Tornado GR1 from 16 Squadron flown by a 31 Squadron crew at low level over the Labrador training area around Goose Bay. (31 Squadron)

en-route from Lockheed TriStar tankers, which also carried the ground crew. During the exercise 617 Squadron worked closely with the Sultan of Oman's Air Force.

Air-to-Air Developments

From mid-1986, the 'standard training fit' for the Tornado GR1 day-to-day low-level flying included an AIM-9L Sidewinder acquisition round. In wartime the aircraft were expected to carry to Sidewinder air-to-air missiles, one on each inboard stub pylon and the acquisition round (basically a seeker head without the rest of the missile body) gave crews the chance to get familiar with using the missile and practising missile tactics. The AIM-9L version of the missile had a head-on capability and it provided the aircraft with an effective form of self-defence. Apart from working with acquisition rounds, Tornado GR1 crews also had the opportunity to fire live missiles against target drones on the RAE Aberporth range on Cardigan Bay. A number of AIM-9G missiles (an older version without a head-on capability) were coming towards the end of their shelf life and were made available, so that each squadron might expect to have an allocation of some six missiles to fire every couple of years. The first Tornado Missile Practice Camp (MPC) was by 20 Squadron in June 1987. They were followed by 14 and IX Squadrons over the summer and by 16 Squadron in the autumn. Like the ACMI, the priority for the Strike Command Air-to-Air Missile Establishment (STCAAME) at RAF Valley was the air-defence units, but even so all the Tornado GR1 squadrons managed to find slots on the range to fire their allocation of missiles.

In January 1987, RAFG squadrons took another step forward with their training as the first detachment by a Tornado squadron to use the Air Combat Manoeuvring Instrumentation

A Tornado GR1 from 27 Squadron. (Geoffrey Lee/ Plane Focus)

(ACMI) Range at Deci. ACMI comprised an air-to-air range off the western coast of Sardinia equipped with a full telemetry system, which tracked data-link pods carried on each aircraft within the range. An ACMI pod was carried on one missile pylon and an AIM-9L acquisition round on the other pylon. Apart from giving the capability to watch each engagement in real time and to assess 'kills' accurately, the system enabled a full debriefing to be carried out after each sortie, so that all the participants could learn from their experience on the range. During a debriefing each engagement could be replayed – and paused at any time – to give a 'God's eye' view of the engagement, or the view from any of the aircraft cockpits. When Tornado squadrons tired of fighting their own kind, the other units visiting Deci – from all four nations as well as the occasional 'guest' air forces, such as the French – were an enthusiastic source of opponents for Dissimilar Air Combat (DACT). The first unit to use the ACMI was 14 Squadron, for a two-week period in January. They were accompanied by a small detachment of Harriers from 3 Squadron to provide some DACT opposition. Thereafter RAFG squadrons could expect two detachments to Deci each year: a fortnight of APC and another fortnight of ACMI.

The Routine Continues

The last years of the 1980s followed the established pattern; a training season starting in Nellis AFB with Exercise *Green Flag* in March and April (XV, 16 and 617 Squadrons in 1987 and 20 and 31 Squadrons in 1988) continuing with the summer months in Goose Bay for each squadron's Exercise *Western Vortex* and then back to Nellis for Exercise *Red Flag* in October and November (14 and IX Squadrons in 1987 and XV, 16 and 17 Squadrons in 1988). The summer months at Deci were filled continuously with APC detachments by RAFG squadrons,

A salvo of eight inert free-fall 1,000lb bombs leave a IX Squadron Tornado GR1 during a loft attack on the range at RAF Cowden. (via Trevor Burbidge)

and, since the air-defence squadrons understandably took precedence in these months on the ACMI range, the annual ACMI detachments for Tornado GR1 units generally took place in autumn or late winter.

The usual diet of exercises and detachments was also interspersed with other visits, some of which were anticipated more eagerly than others. NATO squadron exchanges usually proved to be enjoyable social occasions. Most squadrons could expect an exchange during the course of the year and these might be simultaneous detachments, with both units sending an 'away team' to the partner squadron while the 'home team' hosted the visitors, or they might take place sequentially with one unit deploying *en masse* one week and then hosting a return visit later. There was a wide variety to be enjoyed, for example during 1988 IX Squadron exchanged with a Royal Danish Air Force (RDAF) F-16 Fighting Falcon squadron at Aalborg, 14 Squadron with a Hellenic Air Force F-4 Phantom squadron at Andravida, 17 Squadron with a Turkish Air Force (TAF) F-104 Starfighter squadron at Balikesir, 31 Squadron with a CAF CF-18 Hornet squadron at Baden-Solingen and 617 Squadron with a Armée de l'Air (French Air Force) Mirage 2000 squadron at Nancy. Apart from the social scene, the exchanges were a very useful way to help foster a spirit of co-operation between NATO forces and for each nation to gain an understanding of how the others operated. This in turn made it easier for the air forces of the different countries to operate together effectively, when the time came to do so.

However, if the squadron exchanges were viewed with some excitement, the periodic visit by the Tornado Standardization Unit (TSU) was not so enthusiastically welcomed. Drawn from experienced staff members from TWCU, the remit of the TSU was to visit every squadron to check that both pure and tactical flying were up to standard. TSU visits tended to come around once every two years and during the visit every pilot could expect to fly a formal QFI check with the Central Flying School (CFS) agent and most crews would also fly a routine training sortie, which would be formally assessed by a TSU crew. Although TSU visits were not popular amongst squadron crews, they were a vital in ensuring that the flying standards on the frontline remained at a good, high standard and that crews from different squadrons could work together using the same tactics and procedures.

Tactics

Unfortunately despite the efforts of the TSU, there was a tendency towards non-uniformity across the Tornado Force: for although each squadron had been formed with some Tornado experienced crews, there had also been a large influx of crews with experience – and pre-conceptions – from other aircraft types. Additionally each station, particularly in RAFG where the Tornado squadrons had replaced their former Buccaneer or Jaguar entities *in situ*, brought its own strong tradition of how things should be done. Thus the Marham Wing, the Laarbruch

The Brüggen Wing in 1987 – station commander John Houghton in front of the aircrew and aircraft which formed the most potent strike/attack wing in the RAF. (Terry Fincher/thefincherfiles)

The Laarbruch Wing in 1989 – provides an idea of the number of staff and the facilities needed to support a wing of Tornado GR1 aircraft. (via Tom Boyle)

Wing and the Brüggen Wing had all developed in slightly different directions and each one regarded the other two with some disdain and a little suspicion. Even at Brüggen there was a palpable sense of frustration among the senior station executives that the four Tornado squadrons did not work together in the same seamless way that the Brüggen Jaguar Wing had done. To address this shortcoming, the station commander, Gp Capt R.H. Goodall, initiated a series of 'wing interoperability' sorties, usually four-versus-one evasion sorties, with crews from across all four squadrons; he also instituted a number of short 'exchanges' where crews from one unit would spend a week flying with another. Apart from diversity of tactical opinion, the Tornado force also faced the problem of relative inexperience amongst the high proportion of newly-qualified aircrew. For example at the end of 1989, around half of the crews on 17 Squadron were first tourists and around one third of the squadron aircrews were technically 'dilutees' with less than 400hrs on the aircraft. These figures were typical of most squadrons. In fact this problem was largely solved in time through natural 'cross pollination' as first-tourist crews gained experience and were posted to other Tornado squadrons.

One tactical dilemma that troubled many Tornado crews was how best to employ the JP233 runway denial weapon, which was the main armament for use against Option Alpha targets. The weapon had been conceived in the late 1970s as a means of neutralizing concrete runways. The problem with attacking runways from low level was that conventional bombs hit the ground at a very shallow glancing angle so that when they made a hole it was wide and shallow – and, critically, it could easily be filled in by specialist runway repair teams. The

A close up of the Infra-Red Reconnaissance System (TIRRS) showing the under-fuselage aperture for the Infra-Red Line Scanner (IRLS) and the side window for the Sideways Looking Infra-Red (SLIR) sensors. Until the TIRRS became fully operational the aircraft were issued to strike/attack units. The aircraft carries the markings of 20 Squadron. (BAe Heritage)

idea behind JP233 was to drop large numbers of small cratering munitions (SG357), which would create a number of deep holes and cause 'heave' distortion to the concrete, which would be difficult to repair; a large number of anti-personnel mines (HB876) would also be scattered across the area to handicap the runway repair teams. The theory was sound, but in practice the idea of flying exactly down a runway centreline at 200ft and 450kt (lower or faster and the SG357 would hit the concrete at the wrong angle) seemed tantamount to lunacy: any aircraft carrying out such a manoeuvre would be an easy target for the airfield defences. There was the added problem that any cross-track error would mean that the SG357s missed the runway altogether and would land harmlessly on the bordering grass. Thus there were severe tactical problems with actually using JP233. The general consensus was that the weapon should be used with the shortest selectable stick-length and aimed diagonally across runways and taxiways, with the aim of cutting off access and dividing them into lengths that were too small to be useable. Furthermore, the general view was that an attack speed of at least 540kt would be best.

Tornado Reconnaissance

From the outset, the MRCA project had included a tactical reconnaissance capability and, indeed, the early Con Ops confirmed the intention for two Tornado reconnaissance squadrons in the RAF Order of Battle. Unlike the previous generation of tactical reconnaissance aircraft in RAF service, the Phantom and Jaguar, which carried a reconnaissance pod under the aircraft, the Tornado system was an integral part of the aeroplane. The Tornado Infra-Red Reconnaissance System (TIRRS) was mounted in the space occupied originally in the strike version by the ammunition bay – and for this reason the guns were not fitted to the reconnaissance version. In this configuration, the aircraft was designated the 'Tornado GR1A.' The TIRRS comprised an Infra-Red Line Scanner (IRLS) which 'looked' downwards through an aperture in a small blister under the forward fuselage and two Sideways Looking Infra-Red (SLIR) sensors, which 'looked' through windows on either side of the fuselage. The output from the three sensors was then combined to produce a continuous horizon-to-horizon scan. The imagery was recorded onto two videotapes, one of which recorded the entire flight for post-flight analysis in the Reconnaissance Interpretation Centre (RIC), and the other could be accessed, played back and analysed by the navigator during the flight.

The first Tornado GR1As were modified strike aircraft and, since development of the TIRRS was running somewhat late, the aircraft were initially re-issued to strike/attack squadrons. This short-term arrangement ended in September 1988 when they were all issued to the first Tornado reconnaissance squadron: II Squadron formed that month at Laarbruch under the command of Wg Cdr A. Threadgould. Even so, it was not until July 1989 that the TIRRS was fitted in the aircraft. In September 1989, Flt Lt K.G. Noble and

A Tornado GR1A of II Squadron banks away over northern Germany. Based at Laarbruch, it was the first of the reconnaissance squadrons to convert to the Tornado. (BAe Heritage)

A Tornado GR1A in the markings of II Squadron. (II Squadron)

Flt Lt D. Ledward were able to put the TIRRS through its paces when they followed a trial drop of a JP233 by the TOEU at West Freugh, to see what the TIRRS could record. 'The powers that be wanted a pass over the "runway" test strip shortly after the after drop – twenty-two seconds as it turned out,' recalled Flt Lt Noble, 'then every minute alternating between overhead to capture the image on the IRLS and a stand-off to capture it on the SLIRs. This of course needed pretty tight turning (5g) and loads of burner, so pretty low on gas but we "committed" to West Freugh and landed with not much left after eleven passes.' The second reconnaissance squadron, 13 Squadron, started to form at Honington during 1989: this time, however, the aircraft were fully TIRRS-equipped purpose-built Tornado GR1As, rather than converted Tornado GR1s.

Accidents

The Tornado GR1 enjoyed a relatively good safety record by the standards of the day. One recurring theme, however, was that of mid-air collisions and there was at least one involving a Tornado GR1 in each of the years from 1985 to 1989. Only one of these was between members of the same formation (an attempted join up into night close formation in 1986) and the fact that the rest were random occurrences is a reflection on the intensity of low-level flying particularly in the UK but also on the continent at that period. In 1985, a Tornado GR1 (ZA408) of 45 Squadron from TWCU collided with Jaguar GR.1 (XZ393), from 54 Squadron at RAF Coltishall, off the coast near Sheringham, Norfolk (both crews ejected successfully). Two years later, a Tornado from 20 Squadron collided with Jaguar GR.1A (XZ116) from 41 Squadron near Keswick in the Lake District; sadly the Jaguar pilot (Flt Lt A.S. Mannheim) was killed. In 1988, two Tornado crews (Flt Lt J.N.S. Watts and Lt U. Sayer (GAF) from TTTE and Flt Lt C.D. Oliver and Flt Lt A.D. Cook from 617 Squadron) were killed in an almost head-on collision near Appleby, North Yorkshire while simultaneously and separately using the UK night LFS for auto-TF flying. As a result of this accident, a more proscriptive flow

After concerns about the habitability of the front cockpit without a canopy – in the event of an ejection from the rear cockpit – BAe test pilot Keith Hartley carried out trials of the 'open-top tourer' version in July 1988. (BAe Heritage)

system and a 'slot' system (whereby units had exclusive use of the LFA during their allocated time) were introduced into the night LFS. The only mid-air collision in the continental LFS was during the Mineval at Brüggen in January 1989: Flt Lt M.P. Smith and Flt Lt A.G. Grieve from 14 Squadron were killed when their Tornado hit an Alphajet of the GAF over northern Germany.

Exercises Again

The Brüggen Mineval in 1989 was a precursor to the Taceval, which took place in March. In fact all three Tornado GR1 stations had their Tacevals during the year: Marham in May and Laarbruch in November, so all stations were busy with work-up exercises through the year. Early in the year, 14 and 617 Squadrons both participated in Exercise *Red Flag*, before the aircraft moved to Cold Lake for IX Squadron to fly in Exercise *Maple Flag* during May. Over the summer months both Goose Bay and Deci were visited by all of the Tornado squadrons, for the UK squadrons had also started to use Deci for APC. In April, both 31 and 617 Squadrons took part in the annual French Exercise *Datex*, which involved low flying (250ft) in France and land-aways at Nancy-Ochey. Two months later, the annual Exercise *Central Enterprise* saw all four Brüggen squadrons flying eight-ship missions, as well as participation by 617 Squadron.

Against the backdrop of a busy year for the Tornado squadrons, it was apparent that political cracks were forming across Eastern Europe and, on 10 November 1989 the Berlin Wall was breached. It was undoubtedly a high note on which to end the year and the decade – but it instantly brought into question the future of British forces in Germany and, therefore, the bulk of the Tornado GR1 force.

With the exception of 617 Squadron, all of the Tornado GR1 squadrons celebrated their 75th Anniversaries in 1990. Each unit marked the occasion with a special paint scheme on one of their aircraft: here the 'Anniversary Jet' of 17 Squadron is flying past a Schloss (Castle) in southern Germany. (Chris Stradling)

3

1990-1991
Cold War
to Hot War

After the Cold War

With the formation of 13 Squadron, commanded by Wg Cdr G.L. Torpy, at Honington on 1 January 1990 the strength of the Tornado GR1 force peaked at eleven front-line squadrons, plus an OCU 'reserve squadron.' Four squadrons were based in the UK: 27 and 617 Squadrons at Marham and 13 and 45(R) (TWCU) Squadrons at Honington. Eight squadrons were based in Germany: 2, XV, 16 and 20 Squadrons at Laarbruch and IX, 14, 17 and 31 Squadrons at Brüggen. Although the Cold War was effectively over, the Tornado squadrons continued the routine that had been established over the previous years. The daily flying would reflect the requirements of the annual training syllabus that each crew had to complete, and would also include work-up training for newly-arrived crews, or, for more experienced crews, work-ups to become pairs or fours leaders. Within each year, each squadron could also expect detachments to Deci for APC and ACMI and a deployment to Goose Bay for auto-TF flying or OLF. Land-aways for Exercises *Eastern Vortex*, *Ample Gain* or *Lone Ranger* would be woven into the flying programme, as would participation in periodic exercises like *Mallet Blow*, *Priory* or *Central Enterprise*. The high point of anyone's tour was for the squadron to be given a slot on Exercise *Red Flag*, and that might be expected every two years or so.

However, the driving force behind everything was still Taceval. The regime of Minevals and Maxevals continued, with each station calling exercises almost monthly, but the Cold War scenario began to ring hollow when the Warsaw Pact was so clearly disintegrating. It was difficult for personnel to believe in the reality of Option Alpha followed by two days of on-call tasking, against the backdrop of a rising FGL and culminating in a CLSP mass launch in NBC conditions on the third day. In one Mineval at Brüggen the exercise planners gave vent to everyone's frustration by inventing a scenario that started with a pre-emptive strike

The final Tornado GR1 unit to form was 13 Squadron, which reformed as a reconnaissance squadron equipped with Tornado GR1A at Honington. (Geoffrey Lee/ Plane Focus)

Dick Downs poses next to a 'zap' profile of an F-117 Nighthawk stealth fighter; this had been painted on the tail of his aircraft after he made an emergency diversion to Tonopah test airfield on the Nellis ranges during an Exercise Red Flag *sortie on the day before the US government officially admitted the existence of the F-117 project.*

A Brüggen-base Tornado GR1 practises Air-to-Air Refueling (AAR) with a VC10 tanker: until the crisis in the Gulf the RAFG squadrons had no requirement for AAR and a hasty conversion was needed for all crews. (Tim Marsh)

and ended with 1st (British) Corps advancing across western Poland beyond the range of Brüggen's aircraft. It was apparent even at squadron level that political backing for the status quo was beginning to evaporate: low flying below 1,000ft would be banned over Germany from September and western European governments were clamouring for savings in their defence budgets to deliver them a 'peace dividend.'

For the RAF's Tornado squadrons, the year started much like any other. In March, XV Squadron delivered the aircraft earmarked for the year's North American training, routing via Lajes and Bermuda. This was the first time that the aircraft had been deployed by RAFG crews, rather than UK crews, as had been the case in previous years. The aircraft were then used for *Red Flags* by XV and also 31 Squadrons before moving to Goose Bay for the usual summer run of *Western Vortex* beginning with IX Squadron. Meanwhile other squadrons had begun to cycle through Deci. Then, in July, when 14 Squadron was busy with APC at Deci, 617 Squadron was carrying out an OLF work-up from Eielson AFB, near Fairbanks, Alaska and most of the other squadrons were involved with Exercise *Mallet Blow*, the UK government published the White Paper '*Options for Change*'. Amongst other cuts, this document announced the halving of RAFG's Tornado force by disbanding the three Tornado strike/attack squadrons at Laarbruch the following year and redeploying II Squadron to Marham. In comparison to this dramatic news, the story that Iraq had complained that Kuwaiti was 'slant drilling' into the Rumaylah oilfield hardly registered with the personnel of RAF Tornado squadrons.

Tornado GR1s of 16 Squadron in close formation. The tail of the all-black 75th Anniversary aircraft can be seen in the lead position.(Mal Craghill)

Kuwait

But while most eyes were still on the developments in the central region of Europe, tension was rising fast in the Middle East. On 2 August, Iraq invaded Kuwait and suddenly the world's focus shifted, belatedly, to the Persian Gulf. The UK response, nicknamed Operation *Granby*, was swift: a squadron of Tornado F3 interceptors deployed to the Royal Saudi Air Force (RSAF) base at Dhahran on 10 August and a another squadron of Jaguar GR1 aircraft arrived in Oman two days later.

At the same time it was decided (although the official announcement was not made until 23 August) that a squadron of Tornado GR1s would also deploy to the Gulf region. These were to come from Brüggen, but the crisis had broken over the summer leave period so there was no complete squadron with enough experienced CR crews available as a single unit. The designated the lead unit was 14 Squadron and the commanding officer Wg Cdr R.V. Morris, was appointed to be the detachment commander. Twelve crews were required, of which 14 Squadron could provide five-and-a-half crews, with the remainder coming from the most experienced crews across the Wing. A hasty work-up was initiated, primarily in order to get all twelve crews qualified in AAR. The first conversion sorties started on 8 August with Flt Lt M.J. Murtagh as only the AAR instructor in 14 Squadron. His first trainee was Flt Lt S.H. Cockram and because of a shortage of dual-control training aircraft their first mission was in a 'strike' aircraft (i.e. with no controls in the rear cockpit). Flt Lt Cockram recalled that 'Murts was our only AAR instructor (as his previous tour had been on 27 Squadron). I recall he was

Nige Cookson and John Hogg crew into their Tornado GR1 on the 14 Squadron HAS site at Brüggen for the initial deployment to Bahrain. (Dougie Roxburgh)

simply superb and always made me at ease when moving around and towards the tanker, but the TriStar (my first sortie) was awful (long hose, low wing, poor perspective and only taking fuel off the centre hose so no ability to refuel two aircraft at a time). The Victor on the other hand had a shorter hose; a high wing and wing pods as well as fuselage, so it was much more flexible.' Cockram himself was almost immediately signed off as an AAR instructor and by the time he had finished his own conversion he had already cleared another four pilots on the tanker.

Another AAR instructor pressed into service quickly was Sqn Ldr G.C.A. Buckley, a flight commander on XV Squadron. 'One day I was leading a fourship of Tornados on a low-level training sortie,' remembered Sqn Ldr Buckley, 'when a call on the emergency frequency was broadcast for my formation to recover to RAF Brüggen. This was quite extraordinary and when we landed at Brüggen the reason was made clear... I was an AAR instructor from my days as an instructor at the TWCU and on that day I was the only qualified AAR instructor in RAF Germany, therefore quite an important asset for the AAR training of RAFG crews. I was ordered to conduct an AAR sortie with another pilot in a two-seater Tornado and qualify him as an instructor. We were then to each fly another sortie with another pilot and qualify those pilots. In this way there would be four AAR instructors in RAF Germany and the whole of the Tornado force could be trained in AAR techniques. Therefore, on that day I flew four Tornado sorties before returning home to Laarbruch by car, shattered.' In this way all the crews were swiftly AAR qualified and were ready to deploy to the Middle East by 25 August AAR and combat ready.

Meanwhile engineers Brüggen had prepared twelve Tornados for deployment to the Gulf region, including painting them in a 'desert pink' camouflage scheme. All twelve aircraft, led by

Ramp space for the Tornado GR1s at Muharraq airport, Bahrain was located in the maintenance area of Gulf Air. (Mike Lumb)

Flt Lt Cockram and Wg Cdr Morris, left Brüggen for Akrotiri on 27 August in three fourships, each supported by a tanker. The following day, pausing only to incur the displeasure of the station commander at Akrotiri by delivering a rousing 'beat up' as they left, they continued to Bahrain. Here they were based at Muharraq under the command of Gp Capt R.H. Goodall AFC, who had previously been station commander at Brüggen. The Brüggen crews were joined by another twelve crews and six aircraft from Marham. Almost immediately four aircraft were loaded with JP233 and held at readiness to attack airfields in Kuwait.

In-theatre training began straight away: extensive use was made of low-flying areas in Saudi Arabia and Oman as well as the King Fahd range (just to the south of Dhahran) and the Qarin range on Masirah. The crews also familiarized themselves with flying the aircraft at heavy weights, loaded with two JP233 canisters, the new larger 2,250-litre fuel tanks and two AIM9L Sidewinder missiles. However carriage limitations for live weapons (they were designed to be carried once and dropped, rather than flown repeatedly) meant that each crew got only a limited exposure; the heavier weights were later simulated by carrying two 1,500-litre drop tanks under the fuselage in place of weapons. The heavy-weight flying was not without incident: on 28 October Flt Lt T.J. Marsh and Flt Lt K.A. Smith suffered an engine failure while flying with two JP233 and discovered that they needed to use reheat on the other engine during the landing. To an extent the training carried out in Nevada, involving operational low flying over desert, was a good preparation for low flying in the Gulf region and crews were soon very comfortable at flying operational heights. Evasion training was provided by RAF Tornado F3 aircraft as well as USAF F-15 Eagles and Jaguars from the Omani Air Force. Crews also practised night flying, using the TFR. Previously they had been

Bahrain-based Tornado GR1s flying with live JP233 weapons. Although the JP233 was the principal anti-runway weapon and would have been employed for 'Option Alpha' in the event of war in Central Europe, Tornado crews had never actually flown with the weapons loaded to the aircraft. (Mike Lumb)

A pair of Tornado GR1s at low-level over the Arabian desert. The aircraft are fitted with 2,250-litre under-wing fuel tanks, which gave an extra 15 minutes of low-level flying time. (Mike Lumb)

restricted by peacetime rules to 500ft, but they were now authorized to the lowest selectable height of 200ft. It was during this practice that it was discovered that, rather worryingly, the TFR could not consistently detect some types of sand.

While flying practice continued apace, plans were being drawn up for the increasingly inevitable war. Wg Cdr Morris with Flt Lt Cockram, Flt Lt N.T. Cookson (from 14 Squadron) and Flt Lt L. Fisher (from IX Squadron) were frequent visitors to both the aircraft carrier USS *J.F. Kennedy* and the nearby Bahraini airbase at Sheikh Isa. The latter was home to a USMC Air Wing and the Wild Weasel units from Spangdahlem. Here they planned the initial stages of the air campaign, which would follow the declaration of hostilities. As one of the few assets with an anti-runway weapon, the RAF Tornados were tasked against Iraqi airfields. In the case of the Muharraq-based aircraft the target would be Tallil airfield, to the southwest of An Nasirah on the Euphrates. Rather than a near suicidal run along each runway, the plan was to fly across the airfields, using the JP233 to 'bottle up' the Iraqi aircraft by cutting off the taxiway access from the HAS sites and create minimum operating strips which would be too short for the Iraqi aircraft to use.

Apart from their 'in-house' work-up sorties, the Tornados participated in a number of exercises including Exercise *Shifting Sands*, working with UK forces in the UAE, on 21 October and the huge Exercise *Imminent Thunder* in Saudi Arabia on 15 and 16 November. The latter exercise involved over 1,000 aircraft, as well as naval and ground forces, from the Coalition that had formed in the Gulf over the previous two months. On the two nights of the exercise, eight-ship formations of Tornados from Bahrain were tasked to simulate JP233 attacks against the airfield at King Khalid Military City.

During the autumn of 1990, Tornado GR1 crews at Bahrain concentrated on perfecting their proficiency in flying at ultra-low level, in case they were called on to operate over Iraq in daytime. (Mike Lumb)

The exercise was intended as a 'final warning' to the Iraqis that the Coalition meant business and was also an opportunity for the Coalition forces to practise working together *en masse*.

Meanwhile in the UK and Germany

Posted from Laarbruch to be the weapons leader on 14 Squadron, Sqn Ldr C.J. Coulls arrived at Brüggen in October 'to find a fragmented organization consisting mainly of new crews who were yet to complete a combat-ready workup and were in no way equipped to deploy. The remnants of IX Squadron and 14 Squadron had been amalgamated into a single entity, which had been (much to the disgust of OC IX, who had been left holding the fort) predictably renamed as "11-and-a-half Squadron." This was a frustrating period for all of us; the first-tourists were naturally anxious to get on with their conversion to the frontline and the award of the all-important combat-ready status, and the more experienced were champing at the bit to get involved in the real business that was developing in the Gulf. There were very few aircraft available to us to keep things ticking along and news from Bahrain was sparse; all in all, a deeply unsatisfactory state of affairs.'

Preparations were being made for a more permanent arrangement at Bahrain to replace the Brüggen-based crews who had flown out in August at relatively short notice. Responsibility for this was given to XV Squadron under command of Wg Cdr J. Broadbent. At the same time, the other Laarbruch squadrons were earmarked for deployment to the Royal Saudi Air Force (RSAF) base at Tabuk, in north-western Saudi Arabia. Across the Tornado force that autumn, there was a frantic work-up as the RAFG squadrons hastily carried out AAR conversions and both RAFG and UK squadrons ensured that their CR crews were qualified

A Tornado GR1 at low-level over the Persian Gulf during a training sortie from Bahrain. (Chris Stradling)

Two ALARM missiles carried under the fuselage of a Tornado GR1 on a training sortie over northern Germany. A small cadre of crews had trained with the missile before deploying to Saudi Arabia, but most of the operational work up for ALARM crews was carried out in theatre. (via Pete Batson)

in OLF and were well-practised in weaponry and fighter evasion tactics. Most squadrons also took the opportunity to divide crews into formally constituted fourships. The expectation was that even if squadrons did not deploy *en masse*, the smallest units would be fourships. In the event, this thinking was absolutely correct, and the fact that the fourships had flown and worked together as a team over a prolonged period made it easier for them to slip seamlessly into operational flying.

Peeling Pineapples

One development in the summer of 1990 was the initial introduction into service of the Air Launched Anti-Radiation Missile (ALARM). The missile was originally conceived as one part of a family of anti-radiation missiles, which would provide the RAF with its own Suppression of Enemy Air Defences (SEAD) capability against the integrated air-defence system of the Warsaw Pact during the Cold War. The end of the Cold War might have marked the death knell of the project, but with the possibility of hostilities looming in the Middle East, the first of the new missiles were quickly dispatched to Laarbruch. Flt Lt D.W. Bellamy, a navigator on 20 Squadron was amongst the first crews to be involved with the project; he explained that 'initially XV Squadron were assigned the ALARM role and ground training commenced in

The airbrakes on a Tornado GR1 extend as the aircraft is eased into position during a low-level transit from Bahrain to Tabuk. (XV Squadron)

the late summer of 1990. Fortunately, an executive officer from 20 Squadron had the foresight to recommend one senior crew from 20 Squadron also to attend the briefings just in case XV Squadron was deployed to Bahrain in the offensive counter air role. The XV Squadron weapons leader commenced the ground training with a wise reminder of MoD procurement: 'when you want a missile you specify its requirements, MoD goes off and competes it then buys it, and industry goes away and umpteen years later comes back with a product saying it works as requested. Then it's put in front of you guys and the first thing you will say is ah, but can it peel pineapples.' A few days later XV Squadron was deployed to Bahrain, leaving 20 Squadron to try to peel pineapples. As a pre-production weapon system, there was no published Con Ops for ALARM, no flight reference cards and nor were there any ground procedures. In addition, the only release-to-service authorization originated from test firings conducted by the OEU, with the ALARM missile carried on the inboard under-wing pylons. This meant initial ALARM training flights were conducted with centre-line fuel tanks, which gave some interesting handling characteristics, particularly when air-to-air refuelling or flying at OLF altitudes. For the navigators, training focussed on the mission planning and ground preparation stages of transferring target information, emitter libraries and launch modes from planning consoles to the aircraft using equipment referred to by the manufacturer by obtuse acronyms such as the HUSKY and PUGS... As a stand-off, fire-and-forget missile, ALARM endowed the RAF and the Tornado a radical new capability. It could be launched at considerable stand-off ranges, climbing to high altitude before commencing its descent, giving a window of cover for specified radar targets programmed into the emitter library. Fundamentally there was a choice between targets of known location and area suppression modes, with a trade-off between launch range (maximum and minimum) and the window of cover. Add to this the

The Royal Saudi Air Force (RSAF) base at Tabuk, was to become 'home' to the largest of the RAF's three Tornado GR1 Wings during the Gulf conflict. (Pete Batson)

fact that ALARM could hit any of a number of radars within its library, 20 Squadron crews came to realize that they could fire a "smart" missile and not know where it was going or what pineapples it would peel.'

Preparations for War

The changeover at Bahrain started in November, with the XV Squadron crews' deployment staggered over a three-week period, to allow a smooth handover between units. While there might have been some disappointment amongst the Brüggen crews at the possibility of missing out on some real action, the overwhelming feeling for most of the personnel returning to Brüggen was one of relief that they were getting back home to some form of normality. Some also believed that they might not actually be missing much – suspecting that the crisis would blow over without any fighting. By the beginning of December, XV Squadron was fully settled into Bahrain with twelve CR crews, divided into three constituted fourships.

Nearly 900 miles due west of them, another detachment of twelve crews, led by 16 Squadron under Wg Cdr I. Travers-Smith, had already arrived in theatre at Tabuk. Most of the preparatory work at Tabuk had been done by Sqn Ldr J.W. Crowley and Flt Lt A.M. Randall from 27 Squadron, who had moved across from Bahrain in early October. In contrast to Bahrain, where personnel enjoyed the luxury of the Sheraton Hotel, the accommodation at Tabuk was very basic. 'We lived in "suitable" on-base accommodation and had little help from the Saudi base commander (a Saudi Prince), or his staff, in establishing a Tornado operating base,' reflected Sqn Ldr Crowley. 'Our working "accommodation" was a tent, a single power point and plenty of sand. Meetings with the prince were hard to come by, were strictly formal and at best frustrating. Saudi facilities (operation centre, administration block, empty HAS site and other areas) were strictly out-of-bounds to the RAF. However progress was made, mainly due to much initiative and non-adherence to Saudi rules/guidance... Despite our frustrations, the arrival of a REME party saw ISO containers transformed into an operations block, and numerous tents were erected ready for the arrival of aircrew.' Eventually Tabuk would become the largest of the Tornado GR1 detachment, with nineteen aircraft and thirty crews.

Meanwhile at Brüggen, Wg Cdr J.J. Witts, OC 31 Squadron, had been informed in early November that he would lead a third Tornado Wing which would be based at the RSAF base Dhahran, just across the causeway from Bahrain. Like the other Tornado bases in theatre at the time, this Wing would comprise twelve aircraft and twenty-four crews. Half of the crews would be from 31 Squadron and the other half would be provided by the other Brüggen squadrons. Sqn Ldr Coulls recalled that 'the news certainly gave "11½ Squadron" a new sense of purpose and we set about putting the limited assets available to us to the best use we could. The priorities for training quickly became clear, based on what we could glean from our colleagues in-theatre. The first challenge was to qualify everybody in day and night AAR, a skill that was not normally practised by Germany-based crews... The next priorities were to re-qualify all crews in day OLF... Finally, we also tried to give as many crews as possible some experience of medium-level bombing, from altitudes above 15,000 ft. Again, this was a skill that was not a normal part of the Tornado GR1 force's repertoire, almost to the point of dogma. We saw ourselves as a low-level air force and prided ourselves at being better at low-flying than any of our allies, unquestionably based on our favoured Cold War tactics.' Events a few months later would prove Coulls' insistence on practising medium-level bombing to be prescient.

After a brief work-up, Witts' team deployed to Dhahran at the beginning of January 1991. 'The next major issue,' continued Coulls, 'was to get ourselves tasked onto the Master Air Attack Plan, which was being prepared by a very secretive organization in Riyadh under US leadership. As usual, the UK had excellent access to the planning process due to our position as 'ally of choice' and we had people in key roles in the heart of the organization. However, by this stage there were in excess of 3,500 USAF, USN, USMC and US Army aircraft in-theatre, and the arrival of twelve more Tornados was not necessarily the biggest news in town. The political process had made us very late, albeit welcome, additions and we needed to find our way into a plan that had been under development for nearly six months. It transpired that, because of our late arrival, we had only been tasked for a single, night fourship for the first three days. This was extremely disappointing, if understandable, but there was a promise of expanding our participation, bringing it up to two eight-aircraft formations per day, one timed to be on target just after dusk and the second just before dawn.' Sqn Ldr Coulls also attended a meeting with the UK air commander in the UK facility: 'I recall that this meeting was not the happiest that I have ever attended. There was obviously some disagreement within the UK HQ about our role, rates of effort and weapons selection, amongst other things. One of the biggest bones of contention was the likelihood of a US move to medium-level operations, for which the Tornado GR1 was not best equipped; at a relatively early stage after the Iraqi air-defence system had been neutralized. There was a strong feeling from the operators that we should resist this, but the commander's view was that we would not be given a choice and the options were stark: operate at medium level, or sit on the ground doing nothing. No prizes for guessing who won the argument.'

A Tornado GR1s from 31 Squadron's, with a four-tank ferry fit and armed with live AIM-9L missiles, emerges from an HAS site before departing to Dhahran in late 1990. (Simon Hadley)

At Bahrain, Sqn Ldr N.L. Risdale had been involved in pre-planning the first three days of operations from Bahrain. 'The first issue we had was concern about the overall viability of the task,' explained Sqn Ldr Risdale. 'JP233 was designed specifically with Warsaw Pact runways in mind. The weapon was optimized for a runway about 8,000ft long built on a typical Northern European subsoil, not desert sands. The attack software required very accurate navigation and aiming both for the approach to target and during the lengthy delivery phase. We were well versed in planning and executing these profiles in our routine training, but these were over

A pair of Tornados accompanied by a TriStar tanker photographed in the early morning light as they deploy to Dhahran. (Wally Grout)

A Tornado GR1 flies past ground troops during a low-level training sortie in the Omani desert. (Gavin Wells)

Many training sorties by Tornado crews in the Gulf theatre involved 'hi-lo-hi' profiles to the mountainous areas of Oman.
(Gavin Wells)

familiar, very accurately mapped terrain with a plethora of radar significant navigation and aiming features. The Gulf scenario required us to transit with tankers for about ninety minutes, prior to dropping to low level over a "barren featureless desert" and of course the mapping radar was not brilliant at altitude. The boffins always told us to use JP233 in the along the runway mode, as their computer model showed that only one aircraft with a really accurate delivery would do the job – but to get that one aircraft the plans had two eightships attacking and then repeating this about for hours later. We had an eightship attacking once, and most of the runways were nearer 12,000ft and had usable parallel taxiways. Tallil effectively had four 12,000ft runways. We were really concerned about our ability to produce the accuracy that we would need for these missions to be anything close to successful; we came to the conclusion that the best we could do would be to "harass" the airfield's operations by primarily relying on the area-denial submunitions and if the crater submunitions damaged some of the operating strips, it might stretch their recovery teams. Given all this we came up with plan to cut across the HAS site access taxiways and then spread four other short patterns over the runways/taxiways.'

Both detachments at Bahrain and Tabuk were boosted by last-minute reinforcements from the Marham-based Tornado squadrons of eight crews sent to each location. The last part of the Tornado force into theatre was a small detachment of reconnaissance aircraft under the command of Wg Cdr Torpy. On 15 January, the four Tornado GR1A aircraft arrived at Dhahran, with crews drawn from both 13 and II Squadrons.

The majority of the ALARM training took place in theatre after 20 Squadron crews deployed to Tabuk in October; it was only then that they received the operational software for the weapon. Two dedicated ALARM fourships were formed: Alpha led by Sq Ldr R.I. McAlpine and Sq Ldr R.A. Pittaway, and Delta led by Fl Lt T.J. Roche and Flt Lt Bellamy. According to Bellamy, 'the transition to war phase allowed 20 Squadron lead crews to identify additional constraints in the form of high-level jetstreams that would affect ALARM loiter modes as well as electronic intelligence that indicated how Iraqi air-defence units varied the position of mobile radars used in area defence of airfields. This culminated in the decision to select corridor suppression mode as the preferred method of delivery. Although many solo, pair and fourship ALARM profiles were practised before combat operations commenced, it was not until after the first missile was fired that integration with mission packages occurred.'

In November 1990, the UN Security Council had adopted Resolution 678, which gave Iraq a deadline of 15 January to withdraw from Kuwait or face military action. Unfortunately, despite some high-level diplomacy, by early January it seemed more than likely that Resolution 678 would be ignored by Iraq and that war was inevitable. With the deadline fast approaching the three Tornado GR1 Wings continued with an intense training programme. It was during one typical training sortie that the first Tornado crew was lost on 13 January. 'The 14 Squadron fourship was programmed to fly a practise AAR trail south through Saudi Arabia and into Oman, leave the tanker using night/poor weather procedures, carry out a simulated attack and then return to Dhahran,' recounted Sqn Ldr Coulls, who was leading the formation. 'We had also planned to conduct some additional training events, including the use of flares at very low level to test their effectiveness against infra-red air-to-air missiles in that environment. We had planned to conclude the sortie with a bit of light relief, involving a segment of valley flying in the northern part of Oman, before returning to the tanker for the trip home. We knew that this was to be our last training sortie and were feeling comfortable in the desert environment

The view from the navigator's seat of a Tornado as it overflies an oasis at low level to enter a wadi amongst one of the desert mountain ranges. (Lars Smith)

after four reasonably demanding trips in quick succession. Our Number 3 (Gibson/Glover) unfortunately did not manage to get airborne, but other than that the early part of the sortie went to plan: we rendezvoused with the tanker and made our drop-off point in Oman in good order. Having settled at low level we completed the exercise with the flares and a few minutes later our Number 2 started calling over the radio for the Number 4 to check-in. After several attempts with no reply, and still with no sign of the Number 4, we spotted a large plume of black smoke several miles behind us. We immediately turned around and headed for the smoke. To our horror, we found a very obvious scrape across the desert floor several kilometres long, the smoke rapidly dispersing and numerous unrecognizable items of debris scattered along the line. There was no sign of parachutes or sounds of emergency beacons on the distress frequency. Tragically, Kieran and Norman's aircraft had impacted the ground while travelling at about 500kt, after which there was only ever going to be one result. Thereafter, our long years training took over and we carried out the necessary immediate actions; we were eventually relieved on scene by an RAF Nimrod from an Omani base, then climbed to rejoin our tanker and made our way back to Dhahran.' Flt Lt K.J. Duffy and Flt Lt N.T. Dent were killed instantly when their aircraft hit the ground during a hard turn at ultra-low level.

The Gulf War: The First Wave – Bahrain

Two days later the UN Resolution 678 expired and the personnel at all three Tornado detachments waited for the start of the war. When they arrived to work on 16 January, the Bahrain crews were told that the war would start that night. In the words of Flt Lt N.J.

A pair of Tornado GR1s undertaking a low-level training sortie over a typical desert landscape of barren desert rocks. (BAe Heritage)

Heard, a XV Squadron pilot, 'our mission was to attack Tallil airfield, a large fighter base in southern Iraq, as part of the opening "counter-air" strategy to gain air superiority. The plan was for eight Tornados to drop JP233 runway attack munitions from low level across runways and taxiways at around 04:00hrs [on 17 January] – just before dawn. This was bread and butter to us – night low flying using TFR was our speciality, although tonight we would be down to 200ft, rather than the peacetime limit of 500ft – and we would be releasing weapons as well. After taking off from Bahrain Muharraq at around 02:00hrs, we would meet up with VC10 tankers to take on fuel, routing northwestwards in Saudi Arabian airspace for an hour or so before letting down to low level, entering Iraqi airspace way out in the desert where we knew it would be quiet. Twenty minutes later we would hit Tallil as four pairs, with 30sec between pairs. We would then return to the tanker before heading back to Bahrain, in what would be a four-hour trip.'

The mission would be part of a much larger coalition 'package' of aircraft which would also be attacking Tallil, as well as other Iraqi airfields in a co-ordinated strike on the whole of the Iraqi Air Force and air-defence infrastructure. Each package would be supported by SEAD assets provided by the USAF and USN: this would include EF-111A Raven and EA-6B Prowler electronic-jamming aircraft and F-4G (Phantom) Wild Weasels tasked to take out radar and missile systems with anti-radiation missiles. There would also be fighter sweeps to ensure that Iraqi Air Force fighters could not interfere with the ground-attack packages.

Meanwhile, at Dhahran and Tabuk, more Tornado crews prepared themselves for similar JP233 missions: the Dhahran Wing was tasked to send four aircraft against Mudaysis airfield (halfway between An Najaf and Rutbah) and the Tabuk Wing would send two formations

Gerry Whittingham sits at the operations desk at Dhahran – a scene which would also be very familiar to Tornado crews at Tabuk and Bahrain. (Simon Hadley)

of four Tornados each against the airfields at Al Asad (between Haditha and Ramadi) and Al Taqaddum (near Al Fulljah).

Later that night, it was time for the Bahrain crews to head out to their aeroplanes. 'It was an emotional time,' admitted Sqn Ldr Buckley, who would be leading the rear fourship with Sqn Ldr I.D. Teakle. 'How was the mission going to evolve. Were we all going to get back OK. Most importantly though, was I going to be able to carry out the attack successfully and not let the rest of the squadron down. We were issued with a revolver, a holster and a magazine of bullets also a pack of gold sovereigns (the idea being that if you were captured there would be a reward to your capturers for taking you to safety by receiving another pack of gold sovereigns.)' In the Number 2 position, Flt Lt Heard remembered that 'Rob Woods, my navigator, and I walked out to our aircraft with the other crews with more than a little anxiety, although tonight's mission had hardly come as a surprise. We climbed in and got the jet going … and we were able to sit and wait for taxy time, contemplating again about what we were about to unleash.'

Lining up on the runway at Bahrain, Flt Lt Heard and Flt Lt Woods watched as Sqn Ldr Risdale and Wg Cdr J. Broadbent in the lead aircraft lit their reheat and rolled down the runway. 'Ten seconds later we followed', continued Heard; 'the Tornado was heavy with eight tons of fuel and four tons of weaponry. We got airborne safely and I started easing in on the leader's navigation lights to take up my position on his wing – night close formation had become another newly-acquired skill in the last few months – and we headed for the tanker rendezvous point… we joined on the tanker's right wing. The leader slipped behind the left hose to refuel. I moved behind the right hose and stabilized in the usual position, around

A Tornado GR1 loaded with JP233. This was taken during a training sortie: on an operational mission the aircraft would be armed with AIM-9L missiles on the stub pylons. (Andy Glover)

ten feet behind the basket. We were 'tanking' [refuelling] a lot lower than usual – around 12,000ft – because of the warm temperatures and our heavyweight, so the basket could be quite unstable. However, all went well and with a bit of power I moved in and I plugged into the basket first time – always a satisfying result. Fuel flowed and we were quickly full, so we unplugged and moved to the left wing to watch the other two Tornados of the front fourship take theirs. We were now able to relax a little as we proceeded up the tanker trail. Rob tuned in the BBC World Service on the HF radio which, surreally, was still playing its ordinary schedule – the world was still unaware that the Gulf War was about to start.'

Approaching the drop off point, the Tornados filled their fuel tanks once more and then descended to low level as they headed northwards towards the Iraqi border. The crews busied themselves setting up their EW equipment, arming their weapons and finally switching off all their external lights. 'I had now plugged in the TFR on autopilot,' recalled Heard, 'and we dropped down to 1,500ft above the ground as I checked that the system was behaving itself. I then reset the minimum height in stages down to 200ft, and the Tornado settled beautifully at 420kt over the invisible Saudi desert. On my moving map display I noticed the border approaching, indicating SAUDI ARABIA on one side and IRAQ on the other. This was for real – I was just about to enter the airspace of a foreign country at high speed, low level, with fully-armed bombs, cannon, and missiles – I was about to start a war. At any point the Iraqis were now entitled to defend themselves.

'As we crossed the border, all was remarkably quiet – it was only later in the war that I realized how uninhabited this area was. We were at 420kt, 200ft above the desert, on track, on time, and on speed – all critical elements of night TFR operation. We routinely worked to timing tolerances of plus/minus 5sec. We were now on an AWACS frequency and we could hear occasional reassuring calls of 'Picture Clear' from the controller – meaning no Iraqi fighter activity. We started to see bursts of anti-aircraft artillery [AAA – triple-A] fire in the distance, and we knew that the Iraqis were now awake and alerted, but all remained quiet in our area. We now had some 10min to go to Tallil.'

At the head of the formation, Sqn Ldr Risdale remarked to his navigator, Wg Cdr Broadbent about the impressive triple-A barrage out to the left of their track. 'I should have checked my map before opening my mouth,' he later commented, 'because we were about to turn left and point at that target: Tallil airfield. The US Navy formation attacking before us from medium altitude, had stirred up a furious response which continued unabated for the 4min or so we were approaching it and throughout our eight-ship attacks. About 20sec out we engaged burners to get the speed up to about 520kt, and then went over the target in max dry with the speed washing back to about 480kt. We all took the autopilot out just before the weapon release in case of any TF pull ups. We aimed to deliver at about 180ft radar altitude. The trim change on canister release was significant and I had to push quite significantly to prevent ballooning too much, and then get the TF and autopilot back in.'

In the Number 2 aircraft, Flt Lt Heard's experience was very similar: 'in my ten-thirty position I started to notice a large area of triple-A and was staggered at the amount and intensity of the fire. I had a brief thought of "I'm really glad we're not going there." Just then, we reached another turning point and the Tornado – still on autopilot – turned left onto its next programmed track, and pointed right at the triple-A. It was then that the horrible truth dawned on me – that was Tallil. We were at the back end of a large package attack against the airfield involving the USAF and US Navy, so the defences were up and running. I stared at the interlocking mesh of triple-A and my mouth went completely dry. As far as I could see, there was no way through that triple-A, such was the barrage of incredibly high-energy cannon fire. This was not the sort of stuff that would sew a neat "Hollywood" row of holes in the fuselage – any hit from these shells would blow us to bits. The only thing in our favour was that the RHWR was clear – the Iraqis were aware of our USAF anti-radar missile support aircraft, so were leaving their radars off and just hosing away. We were quite invisible in the darkness, but I could not see how they could miss us with that intense barrage. Rob was now in his attack routine, marking an offset position on the airfield with his radar, and making minor adjustments, which the jet followed. We entered the triple-A, and I was astounded to see that we were still over a minute away from weapon release. This would be a long minute. I watched a gun open up just below and to the right – perhaps just 100yd away from us – but his fire went blindly straight up, and I was astounded at how I could hear nothing of the triple-A – I was still in a warm, quiet Tornado cockpit. At last the time-to-go in my HUD was unwinding – less than a minute to go. Attack speed 480kt – the jet could only just manage that in dry power, but reheat was out of the question in the darkness, as I would become highly visible. Thirty seconds to go… 15sec to go. I disconnected the autopilot and held the Tornado straight and level at 200ft radar altitude, easily achieved using the HUD – we knew the autopilot would not cope with weapon release well, so manual flight was required for the next few seconds. I noticed the leader's JP233 munitions detonating exactly on time, slightly ahead and to our left, the first indication that he was there at all. With 5sec to go Rob and I called "Committing" to each other, meaning we were both pressing the bomb-release buttons

– either button would do, but we did not want a cock-up now and fail to drop the bombs. The munitions started dispensing – a 5sec rumble as sixty runway cratering bombs and over 400 minelets fell away, followed by three large thumps as the canisters fell away automatically afterwards. With all that weight and drag gone, the Tornado leapt forward and I quickly re-engaged the autopilot – that would mean I would not inadvertently fly into the ground in the excitement. Seconds later we emerged from the cauldron of triple-A to the north of Tallil and began our route back to the tanker RV. I looked back to try and watch my colleagues make their attacks, but with so much triple-A I could not make out other JP233 strikes.'

Closely following the first fourship towards the target, Sqn Ldr Buckley could see 'two red lines five or six miles away going vertically upwards and as we continued we could see more of them with similar patterns standing out against the night sky. This was a huge barrage of triple-A – there were large lines and small dots just shooting upwards, some looking like candle lights at the top. We learned later that the small dots and dashes going up in spirals were actually small arms fire and the larger lines were the heavier triple-A. An optical illusion gave me the impression that the triple-A was coming from the top of a hill which would be a sensible place to put an triple-A site so I decided to turn the aircraft slightly to the right to avoid the site, bearing in mind my Number 2 was also on my right. However, no matter where I steered the aircraft, the target pointer showed the barrage. The triple-A was actually the target and we were going to have to go straight through it. As we ran in to the target, I was getting all sorts of comforting remarks from Paddy – we were spot on and all the marks were perfect. We tripped out the terrain-following radar and proceeded to the target. Attack speed was planned at 480kt, which at that all-up weight meant the throttles were almost at

Steve Barnes, Mike Barley, John Broadbent (OC XV Squadron) and Ricci Cobelli, Bahrain-based aircrew from XV Squadron, attend a debriefing after their first wartime mission on 17 January. (XV Squadron)

maximum dry power. We were now flying right into a huge barrage of triple-A with blue and red lines flying past the cockpit. I had been taught right from the start of my front-line career on the Jaguar that if you encounter triple-A go as low and as fast as you can and so I flew lower until the radalt stopped reading (which I knew to be about 100ft) and then levelled using the vertical speed indicator (VSI) in the HUD... To ensure that self-damage does not occur when a bomb is released and explodes on impact with the ground, a minimum height must be flown to enable the bomb to arm. This height for the JP233 was 200ft and therefore I needed to climb the aircraft to 200ft before weapon release.

'As we reached the weapon release point, I eased the aeroplane up, releasing the runway denial weapons in the four JP233 canisters that came off with a machine-gun-like noise, very similar to firing the guns. This was followed by three booms and bumps as the rear canisters dropped off separately, while the front pair went together. With all that weight and drag removed, the aeroplane just shot forward, almost with the same sensation as taking off. Everything had been planned at the aeroplane's mid-speed range, leaving us with sufficient speed flexibility, should we require it, but after weapon release we went to maximum speed just to get out of there. The noise and response of the aircraft to the sudden release of the weapon load was completely unexpected. Coupled with my desire to return to ultra-low level it really felt like we were going over the edge of a large roller-coaster. As soon as we had bomb release I returned to 100ft and put the aircraft in a hard banked turn to the right to get out of all that hullaballoo. I was absolutely buzzing as I flew that target run and subsequent run out and have often thought that if I had been taken out of the cockpit there and then and strapped to a monitor the results would have been extraordinary. On reflection, flying down to 100ft was not the most sensible thing to do. There were occasions when after JP233 weapon release the aircraft's inertial nav system would drop off line and the systems revert to a very unstable secondary mode, which would make the HUD very difficult to read... I didn't use that tactic again. It was only when we got past the target and were on our way out again that we actually had time to actually think about what we had done, going through all that triple-A.'

A few minutes later all members of the formation checked in, indicating that all had made it safely through the target area. Flt Lt Heard later admitted that 'the relief, not just for our own success and safety but for that of our colleagues, was massive.' After crossing the border back into Saudi Arabia, the formation climbed up, in Heard's words 'to greet the beautiful sight of the VC10, faithfully waiting for us on its towline.' After refuelling once more, the eight Tornados headed southeast towards the sunrise, for the hour's transit back to Bahrain.

First Wave – Dhahran

At Dhahran, Wg Cdr Witts and Flt Lt A.J. Smith led their fourship out to the runway at Dhahran for a take-off time of 02:00hrs GMT. The formation climbed out and headed northwest for the tanker tow-lines. Unfortunately during the transit the Number 3 aircraft suffered an ECM equipment failure and had to return to Dhahran, but the remaining three aircraft made their rendezvous with two Victor tankers. After refuelling, this was made more challenging by some severe turbulence in the tankers' height block, the aircraft descended to low level and headed towards the Iraqi border. 'During the descent, I switched on the TFR and locked in the autopilot,' wrote Wg Cdr Witts. 'AJ was busy getting a last radar position fix before leaving friendly territory. He was fretting slightly because of the errors that had accumulated in his

Armourers at Dhahran load JP233 onto a Tornado GR1. They are dressed in Nuclear Biological and Chemical (NBC) protective clothing, which was hot and cumbersome to wear making working conditions difficult. (Les Hendry)

Tornado GR1s under sun shelters at Dhahran being prepared for a night mission. (Les Hendry)

A Tornado GR1 at dusk. All lights on the aircraft would be extinguished just before crossing the Iraqi Border. (Andy Glover)

A pair of Dhahran-based Tornado GR1s armed with JP233. (Andy Glover)

navigation system and he had begun to suspect that our INS was not performing as well as it should. As we dropped towards the desert floor, the night became darker and darker. Cloud cover now obscured what little starlight there was and it was impossible to see anything outside the cockpit, except the lights of our two formation colleagues in the distance. As we crossed the designated "lights off" line, even these small comforting signs disappeared from view.

'The terrain was relatively flat with nothing showing on the radar scope to interfere with our smooth progress. After a while we flashed across the international border and into Iraq itself. AJ and I marked the moment by wishing each other luck and returned to business. Our sortie had been fairly quiet until now. Suddenly, a faint "strobe" began to paint in the one o'clock position. As we sped towards it, the strobe became stronger and the radar-warning receiver computer annotated it as a Fulcrum. My heart sank. The Russian-built MiG-29 Fulcrum was the one Iraqi fighter that we feared the most. Although the Iraqi pilots were an unknown quantity, the Fulcrum was an agile high-performance fighter with a "look down – shoot down" capability. Here we were, 10min inside Iraq, and it looked as though one had shown up. We changed course slightly to the left and the strobe slowly moved around the clock on our right-hand side. Although there were no other threat indications and no warnings from the AWACS, the warning receiver continued to insist that a MiG-29 was transitioning for a tail shot on us. There was nothing else we could do but sit and wait to see what happened. Thankfully, after a tense few minutes, the strobe faded and disappeared.

'I still couldn't see anything ahead, just darkness and the slowly unwinding circle in the fluorescent green symbols on the HUD that indicated time to weapon release. With about five miles to go, AJ took one last look with the radar to make sure everything was spot on. It was and I double checked the last three switches, which would ensure that the JP233s would dispense automatically at the computer-calculated release point. This was really it then. For the first time in my life I was about to drop real weapons on a real enemy target with the

Aircrew 'AJ' Smith, Jerry Witts (OC 31 Squadron), Simon 'Shifty' Young and Adam Robinson, photographed immediately after their first JP233 mission of the Gulf War. (Les Hendry)

intention of doing it as much harm as possible. I was tense but there was no fear. I was far more concerned that we had done everything possible to make the attack successful.

'AJ counted down the seconds to release… "thirty… twenty… fifteen… ten." I had a fleeting impression of a few shapes and lights on the ground ahead and, with about 5sec to go, I held down the commit button with my thumb. AJ continued the countdown and, right on time, the aircraft started to vibrate rapidly as our two JP 233s started to drop their loads. I could see a rapidly pulsing glow in my peripheral vision. I knew that the JPs would take several seconds to dispense fully, but it seemed to take forever. Suddenly, two massive thumps came from beneath the aircraft, so heavy that I thought for a second that we had been hit, or flown into something. Simultaneously, various cockpit alarms sounded, warning lights flashed and the aircraft snapped into a sharp climb as the auto-pilot safety circuits took over control. As I struggled to get the aircraft back under control, I realized that the thumps must have been the empty JP233 canisters being jettisoned and that, somehow, this had had caused the autopilot to drop out. Meanwhile, I could see all kinds of flashing lights and explosions going off outside the cockpit. AJ was shouting at me to get the height down as triple-A tracer arced over and around us. We very nearly hit the ground as I over-controlled the aircraft in my attempts to get the aircraft down too quickly. Now, I was frightened.'

As they re-crossed the Saudi border, it was clear that the navigation system on their Tornado had indeed wandered somewhat; they managed to locate the rest of their formation when the Number 3 aircraft, by now in company with the post-strike VC10 tanker, fired some flares to mark their position. Short of fuel by now, they caught up with the tanker and were able to top up for the last leg to Dhahran.

A JP233-armed Tornado GR1 in a HAS at Tabuk being prepared for a night attack against Iraq. (Dick Middleton)

'It was wonderful to feel *terra firma* beneath the wheels again as we slowed down and taxied back to our dispersal,' continued Witts. 'There, a large group of ground crew were waiting to meet us, huge grins on their faces to match our own. We climbed out of our cockpits to congratulations all round. Jerry Gegg and 'Ob' Long were immediately surrounded by the media pool and gave some memorable interviews for the TV and press. While we waited for them to finish, Les Hendry supervised the ground crew as they stencilled the symbol of a palm tree beneath the cockpit rail of our aircraft. He planned that the aircraft should get one for each mission flown.'

First Wave – Tabuk

The timings for the first formation at Tabuk were almost identical to those at Dhahran: Wg Cdr Travers-Smith and Sqn Ldr J.N. Fradgley also took off at the head of their fourship just after 02:00hrs GMT. Unlike the Tornados from Bahrain and Tabuk which had been supported entirely by SEAD assets of the US military, the Tabuk Wing provided its own support in the form of two more Tornados led by Flt Lt Roche and Flt Lt Bellamy, each armed with three ALARM missiles. These Tornados would work in conjunction with two EA-6B Prowlers (with a F-14 Tomcat escort), which had launched from the US Navy carrier group operating in the Red Sea to provide stand-off jamming to cover the Tornado formation's approach to the target area.

Unfortunately all was not going well in the Number 4 aircraft, crewed by Flt Lt M. Warren and Fg Off C.M. Craghill. 'We encountered technical problems with the stores management system during ground operations, but had no time to run for a spare aircraft,' explained Fg

A Tornado GR1 in full reheat thunders down the runway during a dusk take off at Tabuk. (Lars Smith)

Off Craghill. 'The problem meant that we would be able to dispense the runway cratering munitions from our JP233 runway denial weapon but not the mines designed to hamper clearance operations. With our aim being to put the runways at the massive Al Asad airbase out of use – a daunting task with four aircraft, never mind three – we opted to go anyway. Sometimes these things cleared up once airborne. All ground ops were being undertaken in radio silence to maintain operational security, so at the appropriate time we moved out to join our fourship and taxied to the holding point of Tabuk's military runway. The airfield in north-western Saudi Arabia had two runways; one for civilian airline traffic, the other for Tabuk's resident RSAF F-5 Tiger IIs and their coalition partners – primarily RAF Tornado GR1 bombers and USAF F-15C Eagle fighters. As we waited in the darkness at the holding point, pre-take off checks completed, an arriving airliner came up on the tower frequency and called for landing clearance. Air-traffic control responded: "Cleared to land runway one three, traffic is four Tornados awaiting departure from runway zero six." So much for surprise…

'We received a green light from the tower and took the runway for departure… one by one we thundered down the runway and off into the clear desert night. It soon became obvious that not only would our stores management system not reset; the radar was also not working. As the formation flew to meet our tanker on the Prune Trail refuelling track I tried everything I knew to coax it back to life but to no avail. With no radar we couldn't accurately update the aircraft navigation and weapon aiming system, making us a liability to the other formation members and decreasing our chances of an accurate strike on the runway at Al Asad. Right up to our turn to refuel we tried, but without the radar we were useless. We left the formation and reduced weight before returning to Tabuk, turning the broken jet over to the engineers to work their magic and get her ready for the next day. Mike and I sat quietly in

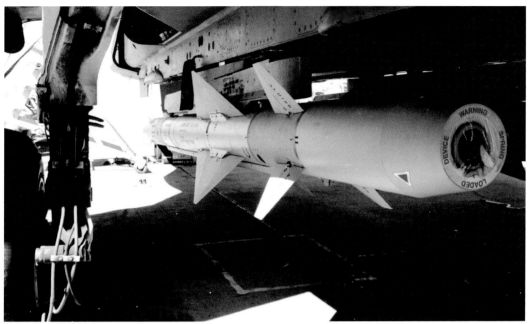

An ALARM missile loaded to an under-fuselage shoulder pylon of a Tabuk-based Tornado GR1. (David Bellamy)

A Tornado GR1 armed with two ALARM missiles. (Geoffrey Lee/ Plane Focus)

The vast airfield at Al Asad: this view gives an idea of the scale of the tactical challenges of neutralizing a large airfield.

the GR1 operations room for the next few hours, playing chess and waiting for news of our formation. Eventually the radio burst into life and three familiar voices checked in to report a successful mission and notify the ground crew that they would be back on the ground in fifteen minutes. A feeling of enormous relief washed over us both.'

Meanwhile, in the lead ALARM aircraft, Flt Lt Bellamy recounted that 'after air-to-air refuelling, we descended to 200ft for a high-speed low-level penetration of Iraqi airspace. With the TFR system performing flawlessly the aircraft passed close to Mudayasis airfield, where we could see Iraqi Mirages being towed into hardened aircraft shelters.' As they pressed towards their target area at low level the ALARM crews also witnessed the first air-to-air kill of the war as an Iraqi aircraft tumbled in flames and crashed near their route. Nearing Al Asad, the ALARM formation manoeuvred around an Iraqi SAM-8 [Sa-8 – NATO name Geko] missile battery and then closed in on the target. Before firing the pilots disconnected the autopilot and the navigators completed the ALARM attack routine. 'We fired off three ALARMs and two immediately plummeted to the deck. To say that was disappointing would be an understatement,' reported Flt Lt Bellamy ruefully.

Tabuk's second fourship was led by Sqn Ldr G.K.S. Lennox and Sq Ldr K.P. Weeks and it took off an hour after the first formation. After refuelling from a VC10, they entered Iraq airspace at low level and flew towards Al Taqaddum. In the Number 3 aircraft, Flt Lt J.B. Klein's two impressions of Al Taqaddum were of a 'heavy dome of triple-A over the target' and the presence of Franco-German built Roland surface-to-air (SAM) systems. Despite the heavy defences, all the aircraft returned safely after a three-hour sortie, although only two of the aircraft claimed to have hit their targets successfully.

At both Tabuk and Dhahran, there was a pause in Tornado operations during daylight hours, during which the ground crew serviced and re-armed the aircraft and the second shift of aircrews prepared for the night wave. This time the airfield at Al Asad would be revisited by an eightship from the Tabuk Wing; meanwhile the Dhahran Wing would send four more aircraft to Mudaysis airfield and another four to Wadi Al Khirr airfield. All of these missions would be armed with JP233. Additionally, the Tabuk Wing would also mount a fourship of ALARM-armed aircraft to provide SEAD support for operations against H3 airfield.

Tornado Down

However, despite the pause at the other two bases and preparations for their own operations that evening, the Bahrain Wing was tasked to launch four Tornados in daytime to harass operations at Ar Rumaylah airfield. The plan was for each aircraft to loft eight 1,000lb bombs into the HAS sites; this weapons fit had been chosen rather than JP233 so that the aircraft would not have to overfly the target in daylight. SEAD support would be provided by two EA-6B Prowler and twenty-four F-18 Hornets (carrying HARM missiles) from the US Navy. One Tornado was unserviceable on start-up, leaving the remaining three aircraft to continue with the mission. After taking off from Bahrain at 04:30hrs GMT, Sqn Ldr P. Mason and Sq Ldr G. Stapleton led their depleted formation west to meet two Victor tankers where the Tornados refuelled close to the Iraqi border. From here the formation followed a route that had been planned to avoid all known Iraqi military sites. 'The Tornados descended in escort formation to ultra-low level in Saudi airspace and crossed the border with their radar altimeters unlocked,' wrote Flt Lt M.A.C. Paisey, who was flying the Number 4 aircraft with Flt Lt M. Toft. 'Evidence of earlier airstrikes was visible from smoking EW sites (which had been attacked by AC-130 gunship aircraft) and the formation proceeded to the target without detection. On the target run Number 2 and Number 4 closed up on the leader, accelerating to 580kt for the loft. At 22sec to go, the lead and Number 4 pulled up deploying chaff and flares on the southern track. During the manoeuvre 57mm triple-A fired at both aircraft, but they successfully returned to low level having delivered their ordnance on the target. Number 2 pulled up behind the leader and Number 4, but failed to release their stores. Number 2 transmitted an unsuccessful attack, quickly followed by the fact that they had a fire in the left engine. The next transmission informed the lead that "we might have to get out." This was the last transmission and occurred at a position approximately fifteen miles southwest of Jalibah airfield. Number 4 passed the position on to AWACS while continuing to egress at low level with the leader.'

During the egress the remaining pair was locked up by SAM-8 and Roland missile systems, which they managed to defeat using a combination of chaff and low flying. The two Tornados made their rendezvous with their tanker and then set off on the return leg to Bahrain, landing after a 4hr sortie. Meanwhile it transpired that the Number 2 aircraft, flown by Flt Lt J. Peters and Flt Lt J. Nichols, had been mortally hit by an Iraqi missile. After the aircraft became uncontrollable the crew managed to eject successfully, but were captured by Iraqi troops. As Flt Lt Paisey noted drily in his diary, 'despite the success of this mission, it served to bring home the reality of aerial warfare.'

A Tornado GR1 loaded with JP233 canisters on the line at Tabuk. (Pete Batson)

A pair of JP233-armed Tornado GR1s starting up outside a HAS at Tabuk, prior to the mission against Al Asad. (Pete Batson)

Second Wave – Tabuk

That evening Sqn Ldr P.K. Batson and Wg Cdr M.C. Heath took off from Tabuk at the head of led Tornados to revisit the airfield at Al Asad. 'With the minimum of radio chatter aircraft taxied at their designated time to arrive at the runway hold in the correct order for take -off at 22:00hrs Saudi time,' recounted Sqn Ldr Batson. 'Departure from Tabuk involved a climb to medium level en-route to meet the Victor tanker in the nominated AAR area. The refuelling was all carried out in silence using light signals but it was a bit turbulent and with the weight of the two JP233 it required much throttle pumping to get the aircraft to close on, and stay in, the basket; as an AAR instructor this was not a recommended technique, but it worked. There was no moon so it was all a bit dark out and about but there were some aircraft lights well below us. After refuelling, checks were completed in preparation for descending to low level and going "sausage side;" this involved switching all the external lights off and switching our EW equipment on. Once at 200ft using the auto-TF, the aircraft was kept on course purely by the navigator keeping the "kit" in order, my job at this time was to change speed as ordered and monitor the TFR to ensure it was doing what it was supposed to. As we crossed the border, looking out the window all I saw was a lot of nothing, just varying amount of blackness. We overflew what appeared to be flaming aircraft wreckage at some point and saw something quite odd at several points along the route. As we crossed major roads a spotlight parked on the road would illuminate, not aimed at us just into the sky. It soon became apparent that it was a very basic but clever system of early warning. No doubt a conscript recruited to switch on the light if he heard an aircraft, but as the lights were quite well spaced along the road it

Nose art on Tornado GR1 (ZA447) proclaims it to be a 'MiG Eater' after Pete Batson and Mike Heath dropped a stick of JP233s, on their first mission, which enveloped an Iraqi aircraft landing on the runway at Al Asad. In fact, the enemy aircraft was a Dassault Mirage F1. (Dick Middleton)

A Tabuk-based Tornado GR1 armed with ALARM missiles transits north towards to Iraqi border. (David Bellamy)

gave a beam of light to the left of us and a beam of light to the right of us forming a surreal corridor of our progression into Iraq.

'The closer we got to the target the faster we went, progressing in stages from 450kt up to about 500kt, the latter needing small bursts of reheat to overcome the drag effect of the JP233. As the leader we were at the front of the package attacking Al Asad. I thought that this could work in our favour as we would well be over the airfield and out the other side before anyone knew that we were there. The target area could be seen from about eight miles out, a minute's flying time, and all I saw was the lights of the airfield and the lights of an aircraft in the visual circuit. At this point I disengaged the autopilot to prevent the TFR giving pull-up commands and was flying manually. Mike and I rapidly discussed the threat the enemy aircraft could be to the rest of Dundee formation so I attempted to lock my air-to-air missile onto it, but no reassuring growl came back. One of the disadvantages of using air-to-air mode when the weapon aiming system is in attack mode is that it cancels it, and that is exactly what it did. It was about this time, 30sec out with no weapon steering in the HUD, that our presence was known to the enemy and the sky was filled with triple-A tracer and bright white star shells exploding just above us. I manually selected pilot weapon aiming and moved my aircraft to ensure the munitions would go over the still lit runway. Out of the corner of my eye I spotted the aircraft that had been in the circuit rolling down the runway so I adjusted the track and hit him as well. As the munitions deployed the most satisfying sound I heard was the two weapon containers departing the aircraft with a 'clunk, clunk'. We were now in the middle of the inferno where it was relatively clear of triple-A but we had to get out the other side. Off target we visually sighted a missile launch so I manoeuvred the aircraft hard to the left to get on to our escape heading ASAP. It was at this point, flying manually at about 150ft in a 60° turn to the left that Mike shouted "roll left, turn left." I didn't really understand why he wanted me to increase the angle of bank so I checked the artificial horizon and kept what I had, only to hear again "roll left, roll left." As I rolled out onto the escape heading and put the autopilot back in, all became clear. As I manoeuvred off target Mike had become disorientated with the stream of tracer around the cockpit and thought we were in a roll to the right, hence his urgent need for me to roll left. We left the target area at a now achievable speed of 520kt racing for the border.

'The gaggle set track for home picking up their respective route and times to make the allocated exit gate to leave Iraqi airspace. At the border the quietly ecstatic formation climbed to medium level and then we checked them in on the radio; all present and correct with no losses, job well done.'

The SEAD support for the mission had been provided by another four Tornados, each armed with three ALARMs, led by Sqn Ldr McAlpine and Sq Ldr Pittaway. 'All went well,' remembered McAlpine. 'As we approached the firing point, I disengaged the auto pilot (200ft auto-TF until then) raised the nose slightly and pulled the trigger to fire the missiles. Immediately the ground below lit up from the very bright missile boost motors – simultaneously there was a shudder through the airframe as one-by-one the missiles left the under-fuselage stations. I recall thinking it was just like looking at *Star Trek* on the TV during a photon torpedo launch from the *Starship Enterprise*. As advertised, following a short period after launch, the missiles' red-coloured sustain motors lit and they entered their steep, slightly divergent, climb to height. I admit to being a bit mesmerized by the display and it was only when Dick Pittaway asked what the hell I was doing at 1,500ft that I sorted myself out, and got us back down to 200ft again. We didn't see any enemy defensive fire that night.'

Ivor Evans (OC IX Squadron) briefs his fourship for a mission from Dhahran. (Les Hendry)

Second Wave – Dhahran

As the Tabuk Wing was returning to base, the two formations of Tornados armed with JP233 were preparing to take off at Dhahran. Sqn Ldr G. Whittingham and Flt Lt K.J. Baldwin were at the head of four aircraft tasked against the airfield at Mudaysis and Wg Cdr I. Evans and Flt Lt R. James were leading the second fourship to Wadi Al Khirr. 'The planning and briefing were carried out without much bother, as the time came to ready ourselves with our flying kit, sanitizing our personal belongings, secreting our supply of gold sovereigns and walking to the aircraft, I remember the chatter subsiding' recalled Flt Lt W. Grout, the navigator in the Number 3 aircraft tasked against Mudaysis; 'we each seemed to withdraw into our own little world thinking "well this is it, years of training and now we have to do the real thing." In the cockpit we both went about our checks as per normal, our Skyshadow pod was playing up, but that was situation normal. It passed the BITE (Built-In Test) and we taxied for take-off. We chatted a little about the prospect of going "sausage side" and what our tactics would be once across the border, lots of weaving and trying to spot missile launches. I started to re-check the Skyshadow pod and found that it would not cooperate at all. It was dead. We continued the sortie with me trying everything to get it to work to no avail. As we approached the border we discussed our next move. I was very adamant that we turn back; the words of the Boss echoed in my ear. "This is not a war worth dying for," "failed ECM is a no-go item, come what may." For me decision made. It took a little persuading to get my pilot to return, but we did. There was silence in our cockpit as we returned to Dhahran (apart from compulsory R/T). We taxied back to the sunshades, shutdown, debriefed and waited in the crew room for our comrades to return. I felt remorse, guilt and worry that we had let the side down, despite the fact that our actions were fully supported. The wait was interminable, pacing around, unable to relax and feeling apprehensive. Several hours later, joy of joy, our team returned following a very successful mission, three pairs of JP233 on the runway and very little resistance. A huge sense of relief followed by the usual banter of "what did you scrub for, Wimps" or words to that effect.'

Theirs was not the only aircraft from Dhahran to suffer technical problems: the Number 4 aircraft crewed by Flt Lt P. Reid and Fl Lt S. Hadley suffered a generator failure. 'We approached the Iraqi border at 450kt and 200ft on the TFR, checks complete and as ready as we would ever be, running north towards the target,' remembered Flt Lt Hadley. 'Then an amber caption went off in the front cockpit; the accompanying flicker of the TV tabs told me it was a generator problem. Sure enough, the right generator had failed. Resets worked only briefly, and so a just over a minute later at five miles to the border we turned back. Our first war sortie was over. Or so we thought.

'In the climb out we managed to contact the AWACS for the return home. Established in the climb at around 10,000ft suddenly everything went black in the cockpit: Everything, black inside and out. It stayed black for a second, maybe less, before lights blared, attention-getters flashed and the whoop-whoop of the lyre-bird warning tone kicked my senses back to life. We had experienced a momentary double-generator failure, except that's not what we expected. It was certainly not like the simulator. Some of the kit was still working, but we had no time to ponder what had happened – we needed to land ASAP.' The crew diverted to the RSAF airbase at Al Jouf.

In the second fourship, both Wg Cdr Evans and Flt Lt James in the lead aircraft and the Number 4 crew, Flt Lt G. Harwell and Fl Lt M.J. Wintermeyer, were also having problems with TFR and auto-pilot systems respectively; both had to abort their sorties. Out of eight aircraft that launched from Dhahran that evening, only four made it to the targets.

Second Wave – Bahrain

At Bahrain, the evening wave consisted of two fourships manned by crews from the Marham squadrons. They were tasked against the airfields at Shaibah, near Basra, and Al Jarra, on the outskirts of Al Kut. The mission against Shaibah was led by Sqn Ldr J. Taylor and Sq Ldr G.E. Thwaites. Unfortunately soon after making its attack, the Number 3 aircraft, flown by Wg Cdr T.N.C. Elsdon and Flt Lt R.M. Collier flew into the ground and both crew members were killed.

The second fourship was led by Flt Lt G.T.W. Beet and Flt Lt S. Osborne. One of the aircraft had to return to Bahrain after the first AAR bracket when it suffered a GMR failure, leaving only three aircraft to press on to Al Jarra. As they approached the target area the Number 4 aircraft, flown by Fg Off N.J.W. Ingle and Flt Lt P. McKernon, accelerated to the attack speed of 540kt. Flt Lt McKernan described what happened next: 'about two-and-a-half miles from the target there was a loud "BANG" from the port wing and the aircraft, which Nige was now flying manually, pitched up to about 600ft. I asked if he had any captions on his CWP. He said "no" and I suggested that we get back down to a more comfortable height. It was very unnerving. I could busy myself with the radar and RHWH but Nige had no such distractions and I didn't envy him watching the orange glow turn into individual lines of tracer. As we crossed the airfield boundary we both pressed our commit buttons thus allowing the aircraft computer to commence dispensing the munitions at the right moment.

'Although we had been given some idea of what the next few seconds were going to be like, we were surprised by the effect of the JP233 system ejecting its munitions. It was like riding over a cobbled street in a cart with wooden wheels. The bang that accompanied the automatic jettison of the empty dispensers was a considerable surprise, despite the warnings we had received. Leaving the target was like going off stage: we left the glow and ran into a wall of darkness. The triple-A continued behind us until we lost sight of it.' After an uneventful transit to the border, the crew climbed to rendezvous with the post-strike tanker.

'In all the excitement,' continued McKernan, 'we had completely forgotten about the impact on our port wing just prior to the target. When Nige selected twenty-five degree wing sweep, the aircraft became unstable, so he swept them back and we refuelled without much trouble with the wings swept at forty-five degrees.' After landing using just mid-flap and without slats, the crew discovered that they had hit a large stork. As McKernan later commented, 'in the excitement of going to war we had quite forgotten the everyday risk of a birdstrike.'

At Bahrain, Flt Lt Heard reflected: 'we had just taken part in the largest air operation for decades, and the Gulf War was now definitely on. We could see that Iraq had taken a real pounding that night, and we wondered if they could sustain that for long. We had become combat-proven crews, and the change in attitude and confidence was clear … but by the time I flew my second mission – the next night – we had lost two Tornados, so we knew that it was going to be tough after all.'

4

January-February 1991
Gulf War

Day Two

The air war over Iraq and Kuwait was now in full swing. The strategic plan was for an intense air campaign to neutralize the Iraqi air-defence system and establish air supremacy before moving on to destroy systematically the Iraqi military infrastructure and its support functions. For the Tornado Force, this would mean, for the time being, continuing with low-level night-time JP233 attacks against the Iraqi Air Force's main operating bases. 'There was no shortage of targets to hit,' commented Fg Off Craghill, 'and the GR1's early role was to keep the Iraqi Air Force fighters and bombers on the ground where they could do no harm.'

Meanwhile Craghill was programmed to be in the Number 4 aircraft for an attack on the massive airfield complex at H3, in the early hours of the morning of 18 January 1991. The mission would be led by Wg Cdr Travers-Smith with Sqn Ldr Fradgley and would be supported by four ALARM aircraft led by Flt Lt Roche and Flt Lt Bellamy.

'Home to a mixed fleet of fighter and attack aircraft, H3 was defended by an aggressive mixture of SAM and triple-A,' continued Craghill. 'Our objective was to sever access to the runways from the HAS dispersals at each corner of the airfield, which was thought to be easier to achieve than putting two runways out of action. In what would become a familiar pattern, we would have "area support" – fighters sweeping a wide area ahead of us for enemy aircraft, electronic-attack aircraft jamming SAM radars and planes capable of shooting anti-radiation missiles at any radars which did threaten. These aircraft were not dedicated to our formation, but knew where we would be at any given time to ensure they could protect us. Refuelling tankers loitered in the airspace of northern Saudi Arabia to ensure all aircraft had sufficient fuel to complete their sorties, and at least three AWACS aircraft fed information constantly to everyone through a series of daily changing radio frequencies.

Armed Tornado GR1s on the line at Tabuk; note the makeshift covers designed to keep heat (and sand) out of the cockpits. (Lars Smith)

A weapon loading team at Tabuk preparing the front section of a JP233 canister for loading under a Tornado GR1. They are wearing full NBC protective equipment including respirators; a scene that would have been typical of any Cold War station exercise. (Pete Batson)

Tornado GR1s of the Tabuk Wing refuel from a VC10 tanker during an operational mission. The aircraft are armed with JP233 and AIM-9L. (Mal Craghill)

'Once airborne we checked in with AWACS on the western refuelling frequency and were guided to our tanker – usually a Victor – to take-on fuel during our northerly transit towards Iraq. Tonight it was the turn of Number 3 to have technical problems, so we departed the tanker as a threeship. Up to this point we could see dozens of aircraft in the refuelling tracks, tanking with their lights on to minimize the risk of mid-air collisions. As we switched to the strike primary frequency and descended to low level, we extinguished our lights and so too did all the other aircraft heading into Iraq; where once we had seen many, we now saw none. It felt lonely, but we knew we were far from alone. Our final radar fix before crossing into Iraq was a customs post at the Saudi/Iraqi border, which we streaked over at 200ft, the terrain-following radar and autopilot adjusting our course as I updated the navigation and attack system.

'The run up to H3 was fairly short; we would be over the target less than 15min after crossing into Iraq. We crossed the border roughly parallel with, and only a few miles from, the Jordanian border, and already we could see sporadic bursts of tracer fire to our east. Word of our approach didn't take long to reach H3, and soon the airfield defences were active; SAM radars began to show on our RHWR and the triple-A became more intense. We were in no doubt where our target was by now. Mike and I completed our pre-target checks and turned eastwards over the main Baghdad to Amman highway. Ahead of us H3 was now alight with dense tracer fire up to around 4,000ft, and SAM radars were searching us out; indications of Roland, then Crotale on our RHWR as I dispensed chaff from our counter-measures suite. Two things happened more or less simultaneously now. A minute ahead of us, and eight miles closer to the target, our formation leader could see no way of

A Tornado GR1 of the Dhahran Wing loaded with JP233. The large size of the canisters is apparent. (Chris Coulls)

prosecuting a successful attack due to the incredible concentration of triple-A, and he called to the formation to abort the attack and egress west from the target area. As we began to turn, Mike and I heard the dreaded radar alarm from our RHWR, and I looked down to see 'SAM-8 target tracker' to our east. I turned on our jamming pod, dispensed chaff and called for Mike to roll out heading north. Almost immediately we were 'spiked' again, and executed another ninety-degree turn, overriding the terrain-following radar and climbing slightly to stay away from the flat desert floor a few hundred feet below us. Finally, with the threat seemingly negated, we turned south and re-engaged the terrain following radar to get back down to 200ft.

'We now had very little situational awareness on the other two GR1s in our formation, but we knew we had to get rid of our weapons to ensure we had sufficient fuel to get back to Tabuk. As we rolled out south a satellite airfield of H3 was directly on our nose about ten miles away; I quickly found it on the radar, Mike lined us up, and we prepared for weapon release. Right then what looked like gunfire erupted just off to our right, between our position and the Jordanian border. We had no time to react, and pressed home our attack. With the JP233 dispensed, the canisters fell away from the aircraft with an almighty thud, and we were able to quickly accelerate to 550kt and run for the border. What we had taken to be ground fire had actually been the Number 2 aircraft dispensing their JP233 around four miles to our west – we had somehow crossed paths in the confused egress from the target area. In a few minutes we had crossed safely back into Saudi Arabia and, turning our lights back on, were able to re-join the formation for the

Douglas Moule, with reading material, awaits the all-clear during a Scud missile alert which regularly punctuated the day. However, Patriot missile batteries proved to be a very effective defence against the missiles. (Douglas Moule)

transit back to Tabuk. For me and Mike, our first combat sortie had been about as busy as were able to cope with – but more was to come.'

Dhahran did not launch any attack missions that morning, but the base reacted to two air-raid warnings in the early hours. 'This time the second was genuine,' wrote the II Squadron diarist. 'Many of us heard the explosion as one of Iraq's Scud missiles was successfully intercepted by a US-supplied Patriot missile.'

Just across the causeway from Dhahran and also in the early hours, Sqn Ldr Risdale and Wg Cdr Broadbent led eight aircraft from Bahrain to Jalibah airfield. 'This time the target layout was about half of Tallil,' explained Sqn Ldr Risdale, 'so just two long operating surfaces and HAS sites in each corner. I guess the target planners had decided that since it was smaller we could attack it by ourselves, which after our experience with Tallil suited us fine. The original plan was basically a copy of the Tallil blueprint with parallel track low-level ingress as an eight-ship gorilla, splitting into two fourships to approach the target from two directions ninety-degrees apart. Given our first night's experience we decided to close up the attack ToTs for each aircraft to try and get the whole attack done in as short a time as possible to try and minimize the threat from triple-A. We decided to adapt the plan and keep six aircraft in one section with just two, myself and Nick Heard, detaching from the front to fly a longer route and make the ninety-degree cut 30sec after the other six had attacked. The first six were to attack essentially in pairs line abreast but the angle of cut across the runways and 10sec ToT separation between the individuals in each pair, and 20sec between pairs, gave what we all considered to be adequate separation.' Leading the rear fourship once again, Sqn Ldr Buckley found this second mission to be 'much harder for us because we knew exactly what we were going to have to face. We decided to forget the medium speed rule and go in at full bore. The Tornado will go pretty fast when you need it, and once you get this train going with a bit of initial burner, not a lot stops it. This mission was a bit hairy because just beyond the airfield was an ammunition dump. The idea this time was for us to run through from south to north, turn left and left again and head straight back home. But because we'd decided to go max-chat [maximum speed], our turning circles were obviously going to be that much wider and although were briefed to compensate by tightening the turn, in the heat of the moment I forgot, as did the Number 7 behind me.

'Running into the target I looked out of the left side of the cockpit and although I couldn't see an aircraft I saw the unmistakable trail of a JP233 weapon exploding towards me. The aircraft that delivered that weapon must have only just passed behind me. We dropped our weapon, but this time I was ready for the kick in the back as the aircraft shook off its heavy load. I allowed the speed to stay high which was a mistake because of the increased size of the forthcoming turning circle that was, this time, flown by the autopilot. Off the target we had, in fact, to complete two 90° turns to achieve the run-out for home with about a two minute leg between turns. After the first turn, with autopilot in and TFR engaged I looked in amazement at the target we had just attacked. The triple-A was incessant and there were several explosions going off. But whilst I was exuding enthusiasm at the results of our efforts a nasty event was brewing up for us: suddenly we were looking right into a fantastic fireworks display; we were right over the top of the ammunition dump with triple-A coming at us from all directions. The dump was heavily defended and it seemed to be firing all of its weapons at once.'

Reconnaissance

The second day of the war marked the first missions by the Tornado reconnaissance detachment at Dhahran. There had been some speculation the previous day that the Air Headquarters intended to use the Tornado GR1A to carry out bomb damage assessment of the JP233 targets, but in the words of the diarist 'sense prevailed and we weren't tasked.' However on the evening of 18 January two aircraft, crewed by Wg Cdr Threadgould and Flt Lt T. Robinson and Sqn Ldr R.F. Garwood and Sq Ldr J. Hill, took off at 19:00hrs GMT and set off to search for Scud launchers. 'All had safe and successful sorties, which were achieved without tanker support using two 2,250-litre tanks and two 1,500-litre tanks per aircraft,' recorded the II Squadron diarist. 'but Wg Cdr Threadgould had a bit of excitement over the other side when just before the target it became clear that as the 1,500 litre tanks were jettisoned, the 2,250-litre tanks stopped feeding. Instead of having 4,200kg of useable fuel over target, only 1,700kg was available. A quick dash to the border, followed by jettisoning of the big tanks and some super help from AWACS resulted in a diversion to King Khalid military strip.' The pattern continued over the next few evenings with pairs of reconnaissance aircraft dispatched over Iraq to search for Scud missile sites.

Also that evening the Tabuk Wing attacked H2 airfield. In a change of tactics, only four aircraft led by Sqn Ldrs Lennox and Weeks, were armed with JP233 but they were supported by a six-aircraft SEAD formation, led by Sqn Ldr McAlpine and Sq Ldr Pittaway, which carried a mixture of ALARM and also 1,000lb bombs. 'For the first few nights of combat operations the triple-A fire over Iraqi airfields was intense,' explained Flt Lt Bellamy, 'and at times seemingly initiated when an ALARM formation launched their missiles. For this reason,

Two of the Tornado GR1A reconnaissance aircraft at Dhahran. To many it seemed odd that the older aircraft on II Squadron were sent to the Gulf, rather than the new aircraft on 13 Squadron. (II Squadron)

Loading the rear half of a JP233 canister onto the shoulder pylon of a Tornado GR1. (BAe Heritage)

several ALARM packages changed their weapon loads to conventional 1,000lb bombs to attempt to suppress triple-A sites and cut a path for other Tornados targeting airfield runways.' Although two of the SEAD formation dropped out due to unserviceability, the tactic proved successful and all four of the JP233 aircraft were able to deliver their weapons successfully. Another six aircraft, this time led by Flt Lt P.A. Fenlon-Smith and Flt Lt R.L. Hawkins visited H2 the following evening. In another departure from the tactics of the previous two days, this time the aircraft were loaded with eight 1,000lb bombs to be lofted into the airfield.

Also on 19 January, the Bahrain Wing revisited Tallil, which had been their target on the first day of the war. This time, like the Tabuk Wing, some of the aircraft were armed with eight 1,000lb bombs, in an attempt to clear a path through the defences for the JP233-loaded aircraft. One of the pilots later wrote 'I found myself tasked with targeting a Roland sight on a SEAD mission (one of four aircraft targeting suspected air defences with four "slick" 1,000lb bombs before eight far braver chaps were to follow through close behind and deliver JP233). The highly-questionable decision to perform "in-house" SEAD was primarily based on a lack of confidence in the SEAD that had been provided by US assets on earlier missions. Needless to say, this mobile system was over four miles away from the location that had been provided by RAF intelligence. We discovered this during the run in to the target when Bob and I had a Roland lock in our two o'clock. The lock up was shortly followed by a plume of white flame going upwards in our two o'clock – and to our annoyance, not moving left or right. After missile time of flight of less than 3sec, an explosion occurred which produced a silhouette of Dave and Robbie's Tornado. Bob suggested that some sort of evasion manoeuvre might

Free-fall 1,000lb bombs ready to be loaded at Tabuk: these weapons could be loft-dropped from low level or dropped from medium level.

be appropriate so I duly obliged whilst he let off chaff plus some flares that helped me to see terrain ahead, before the airfield batteries started firing such that night vision was no-longer an issue. Regrettably, quite a lot of speed had washed off as a result of the hard (reasonably level) manoeuvre and reversal back towards target, plus it was now clear that our target was not underneath Bob's mark. The tracer above us resembled sheet lightning in daylight in the thin stratus above us. We pulled up into it to loft out bombs on what had once been a Roland battery, but what I guessed was now desert, before we focussed on getting back to low level and getting home.'

Unfortunately during this sortie Flt Lt D.J. Waddington and Flt Lt R.J. Stewart's aircraft was hit by a Roland missile. The crew managed to eject and were quickly taken prisoner by the Iraqis.

Day Four – Tactics Evolve

By 20 January, the three Tornado bases had begun to experiment with their own separate tactical approaches. At Tabuk, JP233 was abandoned in favour of 1,000lb bombs delivered from lofted attacks. Although these weapons would not be effective against the operating surfaces, they would cause damage against other parts of the airfield infrastructure, including HASs. The six aircraft tasked against Ruwayshid airfield, close to the Jordanian border, in the early hours of the morning each lofted eight bombs onto the airfield.

At Bahrain, Sqn Ldr Buckley reported that 'we heard from another base that they had a reasonable amount of success lofting bombs with an airburst setting on the fuze. Our initial sorties adopted the tactic of going into the airfield target behind the USAF; unfortunately

The crews of a fourship from XV Squadron who flew from Bahrain throughout the Gulf War: Bruce MacDonald, Paddy Teakle, Mike Barley, Steve Barnes, Glynn Harley, Dave Cockerill, Tony McGlone, Gordon Buckley. (Gordon Buckley)

on the first two sorties, by the time we reached the target they were well and truly stirred up like a hornet's nest, with heavy triple-A going off in all directions. No, it was better to be on our own with the first two aircraft loaded with JP233, the next four with 1,000lb bombs set for airburst, and the last two with JP233, again, to run through the black holes that would be left. This was the tactic for the third sortie.'

'This mission was one of those trips where just about anything that could go wrong did go wrong,' wrote Sqn Ldr Risdale afterwards. 'The Number 8 (JP233) went unserviceable on the ground, but the remainder got together and we rendezvoused with the tankers for our first of two brackets. I was about three-quarters full when we flew into a big bumpy cumulonimbus cloud. Despite using burner I dropped out, as did Nick on the other wing. We then spent some time bouncing up and down trying to synchronize the bounces with the hose. Nick spooked, I managed to get back in and fill then Nick completed his refueling on my hose. The rear tanker team was having similar problems.'

'This whole sortie was an absolute nightmare,' agreed Sqn Ldr Buckley. 'The weather was bad, the two tankers would not come out of the cloud and trying to tank in cloud at night is bad news. One aeroplane had to turn back as his fuel would not transfer correctly and my Number 2 just could not physically get his probe into the tanker's refuelling basket so I had to send him home. Eventually only four of us got to the target.

'When we left the tanker and dropped down to low level there was ground fog everywhere. So, once again we found ourselves at 200ft and 420kt relying totally on the aircraft systems. As we ran into our initial point for the attack, I could actually see the effect of the other aeroplanes' weapons, but the results were disappointing. The final run in to this target was after a ninety-degree turn onto the final attack heading and so for some time I was flying along the perimeter of the airfield with a good view of the attacks made by the rest of our lead formation. The idea of the loft attack was to suppress the triple-A to create a hole into which the rear two of the formation could fly through unimpeded and drop their bombs. If the mission had gone ahead as planned there would be thirty-two 1,000lb bombs air-bursting over the heads (literally) of the Iraqi forces that were throwing up the triple-A. However, due to the un-serviceability problems en-route there were only four aircraft now attacking the airfield.'

In the lead pair Sqn Ldr Risdale was approaching the target and, in his words, 'looking forward to having a quiet JP233 attack rather than flying through the Flak firestorm. Unfortunately, the air defences at Al Jarrah must have been more sophisticated than the other airfields we had attacked, because the triple-A started up about 30sec before our arrival, and for a third time we went through on a wing and a prayer. But of course this was our third attack and both of us were convinced that the barrage was more aimed and consequently more threatening. I was also convinced that John had selected long stick since I had the impression that I could feel every single sub-munitions come out slowly, rather than the almost machine-gun rattle I recalled from the first run. How the brain plays tricks.

'The first two aircraft had run through as planned, delivering their JP233 weapons,' continued Sqn Ldr Buckley. 'The next aircraft through, just ahead of my planned attack, was a loft attack of eight 1,000lbs bombs. The sight of these bombs exploding mid air was shocking to the senses, but amazingly the triple-A did not diminish and I realized that I was going to have to make the same attack into the maelstrom that was the target. I got the burners going until I had no more spare fuel left so I shut them off, but then I didn't have the speed. Then the triple-A started whistling past the canopy and I told Paddy, "We're here, we're here", but he said we still had 50sec to go. At that stage I tripped out the TFR and just went on in. When I looked at the film afterwards, I'd actually allowed the aeroplane to climb to 600ft. I thought this was suicidal because all my teaching had been to go as low as possible when facing triple-A.

'At least I had got some speed on. With the acceleration that the short burst of reheat gave me we were now doing about 600kt but with the reheat out the speed started to wash off alarmingly. By the time I pulled up for the attack we were back to around 550kt which was more than enough for an attack with reheat, but no reheat to sustain the speed during the upwards manoeuvre there was a chance the aircraft computer would not get a release solution and the bombs would not be released. The Iraqis had pushed the defence line of the airfield out to about three to four miles, which is right in the heart of the loft envelope. In effect we were pulling up right into the teeth of the triple-A. Fortunately, the bombs did release with an almost normal profile. At weapon release, the aircraft pitch attitude was about twenty degrees and around 1,500ft. The idea is then to get the aircraft back down to low level as quickly as possible whilst turning away from then target… A tricky manoeuvre at the best of times, but when executed at night, with triple-A flying past the cockpit, the pressure of not having enough fuel to return home and the ever present nightmare of disorientation it was even more hazardous.

'Paddy realized we didn't have enough fuel to get home so we jettisoned the twin store bomb carriers and "clean" the aeroplane. We got home all right, but upon walking in

A Bahrain-based Tornado GR1 recovers to Muharraq airfield after releasing its weapons. After 20 January the Bahrain Wing tried using 1,000lb bombs in preference to the JP233. (XV Squadron)

to the debriefing room I met the pilot from the lead formation who had just carried out the same loft attack as me. "I don't have too many more of those inside me," he said which came as quite a shock to me. He was the last person I expected to hear that sort of comment from. It made me assess my feelings. Although I felt as though I could continue for some time to come it was apparent that something had to done about our tactics and how they relate to the incredible triple-A barrages that we faced each time we went and attacked an airfield. The meeting to modify our tactics was held in a briefing room with the senior members of the Bahrain detachment. The consensus was that since we considered ourselves to now have air superiority there was no need to risk further operations at low level through triple-A barrages particularly if the Americans would agree to provide air support for us.' For Sqn Ldr Risdale, too, 'this third mission was an emotional watershed. After returning to my room, I mulled over what we'd been through had a bit of a cry. As a team, we were all quite private about such emotional hiccups but I don't think any of us were immune.'

Later that day, Bahrain's second eightship launched to attack the airfield at An Najaf from medium level. A single aiming point was chosen in the middle of the parallel runways: the idea that ballistic dispersion would scatter the bombs and blanket the entire airfield area. The formation, led by Sqn Ldr Mason and Sq Ldr Stapleton, rendezvoused with two Victor tankers, which led them along the 'Olive Trail,' a 200-mile tanker-trail route towards the Saudi/Iraqi border. The ingress route to An Najaf took about 40min and a strong upper wind caused some problems, because the Tornados were forced to fly at an uncomfortably low airspeed in order to keep to their pre-planned timings. A further snag was that both the lead and Number 3 aircraft reported that their GMRs had failed, so that they would have to fly in close formation on their wingmen (at night) and release their weapons when they saw the wingmen drop theirs. However, despite these setbacks, all eight aircraft arrived over the target on time. Until then, the formation had been unopposed, but Flt Lt Paisey described how 'the defences

A Tornado GR1, loaded with 1,000lb free-fall bombs, AIM-9L and 2,250-litre fuel tanks, taxying out for a mission from Dhahran. (Les Hendry)

opened up only after the first bombs impacted. The triple-A was heavy and consisted of both tracer and airburst, reaching a height of approximately 18,000ft. No SAMs were launched and there were no RHWR indications. Eight Tornados had dropped sixty-four 1,000lb bombs on the target in one minute.' For the egress from the target, the effects of the winds were reversed and this time the crews had to use reheat to accelerate to a fast enough speed to keep to the planned timings.

At Dhahran, Sqn Ldr Moule and Sq Ldr Coulls had spent a frustrating evening planning to use cluster bombs (CBU) for an attack on a Scud battery, which had been located by a reconnaissance aircraft. Unfortunately by the time all the work to co-ordinate the mission was completed, it was daylight and the sortie was cancelled. Instead the crews were re-tasked for the following night. 'The target was another major Iraqi airfield, Jalibah, which looked like a relatively unpleasant place to go to,' recalled Sqn Ldr Coulls. 'As the mission was to "harass" operations from the airfield, we opted for the first four aircraft lofting 1,000lb airburst-fuzed bombs along the line of the triple-A defences, closely followed by the second four attacking the runways and taxiways with JP233 from an entirely different direction. We were packaged with other units attacking targets in the general vicinity and would, therefore, benefit from their support.' In fact the second pair was later re-tasked to carry 1,000lb bombs as well. The Dhahran Wing had taken a slightly different tactical solution to that at Bahrain, by opting to loft five, rather than eight, 1,000lb bombs. This gave the aircraft a little more performance margin during the run in for the attack and the loft manoeuvre itself.

The mission did not start well. One of the pilots cut his head badly while walking out to his aeroplane and could not fly the sortie, and when Sqn Ldr Moule and Sq Ldr Coulls got airborne they suffered a number of systems failures in their aircraft. However, they decided to press on. Coulls continued the story: 'the rendezvous with our tanker was successful and we were finally on our way. At this point, it is worth mentioning that the weather during the first week of *Desert Storm* was very poor. Our transit altitude was at about 10 to 12,000ft, which tonight was exactly coincident with the cloud tops, which put us in and out of cloud when on the tanker, and also suffering moderate-to-severe turbulence for most of the transit. It was very uncomfortable, and a real testament to the skill of the pilots to get safely into contact with the refuelling basket. However, we eventually got to the drop-off point, still in bad weather, and turned north towards the Iraqi border, lights out and in radio silence. We started our descent and actually broke out into some clear air for a while. We were still concerned about the accuracy of their navigation system and tried to spot one of the other formation members, not surprisingly without success.

'At this point we decided that the best thing to do was to get to low level earlier than planned, thus keeping us clear of the rest of the formation. We were also running a little early on our timeline and consequently were flying much slower than our planned cruise speed, but were still in friendly territory. As we approached the border, we accelerated and dropped down to 200ft using the automatic terrain-following system, straight into dense fog, probably the last thing we were expecting to find in the desert. Then, as we accelerated through exactly 400kt, the aircraft entered what was known as an open-loop pull up, which is pretty much like it sounds, climbing the aircraft steeply away from the ground. This necessitated cancelling the automatics and manually settling the aircraft back down to low level. Unfortunately, the automatics refused to remain engaged above 400kt, and Douglas had to fly the aircraft manually,

Douglas Moule and Chris Coulls about to lead their fourship on a bombing mission from Dhahran with eight 1,000lb free-fall bombs loaded to their Tornado GR1. (Douglas Moule)

Battle damage to a Dhahran- based Tornado GR1. (Les Hendry)

very close to the ground, in cloud, with both us using the radars to monitor our ground clearance. This was something that we had practised in the simulator (Cold War mentality), but should really have stayed there. We pressed on like this for far too long until we finally saw sense. We were a hazard to ourselves and the rest of our team, so we turned and headed back to the south just before we were planned to converge on the target, thoroughly disappointed.'

The remaining aircraft prosecuted their attack successfully, although two aircraft received battle damage.

That evening another eight-ship formation took off from Tabuk, bound for Al Taqaddum airfield, however it seemed to be plagued with bad luck. 'We had a full bomb and fuel load, got airborne, then hit a snag,' recalled Sqn Ldr Batson, in the lead aircraft; 'the control column would not move much to the right. I handed over the lead of the sortie and then went to a pre-designated area to jettison the bombs and dump some fuel, the idea being that if we lightened the aircraft, we might be able to invert it; if there was something just jamming the controls, we would shake it out. We shook the aircraft around for about half an hour but could not fix the problem so we flew back to base to attempt a landing. Every time I lined the aircraft up with the runway, the wind blew us off. I'd been trying to land for about an hour, making several approaches to a variety of runways at Tabuk, but all to no avail. The senior RAF supervisor at Tabuk then ordered us to abandon the aircraft. The transit to the abandonment area was occupied with running through the drills in the FRCs, with both of us preparing for an ejection from about 6,000ft above the ground. The Saudis launched a rescue helicopter when they knew we were just about to eject, presumably to avoid it being hit by anything raining down from on high. I discussed with Mike who would do the countdown, but as he

The scattered wreckage of Tornado GR1 (ZD893) after Pete Batson and Mike Heath were forced to eject after a control restriction prevented them from landing the aircraft on 20 January. (Pete Batson)

was going to initiate command ejection for us both it was decided that he would do the count – we agreed a countdown of ten.

'I remember the ejection as if I were watching a slow-motion film. It seemed like a lifetime before anything happened – although in fact it only took 0.6secs between Mike pulling the handle and the cockpit canopy flying off. There was an enormous bang and I was hit in the right eye by something as my head was forced into my lap; then I remember that although it was pitch black, there was this vast pool of white light from the flash of the ejection rocket's explosion. As we were taught, I started checking from top to bottom to ensure the parachute had deployed and then located and released my dinghy pack once I saw the ground approaching. I had seen Mike some distance off during the descent but he was above me and rightly, as he went first, he should have been below me. I checked the parachute again and found it had a rip in one gore allowing me to descend a spot quicker than normal. It was quite a pleasant descent really; I was able to see the circular irrigation fields and several small lights dotted around the area. As the ground appeared closer I got into the parachute landing position and waited for the inevitable; after several seconds it did not come so I relaxed as I presumed I had estimated the closure incorrectly. Then I hit the ground and landed like a bag of spuds, no front left or right parachute landing for me.'

Meanwhile something of a shambles ensued with rest of the formation. 'The Number Two took over and then AWACS delayed the mission by twenty minutes. There was indecision,' declared Flt Lt Hawkins in the Number 5 aircraft, 'and it ended up with me calling over the radio "who wants to come with me?" We proceeded as a fiveship and completed the task against Al Taqaddum.'

The Move to Medium Level (21 to 24 January)

Eight aircraft from Tabuk led by Sqn Ldrs McAlpine and Pittaway carried out a low-level attack against the airfield facilities at H3 airfield in the early hours of 21 January. Once again the aircraft carried eight 1,000lb bombs, which they delivered successfully from a loft profile. However, the Tornado missions flown that evening reflected a move towards operating at medium level.

In Sqn Ldr Coulls' view, 'to say that this was something of a culture shock to us is an understatement; medium-level tactics had not been widely practised by the Tornado force and the majority of the crews had no experience whatsoever. The facts were that the RAF had lost a number of aircraft during the opening week and we knew that the low-level tactics had been at least a contributory factor in all cases, whether the cause of the loss had been due to enemy action, or controlled flight into the ground. Flying above 20,000ft would obviously negate the risk of hitting the ground, and also take us above the reach of triple-A and the tactical SAMs; or so the intelligence told us.'

'When I flew in the first medium level mission of the war I was very uneasy,' agreed Sqn Ldr Buckley. 'All of our training during the Cold War and up to now had been at low level and night medium-level tactics are quite different. It all hinges on keeping a safe distance from the rest of the formation around you. At the altitudes we were flying and the all-up weight of the aircraft meant that speed control was critical and keeping formation position was quite difficult to achieve.'

For that evening's sortie from Bahrain, eight aircraft, each armed with eight 1,000lb bombs were tasked against the airfield facilities at Jalibah. The mission was flown at medium level

A Tornado GR1 from the Dhahran Wing, loaded with eight 1,000lb free-fall bombs, climbs through the clouds to attack Iraq. Having concentrated exclusively on low-level tactics during the Cold War, the RAF was not particularly well prepared for medium-level operations over Iraq. (Andy Glover)

Loaded with 1,000lb free-fall bombs, the Tornado GR1s from the Bahrain Wing wait as their Victor tanker taxies past. (Gordon Buckley)

and was supported by four F-4G Wild Weasels and a fighter escort of two F-15C Eagles. After refuelling the Tornados left the two VC10 tankers for the 30min flight to Jalibah; once again they encountered the strong upper winds, which forced them to fly uncomfortably slowly on the way into the target. On the route in, the Tornados were unchallenged, but the triple-A barrage started as soon as the first weapons impacted. A number of SAMs were also launched ballistically, with no indications of guidance. All the aircraft dropped their weapons inside a 2min window and started to head to the safety of the Saudi border, but the effects of the wind meant that they had to use reheat to keep to their time plan. The egress was made all the more exciting by radar lock-ups, which the RHWR identified as MiG-27 Fulcrum and Mirage F1 fighters – the two types in the Iraqi Air Force inventory with a night capability. Later analysis showed these in reality to be other friendly fighters – but in the heat of the moment most of the formation had jettisoned their fuel tanks and twin-store carriers in attempts to break the lock. Two Victor tankers were on hand as the formation crossed back into Saudi airspace. However the drama was far from over: as the Tornados approached Bahrain they found themselves in the midst of a Scud missile alert.

A few hours later, Sqn Ldr Whittingham and Flt Lt Baldwin led the first medium-level mission from Dhahran. Following a similar profile to the Bahrain-based Tornados, the six aircraft also attacked the airfield at Jalibah, each dropping five 1,000lb bombs on the HAS sites. Flt Lt Grout, the navigator on the Number 3 aircraft described the sortie: 'planning and briefing complete, the crew-in went well, we were all serviceable and we took off in good order. The tankers were exactly where we expected them and the AAR went according to plan with all aircraft plugging in and getting the correct fuel. All was well in our little dark world. We checked in with AWACs turned off the lights and crossed the border. As we approached

Two Tornado GR1s from the Dhahran Wing, loaded with eight 1,000lb free-fall bombs, refuel from a VC10 tanker of 101 Squadron. (Andy Glover)

the built-up areas, initially we were over desert, the sky ahead lit up with a myriad of swirling anti-aircraft fire, mainly tracer. It looked like a deadly fourth of July party. I remember the odd expletive issuing from my mouth, as we steadily got closer. We had to go through this fire as there was no alternative direction to attack from, other formations to avoid et cetera. I was now half heads-in looking for offsets and half out watching the tracer display, whilst in between tightening my straps and making sure all my kit was stowed snuggly in my flying clothing, I'm sure there was some buttock clenching in the mix as well. The feeling was more apprehensive than frightening.

'As we progressed nearer to the target it became clear that the triple-A was of small calibre and was not reaching our altitude, phew, relief. However, no relaxation as we still kept a good lookout for any missile launch as the Iraqis had by now started to launch without using radar. Bombs away… lots of bright flashes from the forty bombs dropped by our eight jets; now the run for home. As we crossed the "lights on" line the sky became a mixture of stars and aircraft lights. Our accurate plan in-bound the target had become a bit of a shambles out-bound and we were not sure which aircraft were ours; this, added to the fact that there were numerous tankers waiting for several different missions made the initial part of recovery somewhat haphazard. Some bright spark transmitted for his formation to drop a flare, he got more responses than he bargained for. Eventually we all got our acts together, refuelled and came home. Four hours and 25min passed in a flash. Then a great sense of relief that the mission had been successful and that we had all survived another day.'

In the Number 4 aircraft, Flt Lt P. Reid and Flt Lt S. Hadley were also experiencing the Iraqi air defences for the first time. 'I took fix/attack mode at forty-six miles to make sure

An ALARM-armed Tornado GR1 from Tabuk heads towards the Iraqi border. (David Bellamy)

that I nailed the target,' recalled Flt Lt Hadley. 'A minute or so later we saw our first triple-A: a massive red bursting carpet of small explosions at around 10 to 15,000ft, perfectly visible against the total blackness of the empty desert. Then some more, this time white streaks snaking up from some sort of rapid-fire triple-A, much lower in altitude. It wasn't scary, but at the same time rather mesmerizing. Just as we were about to drop as part of the lead fourship, the bombs from the Numbers 1 and 2 aircraft impacted, with a series of brilliant white flashes in rapid succession marking where the sticks of bombs hit. They really lit up the night.'

Meanwhile at Tabuk Flt Lt Roche and Flt Lt Bellamy had been tasked lead an ALARM formation to provide SEAD support for an operation by F-15E aircraft. 'On the night of 21 January, four ALARM-equipped Tornados performed a graceful fan-split at low level to spread-launch 12 missiles at radars located around Al-Qaim, close to the Syrian border,' recounted Flt Lt Bellamy. 'This mission was in support of fourteen F-15E Strike Eagles who released weapons from an altitude of 30,000ft. On return to Tabuk, the ALARM crews were greeted with ground crew in full NBC attire and the eventual realization that the F-15Es had bombed a very suspicious target; an anthrax production facility.'

As the ALARM formation was recovering to Tabuk, one of the last low-level missions was about to get airborne, with a ToT in the early hours of 22 January. The eight aircraft led by Sqn Ldr Lennox and Sq Ldr Weeks, and each armed with five 1,000lb bombs, were bound for the radar facility at Ar Rutbah. Unfortunately this mission was not blessed with good luck: firstly, three aircraft had to pull out before crossing the border because of systems failures and then the lead Tornado was shot down over the target and both crew members were killed.

A Tornado GR1 from the Tabuk Wing, armed with 1,000lb free-fall bombs carries out pre-strike AAR from a VC10 tanker over northern Saudi Arabia. As the campaign progressed the ALARM crews also flew conventional bombing missions as well as the SEAD sorties. (David Bellamy)

That afternoon Flt Lt Fenlon-Smith and Flt Lt Hawkins led another eight aircraft from Tabuk at medium level, supported by two ALARM Tornados, against an ammunition storage facility at Qubaysah, to the west of Ramadi. However the other Tornado missions over the next three days, all of which were carried out at medium level and at night, continued the work of harassing and neutralizing the main operating bases of the Iraqi Air Force. Sqn Ldr Risdale and Wg Cdr Broadbent led an eightship from Bahrain against Tallil, Wg Cdr Witts and Flt Lt Smith led an eightship from Dhahran against Shaiba on 22 January. 'At this higher altitude things seemed much more pedestrian,' thought Witts, 'and, of course, there was the added grandstand view of southern Iraq and Kuwait, where the darkness was periodically punctuated by fires and explosions. Triple-A was still trying its best to reach us but, now, we could look down almost contemptuously on the streams of tracer as they whirled about beneath us. There were a few pockets of heavy-calibre triple-A that could reach our operating altitude, but we tried to stay well clear of those. On the other hand, SAMs were now much more of a threat, although the campaign to defeat them was having considerable success. USAF Wild Weasels would attack any missile radar that threatened and the Iraqis were starting to fire their SAMs in an un-guided mode rather than turn on their radars and attract the' lethal attention of the Wild Weasels. On this trip, we saw a few missiles arcing up nearby, but nothing that threatened us directly.' The following day the Bahrain Wing had bombed Mudaysis airfield and formations from Tabuk (led by Flt

Lt M. Williams and Flt Lt Goddard) and Dhahran (led by Sqn Ldr Moule and Sq Ldr Coulls) attacked Al Taqaddum. Sqn Ldr Coulls remembered that 'the target ingress and egress involved a lengthy transit over the heavily built-up areas to the south and west of the city of Baghdad, and whilst the air-defence network was no longer integrated, individual SAMs were capable of autonomous operation. As we proceeded north, with about sixty miles to run to the outskirts of Baghdad, all hell broke loose below us. We had some collective experience of ground fires at this point, but had seen nothing like this. We could make out triple-A, with numerous colours of tracer and trajectory. There were missiles, presumably unguided, again with different coloured trails, fortunately all topping out below us; it looked like the intelligence might be right after all. Some of the fires looked like they might only be flares, fired for effect, but we had no real way of knowing. This intense display continued for at least the next 15min, until we were well clear of the target, and is a sight that we will never forget. We were also happy that our bombs had impacted close to the aim point; there was enough ambient light to see the ground and make out the features on the airfield and we managed to arrange our off-target manoeuvre in order to see the bombs strike. To help, there was some low-lying mist on the airfield and we could see the shockwaves travelling outwards from the impact points. As we manoeuvred off target, we were locked-up by an SAM-3 [Sa-3 – NATO name Goa] target-tracking radar, which we knew was there, but our countermeasures procedures seemed to work and the lock was broken.'

On 24 January the Tabuk Wing bombed the barracks at H3 airfield. The mission was successful, but Flt Lt Hawkins recalled that 'there was very heavy large-calibre triple-A coming up to 20,000ft plus. I found myself trying to stand up to get my backside away so I told myself "sit down you silly fool." (As if another 3in would have helped);' in the Number 5 aircraft Flt

Crews make a time check during a pre-mission briefing of the Dhahran Wing. (Douglas Moule)

Phil Reed inspects damage to Tornado GR1 (ZD843) on IX Squadron caused by the premature detonation of its bombs on 24 January. The crew, Stu Gillies and Pete Rochelle, were lucky to be able to recover the aircraft to Dhahran. (Les Hendry)

Lt Klein also noted 'heavy triple-A up to 21,000ft' and Flt Lt T.J. Marsh, on his first operational mission, with Flt Lt K.A. Smith, remembered 'lots of fireworks that night, very colourful with red and orange tracer (apparently Soviet supplied or home produced was the difference).'

The mission flown from Dhahran that evening against Al Rumaylah was less successful and resulted in the loss of one Tornado and the near loss of another. The first four of the eight aircraft had been loaded with 'proximity' fused bombs, with the intention that the weapons would explode above the ground to keep down the heads of the triple-A gunners so that the rear four could concentrate on the HAS areas with impact-fused bombs. Perhaps luckily for them, two of the first four aborted their sorties after technical difficulties and had to return to Dhahran; the remaining two pressed on to the target and were severely damaged over the target. Flt Lt S.J. Burgess and Flt Lt R. Ankerson were forced to abandon their aircraft immediately and they became prisoners of war. Meanwhile, Flt Lt S. Gillies and Flt Lt S.P. Rochelle coaxed their badly damaged Tornado back to Dhahran. It was only when the aircraft was inspected after landing at Dhahran that the awful truth became apparent: the proximity-fuses had detonated right under the aircraft and both Tornados had been damaged by their own weapons.

New Targets (25 January to 2 February)

By 25 January, the Iraqi Air Force had been effectively neutralized and the targeting for the Tornado force switched to the Iraqi communications systems, power distribution and ammunition storage. On that day Flt Lt Fenlon-Smith and Flt Lt Hawkins led an eightship from Tabuk against the petroleum storage facility at H3 and the following day the same crew led another eight aircraft, at low level this time, against the tropospheric scatter aerials at Ad Diwaniyah and Al Kufah. Both of these missions were supported by ALARM-carrying Tornados, although by now stocks of these missiles were depleted, so each SEAD aircraft carried only two missiles each. Of the low-level loft sortie against Al Kufah, the newly-arrived Flt Lt T.J. Marsh commented that 'this attack was planned for accuracy at low level as a loft delivery, due to the analysis of the likely defences; it was not an unexpected change of tactics just a rational decision by the lead crews. The attack was extremely distracting for me, being at the back of the package and experiencing the reflections and flashes in the HUD and on the canopy plus all the triple-A.' Meanwhile, Flt Lt C.C. Drewery and Sqn Ldr H.E. Newton led eight Tornados from Dhahran against the power station at An Nasiriyah and, after their leader aborted, Flt Lt Scott and Flt Lt M.A. Jeffery found themselves at the front of five aircraft bombing the ammunition depot at Khan Al Mahawil. The Bahrain Wing was tasked against Al Zubayr oil-pumping station, close to the Iranian border on 25 January. In a departure from the practice until then, it was decided that this mission would not carry out AAR on the out-bound leg and instead would rendezvous with the tankers on the return leg. This had the advantage that without full fuel tanks the Tornados were much lighter and could therefore climb higher for the ingress to the target area. The routing to the target was along the coast and Flt Lt Paisey in the Number 4 aircraft wrote that 'very little triple-A was

A Tornado GR1 armed with two ALARM missiles starts its take-off roll from Tabuk. (David Bellamy)

encountered on coasting into Iraq, but the Tigris-Euphrates delta lit up with pinpoints of flashes denoting light triple-A. However it was not until weapons started falling on the target that heavy triple-A opened up with snaking lines of tracer weaving through the sky beneath the formation. Some shells exploded around 18,000ft. Several crews saw un-guided missile launches, which arced above the aircraft.' The target stood out well on radar and all crews were confident of good hits. The next day Sqn Ldr Risdale and Wg Cdr Broadbent led the Wing against the ammunition depot at Tall al Lahm, near Jalibah.

After attacks the previous day by eight aircraft from Tabuk on the communications facility at Ar Rutbah and by eight aircraft from Dhahran on the ammunition depot at Rumaylah, a concerted effort started on 28 January against Iraqi fuel storage depots. The store at H3 was attacked by ten aircraft from Tabuk in the morning and a further twelve aircraft from Tabuk attacked the storage at Haditha that evening. Eight aircraft from Dhahran attacked the storage at Uwayjah and eight from Bahrain attacked An Najaf. After impressive explosions gave evidence of direct hits, Sqn Ldr Risdale, who led an eight-ship from Bahrain to the oil refinery at As Samawah, commented that 'there was no need for the BDA pictures.' The following day an eight-ship from Dhahran bombed the Sayyadah petroleum facility, Al Taqaddum airfield was revisited by ten more Tornados from Tabuk and eight aircraft from Bahrain attacked the petroleum facility at Ad Diwaniya.

The pattern continued over the next four days: in that period, the Tornado Force from all three bases attacked airfield facilities at Al Jarrah, Taqaddum, and Q'alat Salih the SAM supply facility at Shaibah, the EW site at Wadi Al Khir and petroleum storage and pumping stations at

Tim Marsh and Ken Smith recover from a steep-dive attack on the oil refinery at Haditha on 7 February: their stick of five 1,000lb bombs can be seen impacting just above the wingtip, with black smoke coming from the centre bomb strike. (Tim Marsh)

A Dhahran-based Tornado GR1 loaded with three Paveway II 1,000lb Laser-Guided Bombs (LGB). The introduction of LGBs into RAF service marked a quantum leap in the accuracy of bombing attacks from medium level. (Chris Coulls)

Ar Ramadi, Al Hillal and H2. The Bahrain Wing also attacked the Republican Guard barracks in Kuwait on 30 January. However, while these attacks caused a degree of 'harassment,' the Tornado weapon aiming system was not precise enough from medium level to ensure that small targets, such as individual buildings within a complex, were hit with accurately enough to do lasting damage. Radar-aimed bombing at night had reached its limitations and new tactic was clearly needed.

Laser Guidance 1 – Pave Spike

From its earliest days at Laarbruch, the Tornado GR1 had demonstrated the ability to drop LGBs, in co-operative attacks with Pave Spike-equipped Buccaneers. Perhaps this low-level technique could be adapted for medium-level operations. Six Buccaneers had deployed to Bahrain in the last week of January and on 30 and 31 January, a number of training sorties were flown over Saudi Arabia with Tornados from both Bahrain and Tabuk to iron out the tactics. Referring to the Cold War Option Lima, Sqn Ldr Coulls found that 'interestingly, when we eventually got into the LGB business with the Buccaneers in Iraq in 1991, the tactics that we had developed for low-level operations in Germany formed the basis for what we used at medium level there. And many of the characters were the same on both forces!'

The first LGB mission was flown on 3 February. Sqn Ldrs Mason and Stapleton led a mixed formation of four Tornados and three Buccaneers against the highway bridge at As Samawah, one of three bridges across the river Euphrates within the city. Each Tornado was armed with three LGBs and the intention was to operate as sub-formations operating two

A typical bombing formation during the final stages of the Gulf War air campaign: LGB-armed Tornado GR1s from the Dhahran Wing, accompanied by a Pave Spike Buccaneer S2B, refuel from a VC10 tanker of 101 Squadron. (Simon Hadley)

minutes apart, each comprising two Tornado bombers and one Buccaneer designator. The third Buccaneer acted as an airborne spare, but was not needed. After AAR from two VC10 tankers, the formations crossed into Iraqi airspace. Initially the crews found themselves in thick cloud, which forced each three-ship into close formation. The discomfort of being in close formation in enemy airspace was exacerbated by the disparity of speeds between the two different types, but the skies soon cleared, giving ideal clear weather for laser operations. Unfortunately three of the bombs dropped by the first pair did not guide because the wrong laser codes had been set. However, all of the remaining attacks were successful.

Later that day Sqn Ldr Taylor and Sq Ldr Thwaites led another four Tornados and two Buccaneers from Bahrain to attack another of the Euphrates bridges at As Samawah. This attack was entirely successful, as was another one carried out by the same crews the following day against one of the bridges at An Nasiriyah. Sqn Ldr Mason and Sq Ldr Stapleton also led their second LGB attack on 4 February, this time against the road bridge over the Euphrates at Al Madinah, just to the west of Qrna. Although one of the four Tornados and one of the Buccaneers became unserviceable, the remaining aircraft pressed home successful attacks, the first two aircraft dropping the southern span of the bridge and the last one dropping the northern span. 'During the bombing run traffic was seen on the bridge,' noted Flt Lt Paisey. 'At the first impact the traffic stopped and was seen to reverse, only to see the other end of the bridge explode. He remained on the intact centre span, no doubt surprised and relieved.'

On 5 February, Sqn Ldr Risdale and Wg Cdr Broadbent led their fourship against the remaining suspension bridge over the river Euphrates at As Samawah and then visited An Nasiriyah the following day. Sqn Ldrs Moule and Coulls led the first LGB sortie from Dhahran

A Tornado GR1 from the Bahrain Wing armed with LGBs as it prepares to refuel from a Victor K2 from 55 Squadron. The Pave Spike-equipped Buccaneer is in the background. (XV Squadron)

on 5 February. The target for the four Tornados was a large road bridge over the river Tigris at Al Kut. 'The rendezvous, tanking and target ingress went like clockwork,' recalled Sqn Ldr Coulls, 'and we settled on the target run. All was going well shortly before weapons release, when there was a radio call from our designator, asking which bridge we were aiming at, and with seconds to go until weapons release confusion reigned. However, we were cleared to drop just in time and as we manoeuvred off target, it was suddenly apparent what the problem had been. The target bridge had already been hit and one end of it was lying in the river. The Buccaneer navigator had been able to see all of this with his targeting pod. There was another large bridge in the city, about a kilometre from ours. In the event, our bombs were guided into the buttresses at one end, completing the job that somebody else had started.'

Daylight Operations

Since Pave Spike was a purely optical system it was limited to daylight only, so the LGB missions were all flown during the hours of daylight. In fact the Tornado Force had already begun to shift towards daytime operations by 3 February. This was mainly to try to improve the accuracy of the bombing by delivering the weapons visually from a high-angle dive where possible. The new tactics were also used for the first time on 3 February, when day waves were launched, carrying free-fall bombs, from Dhahran and Tabuk respectively against storage warehouses at As Samawah and ammunition storage at Qubaysah and from Bahrain against the ammunition storage facility at Tall Al Lahm. On 4 February, Tabuk launched three fourships to attack the ammunition depot at Karbala and on 5 February the Wing attacked the power station at Al Musayib and later the petroleum production plant at Al Hillah. Meanwhile, the

A Dhahran-based Tornado GR1 as it carries out pre-strike AAR. The graffiti written by the ground crew is visible on the fins of the LGB. (Andy Glover)

Although LGB operations were in full swing, a number of attacks were also mounted against area targets using free-fall 1,000lb bombs. This aircraft, in the sun-shade revetments at Dhahran is about to taxi with eight bombs loaded. (Andy Glover)

Dhahran Wing took on airfield facilities at Al Jarra and joined the Bahrain Wing in a mission against the petroleum storage at An Nasiriyah.

Although the weapon accuracy was improved, the new tactics were not without their own problems. Flt Lt Klein, leading the attack on Al Musayib, reported missing the target because of high winds and unfamiliarity with the high-angle dive manoeuvre. Unfortunately, too, the weather was not always suitable for this delivery profile because of cloud obscuring the target area. Night attacks continued, as well, with targets including Shaik Mazhar ammunition depot (Dhahran), Al Iskandariyah ammunition plant (Tabuk), As Samawah petroleum storage (Dhahran).

On 6 February there were daylight raids by Tabuk against the airfield facilities at H3 Southwest, by Dhahran against the Al Jarrah SAM support facility; the Bahrain Wing also attacked Al Jarra that day, concentrating on the hangar buildings. That evening eight Tornados, with support from a pair of ALARM aircraft, took off from Tabuk to revisit the power station at Al Musayib. 'The refuelling and transit were uneventful as we crossed into Iraq and headed for Baghdad on another clear night. This would turn out to be to our advantage,' recalled Flt Lt Craghill in the Number 4 aircraft. 'As we entered what had become known as the "super-MEZ" (the Missile Engagement Zone of the many SAM sites around Baghdad) it became clear that our presence would not go unchallenged. Despite the pre-planned firings of a number of ALARMs, the Iraqi defences were very active. Part of our pre-war training had been a focus on not just the capabilities of Iraq's many SAMs, but their key visual characteristics at launch. Knowing the colour of the missile's rocket flame, and typical salvo sizes of missiles fired, meant we would be able to identify what was being

A pair of Tornados from the Tabuk Wing, armed with ALARM missiles, refuel from a VC10 tanker at the beginning of a SEAD sortie. (David Bellamy)

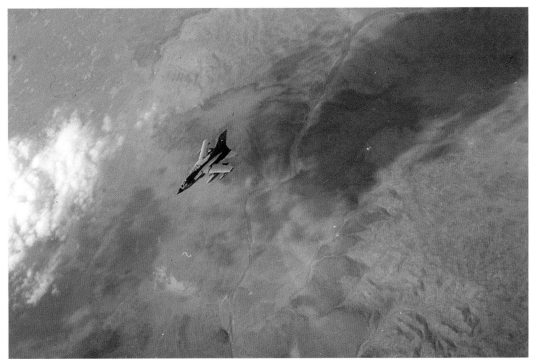

A Tabuk-based Tornado GR1 flies over Iraq. Much of western Iraq was empty desert devoid of landmarks, which could make accurate navigation difficult. (Lars Smith)

launched. On this particular night we watched in amazement as, far below us, salvos of SAM-8, SAM-3 and SAM-6 missiles were fired off, seemingly without guidance due to the threat of anti-radiation missile attack. The Iraqis wanted to be seen to be doing something, but did not want to get killed in the process.

'Not all operators were so timid. As we ran in towards the target, with armament safety switches live, bombs primed, and the target identified on radar, Mike and I received indications on the RWR of SAM-2 target acquisition radar. This had become relatively common, but as we monitored the display the audio alarm sounded to warn of SAM-2 target-tracking radar. I dispensed chaff and confirmed to Mike that the jamming pod was responding correctly. We now had only a few miles to run to weapons release – perhaps ten seconds – when the unthinkable happened. The alarm switched to a ferocious warble, the display changed to SAM-2 missile guidance, and as we looked out in the direction of the 'spike' we saw an almighty flash as a single massive missile came off the launcher. There could be no doubt that a SAM-2 was coming straight for us. We quickly agreed to complete the attack, now only seconds away, and then defend against the missile; I made a call on the strike primary frequency that we were defending against a SAM-2, with our location, to cue our electronic attack support. One thing on our side was that the missile had been fired at fairly short range, so we were able to track its position from the burning rocket plume throughout most of its flight. I kept dispensing chaff, and as soon as we felt our bombs release Mike hauled the aircraft into a descending right-hand turn towards the missile as I called out heights

Sticks of free-fall bombs fall on a large Iraqi storage area. Although crews could use visually-aimed high-angle dive profiles for weapon delivery on daylight missions, attacks using free-fall bombs were not particularly accurate. (Lars Smith)

and speed. Our aim was to turn tight inside the missile's flight path, making it pull hard to keep track of us and hopefully increasing its miss distance. Somewhere close behind us there was a bright flash as the missile detonated, whether on proximity to us or based on a pre-programmed altitude we didn't know, and somehow we had escaped unscathed. Mike put the aircraft into a climb in full afterburner – uncomfortably high-lighting our position in the darkness, but essential to regain height and energy in case of another attack – and we re-joined the formation for the egress southwest across Iraq. Luckily for us there was an emergency refuelling track just south of the border where we were able to replace the fuel lost in defending against the SAM-2, and we made an uneventful recovery to base. Back on the ground, debriefing with our colleagues, it hit home just how close we had come to being hit by that missile when several of the aircraft ahead of us on the attack claimed that it had gone off "just behind" them. What saved us was our training and the fact that we knew each other so well by this point, each trusting the other to do whatever was required; that, and a huge dose of luck.'

Operations on the next two days consisted entirely of daylight raids against oil or petroleum facilities by aircraft dropping free-fall bombs or against bridges by aircraft dropping LGBs. When the Tabuk Wing sent eight aircraft to Haditha, Flt Lt Hawkins commented: 'we went against Haditha petrol facility using a steep dive/toss profile. We were leading and achieved a direct hit with five 1,000lb bombs, which set it alight with Pete calling over the radio "it's a burner." Very satisfying…'

A Dhahran-based Tornado GR1 armed with LGBs refuels from a VC10 tanker of 101 Squadron. (Martin Wintermeyer)

Reconnaissance Continues

Although the ground–attack wings had shifted from low level to medium level and from night to daytime, the reconnaissance detachment at Dhahran continued to operate under cover of darkness at low level. Typically two or three Tornado GR1As would launch each night: the sorties were planned to be flown at between 550 and 600kt and the usual tasking included line searches along 'standard routes' in the desert to the west of Kuwait on the way to cover areas deeper in Iraq. It was not until the outbreak of the land war that crews realized that those line searches had been intended to ensure that the area was clear of Iraqi forces. Most of the early reconnaissance sorties were 'Scud Hunting' aimed at locating Iraqi Scud missile batteries, which were deployed somewhere in the vastness of the desert. A number of the batteries were successfully found, but the images brought back by reconnaissance aircraft also included other systems and equipment such as Soviet-supplied P-14 (NATO name Tall King) radars, T-55 main battle tanks (MBT), SAM-8 surface-to-air missile batteries and also towed artillery.

Some of the crews experienced exciting moments, like Flt Lt B. Robinson and Flt Lt G. Walker who suffered a generator failure and temporary loss of the entire electrical system when operating to the southwest of Tallil on 31 January. Having lost all of their EW self-protection and most of their navigation systems, the crew managed to zoom–climb and dash for the sanctuary of Saudi Arabian airspace. Two nights later the same crew had more excitement when their aircraft was in collision with a Tornado GR1A flown by Wg Cdr Torpy and Flt Lt Perrem; fortunately no lasting damage was done to either aircraft.

A Tornado GR1 performing a non-operational sortie over the Saudi Arabian desert. (Les Hendry)

An LGB-armed Tornado, crewed by 'Shifty' Young and Adam Robinson, about to taxi out for mission from Dhahran. (Les Hendry)

Laser Guidance 2 – TIALD

During the 1980s, Ferranti had been involved in a project to provide the RAF with a 'home-grown' laser-designating capability. The result of their research was the Thermal Imaging Airborne Laser Designator (TIALD) pod and the project was at a research and development stage in late 1990. With deployment to the Gulf looming later in the year, the RAF asked Ferranti to accelerate development so that it could be used operationally if needed over Iraq. This they managed to do and on 24 January 1991, four crews from 13 Squadron deployed to Boscombe Down to take part in Trial *Albert* to prove the TIALD pod for operational service. Among the crews were Flt Lt K.G. Noble and Flt Lt J.M. Cass, who had just graduated from the QWI course. Noble and Cass designated the first successful LGB drop at Garvie Island on 2 February and four days later the crews of 13 Squadron left Honington behind a TriStar tanker for the long trail to Tabuk. At this stage only two prototype TIALD pods existed and they, too, were dispatched to Tabuk.

Once at Tabuk the TIALD project was taken over by Wg Cdr R. Iveson and his navigator Flt Lt C.C. Purkiss. After a trial drop on the nearby Badr range on the night of 8 February, TIALD was cleared for operations and Iveson and Purkiss flew the first sortie on 10 February. The targets were all the HAS on H3 Southwest airfield and the tactics mirrored those already being used successfully by the Bahrain and Dhahran Wings, with one designator working with two bombers. By now the stock of ALARM had been almost used up, and with the Iraqi air-defence system virtually shut down the ALARM-qualified crews found themselves back in the conventional bombing role. Noble and Cass flew their first operational TIALD sortie on the night of 11 February, targeting HAS on H3 Northwest airfield. By now it was clear that just two LGBs were enough to destroy a HAS, so weapons loads were reduced accordingly. The advantage of TIALD over Pave Spike was that its infra-red sensor enabled it to be used at night. Some more crews were hastily trained to use the equipment to provide ten TIALD-qualified crews, which would allow almost round-the-clock operations. Thus the two TIALD pods, by now nicknamed 'Tracy' and 'Sandra' after the 'Fat Slags' characters in the satirical magazine *Viz*, were used almost continuously.

From 9 to 11 February, while the Pave Spike/LGB formations had continued the work of destroying the bridges over the Euphrates and Tigris rivers, all three bases had also been launching four- or eight-ships armed with free-fall bombs against ammunition depots and petroleum storage facilities. The ammunition stores at Al Iskandariyah, Tall Al Lahm, Habbaniyah and H3 were all attacked and Sqn Ldr Buckley and Sq Ldr Teakle led eight aircraft from Bahrain to the petroleum storage facility at Uwayjah on 9 February. Sqn Ldr Whittingham and Flt Lt Baldwin led eight aircraft from Dhahran to the storage tanks at Basrah the following day; during this mission, Flt Lt Turnbull and Flt Lt Grout dropped the 1,000th 1,000lb bomb of the campaign. However, the fact that all of these targets had been attacked previously is perhaps an indication of the overall inaccuracy and ineffectiveness of dropping free-fall bombs from medium level. On 12 February, eight Tornados from Bahrain led by Sqn Ldr Taylor and Sq Ldr Thwaites, plus a further eight from Dhahran led by Sqn Ldr W. Hartree and Flt Lt R.J. Wesley, bombed the liquid propellant production plant at Latifiya and Flt Lt Fenlon-Smith and Flt Lt Hawkins led seven aircraft from Tabuk to attack the EW site at Ar Ruwayshid. These were the last missions in which free-fall weapons were used, and for the rest of the conflict Tornados operated in pairs or fourships dropping LGBs in co-operation with Pave Spike or TIALD designators.

A Thermal Imaging and Laser Designator (TIALD) pod loaded on the shoulder pylon of a Tabuk-based Tornado GR1. (Tim Marsh)

Kev Noble and Jerry Cass of 13 Squadron carried out much of the trials work to introduce the TIALD into service: they went on to fly operational sorties from Tabuk. (Kev Noble)

There were only two TIALD pods available, and this forced the Tabuk Wing to depend on the incredible work of engineers from the RAF and GEC-Marconi to keep the equipment serviceable. (Kev Noble)

A TIALD-equipped designator aircraft is in the background as an LGB-armed Tornado refuels from a VC10 tanker of 101 Squadron. (Lars Smith)

The TIALD pods were named Sandra and Tracy, after the 'Fat Slags' characters in Viz, *the satirical magazine.* (Kev Noble)

Precision Attacks

Although laser guidance solved many of the weapon aiming problems from medium level, it was no panacea. Weapons still had to be dropped accurately into the 'laser basket' – the relatively small area of sky in which the laser energy was reflected back. The correct laser codes had to be programmed into the weapons and the bombs had to be dropped within the tight timing schedule within which the designator marked each individual target. Even assuming that the weapon was dropped into the laser basket at the right time with the right codes set, there was always a chance that it still might not guide; there was also the chance that smoke or

Pre-strike refuelling for a Tabuk Wing attack mission: the TIALD designator aircraft refuels from a VC10 of 101 Squadron while the LGB-armed bomber waits. (Lars Smith)

A Buccaneer Pave Spike designator with a pair of Dhahran-based Tornado GR1s. (Andy Glover)

cloud might interrupt the laser lock and seduce the bomb away from the target. This might in any case occur if two targets were close to each other and the debris from one was blown into the laser field of view for the second. And, of course, the premise for all laser operations was that the weather was good enough for the designator actually to see the target.

Many of these points were driven home during an ambitious sortie from Bahrain on 12 February. Sqn Ldr Mason and Sq Ldr Stapleton lead fourship of Tornados and a pair of Buccaneers against HAS sites at both Taqaddum and Al Asad airfields. Each aircraft was loaded with three LGBs and the intention was to drop two bombs on targets on the first airfield and then remaining one on targets at the second airfield. Each Pave Spike designator would mark two targets on each airfield. In the end, because of various mix-ups between designators and

A Tornado GR1 from the Dhahran Wing, with a Buccaneer and a Victor K2 tanker gives some idea of the challenges of AAR in cloudy conditions, which also were often very turbulent. (Chris Stradling)

bombers only one of the eight targets was hit. The problems, which included most of the 'gotchas' with laser-guided weapons, were largely caused because the crews had allowed too little time between individual attacks to allow the designators to find each specific target. But it was only through bold experiments such as this that the lessons could be learnt.

Over the next six days the Tornados from all three were employed in systematically destroying every individual HAS on all Iraqi Air Force main operating bases. The airfields at H2, H3, Al Amarah, Al Asad, Al Taqaddum, Al Jarra, Tallil, Kut Al Hayy, Mudaysis, Jaliba, Q'alat Salih were all attacked over this period.

In comparison to the incredibly high-risk low-level operations, the medium-level LGB operations might, in the minds of some, to have become something of a 'milk run.' The Iraqi defences seemed to have been reduced to sporadic triple-A and the occasional launch of an unguided SAM. 'I think we must have got a bit complacent at that point,' admitted Sqn Ldr Buckley, 'because we thought we could deal with these threats.' Buckley's own 'wake-up call' came on a mission to the west of Baghdad. 'This was a very hairy moment for Paddy and me,' he later wrote. 'Not one SAM-3, but four were fired up to us. It was perfectly clear day with no cloud and I watched the trail of each missile as it raced upwards towards us. My intention was to roll the aircraft and pull towards the missile at some predetermined point that I couldn't specify if asked (I would have to apply a bit of "that looks about right"). However, happily for Paddy and me the missiles all arched over well below the level of our aircraft and we were unscathed.'

Any complacency amongst the Tornado Force was certainly shattered on 14 February during a mission to destroy the HASs at Al Taqaddum. Led by Sqn Ldr Mason and Sq Ldr Stapleton, twelve aircraft from Bahrain, comprising eight Tornados and four Buccaneers, were supported by four F-4G Wild Weasels and two EF-111A Raven jammers. After joining two VC10 tankers to follow the 'Olive Trail' the formation pushed northwards into Iraq. All eight Tornados followed the same attack track at 90-sec intervals and all scored direct hits on their target, however as they turned off target the Buccaneer designating for the last Tornado, reported a double missile

Flying in clearer conditions, two LGB-armed Tornado GR1s from the Dhahran Wing refuel from a Victor tanker of 55 Squadron; a Pave Spike Buccaneer is in attendance. (Andy Glover)

A LGB dropped by a Tornado GR1 of the Tabuk Wing falls towards a target in Iraq. By the end of the air campaign, the Tornado force was dropping single LGBs onto point targets. (Tim Marsh)

A pair of Tornado GR1s recovers to Tabuk after a mission over Iraq. (Kev Noble)

launch. Some 17sec later, the Tornado, which was crewed by Flt Lt R.J.S.G. Clark and Flt Lt S.M. Hicks, was hit by a SAM, and was seen to enter a shallow dive trailing smoke until it hit the ground to the east of the target area. Although no parachutes were seen by the rest of the formation, Flt Lt Clark was able to eject, but was captured; Flt Lt Hicks was killed. It was a sobering reminder that the Iraqi air defences should never be underestimated.

The next day, after leading his fourship to destroy HAS at Tallil, Wg Cdr Witts commented that 'After the previous day's shoot down, we were a bit warier of the Iraqi defences and with some cause at it turned out. We had attacked Tallil once again and, just after releasing our bombs, had been locked up by a SAM-6 which had taken a great deal of evasive effort to shake off.'

However, despite the loss of another Tornado, the campaign against the HAS sites was entirely successful. On 17 and 18 February there was a brief return to finish off the bridges over the river Euphrates at As Samawah, Ramadi and Fallujah, but from 18 February the focus for operations moved to the operating surfaces and ancillary services on the airfields. Placed on critical points of the taxiways and runways, a single LGB could create a crater large enough to render the concrete unusable – far more effectively that could a JP233. Furthermore, other small buildings which had been unscathed by earlier attacks, could also be pinpointed. Over Tallil once again on 18 February, Wg Cdr Witts reported that 'we were aiming at communications buildings, fuel storage areas and weapons storage. Despite some fairly active defensive triple-A and SAM defences, we achieved some very satisfying explosions.' For Flt Lt Noble 'the most memorable sortie was Al Jarrah on 19 February against the ammunition dump – Jerry would normally just call "Splash" over the radio, which he did again this time, but immediately called "cor… that went up" over the intercom. I dipped the wing to have a look and it was like a small atom bomb had gone off.'

Sqn Ldr Whittingham and Flt Lt Baldwin led another fourship to Al Jarrah that afternoon. 'I was playing Billy Idol on the CVR [Cockpit Voice Recorder] as we flew towards the target,'

'Cor… that went up' – an impressive secondary explosion as an LGB dropped by a Tornado GR1 from the Tabuk Wing hits an ammunition store at Al Jarrah on 19 February. (Kev Noble)

The part played by the media in reporting the progress of the Gulf War was not lost on the ground crew of the Dhahran Wing, who thought it would be amusing to rename aircraft 'CN' as 'CNN'... (Andy Glover)

... and another aircraft as 'SKY.' (Simon Hadley)

recalled Flt Lt Hadley. 'I would turn it off before we got to the target area, where we had two SAM-2s straddling the target so that we had around 100 miles of SAM belt to thread our way through. Fortunately, the Ravens and Wild Weasels had been doing their job, and the Iraqis were scared to turn on their radars.

'That day, the mayhem began slowly. First the radar started to fail. After working at it I got it up and running again, but then the HUD failed, and other bits of navigation kit, and very quickly we got sucked into the drills to try to get the jet working so that we could drop our bombs on target. Then we were into the SAM MEZs. Twice before target we were locked on by the SAM-2s, twice we broke lock. Bombs dropped, the other SAM-2 lit us up twice, again causing us to go defensive to break lock. Eventually, after around twenty minutes of equipment failures, evading SAMs, and bombing the target everything went absolutely calm, almost in an instant. And as we powered away from the threats towards the tanker, I was suddenly aware of some music playing. It was Billy Idol. Still. I had tuned out the music the instant that the kit started failing, and had not noticed it at all as we fought to break radar lock and press home the attack. Now that all was back to normal, a high-level transit to the tanker and home, the music suddenly became audible again. I had just completed a highly intense war mission with rock music blaring in the background but did not even notice. My brain just tuned it out to concentrate on the task in hand.'

Most of the missions on 20 February against Shaibah, Q'alat Salih, Rumaylah and Kut Al Hayy brought their weapons back because of poor weather obscured all of the targets. The cloudy weather continued into the next morning, but the skies had cleared enough on the afternoon of 21 February for successful sorties against Rumaylah by the Dhahran-based aircraft; however, missions against Shaibah (by Tabuk-based aircraft) and against Q'alat Salih and Kut Al Hayy (by Bahrain-based aircraft) were thwarted by the clouds. Two days of relatively good weather then followed, allowing the Tabuk Wing to neutralize Al Jarra and

A Tornado GR1 from the Dhahran Wing, with a weapon load of three LGBs, heads towards Iraq. (Andy Glover)

A Dhahran-based Tornado GR1 returns from a LGB mission over Iraq, accompanied by a Pave Spike-equipped Buccaneer. (Andy Glover)

Simon Hadley (navigator) and Paul Reid (pilot) in a Tornado GR1 armed with LGBs, from the Dhahran Wing. (Simon Hadley)

A pair of LGB-armed Tornado GR1s from the Dhahran Wing set off for a mission over Iraq. (Andy Glover)

Mudaysis, the Dhahran Wing to complete their work at Rumaylah and the Bahrain Wing to attack Kut Al Hayy and Q'alat Salih.

The ground war started on 23 February and from this day the skies began to fill with thick black smoke after Iraqi forces set light to the Kuwaiti oil wells. 'The sky was full of ominous black smoke up to about 9,000ft, all coming from Kuwait,' wrote Wg Cdr Witts. 'We successfully attacked the airfield at Q'alat Salih north of Kuwait and not far from the Iraq-Iran border. It was a god-forsaken area, bearing indelible scars from the Iraqi's previous long-standing conflict with Iran.' A formation from Bahrain led by Flt Lt Beet and Flt Lt Osborne was also tasked against Q'alat Salih that day. All three bases flew missions against Tallil, but only a handful of aircraft were able to drop their weapons. Sqn Ldr Risdale commented, tongue in cheek, 'the target was totally obscured by black smoke so we took our bombs home, stacked for the day and went water skiing... hey ho' The Tabuk and Dhahran Wings both attacked Jalibah on this day, but with mixed results.

The clouds returned over Iraq for the next two days and daily missions mounted by Tornados from both Dhahran and Bahrain against Al Taqaddum on 25 February were unsuccessful because of the weather conditions in the target area. Further sorties against Shayk Mazhar by Bahrain-based aircraft experienced similar difficulties the next day, as did the Tabuk Wing in trying to attack Al Asad airfield and the bridge over the Euphrates at As Samawah. On 27 February the weather cleared enough for LGB operations to continue. During the day, the airfields at Al Asad, Shaykh Mazhar, Al Taqaddum and Habbaniyah were all attacked. In the evening the last Tornado mission of the war was flown from Tabuk against the airfield at Habbaniyah. It fell to Flt Lt M. Warren and Fg Off Craghill drop the last bomb of the campaign, TIALD designated by Flt Lts W.P. Bohill and J.W. Ross.

In the early hours of 28 February came the news that Iraq had capitulated. 'We were all woken from our beds at five o'clock in the morning by the four-ship crews who had been

Thick clouds of black smoke, from oil wells in Kuwait deliberately set alight by retreating Iraqi forces, fill the skies. These conditions made LGB operations difficult in the south-eastern areas of Iraq. (Mike Lumb)

Two Tornado GR1s, still carrying their weapon load of LGBs, break into the circuit at Dhahran. Towards the end of February weather conditions in the target areas often meant that aircraft could not drop LGBs. (Andy Glover)

A Tornado GR1 from the Dhahran Wing, loaded with LGBs, heads into Iraq. (Chris Stradling)

cancelled due to Saddam's capitulation,' recalled Flt Lt Marsh at Tabuk. It was the start of a party, which continued for the rest of the day. Marsh's feelings, probably shared with the other personnel were '... about bloody time... it had started to drag a bit.'

'So was it worth it' wondered Flt Lt Hadley, doubtless echoing the thoughts of others. 'Was the liberation of Kuwait worth the loss of Kieran, Norman, Steve Hicks and the other aircrew. For a long time I had doubts... Then in July 1999 I was posted to IX Sqn at Brüggen and within months we were back down to the Gulf, this time to Ali Al Salem (AAS) in Kuwait for a three-month stint.

'The arrival briefs included a tour around the base. We were shown the room in a HAS in which a number of Kuwaitis had been held prior to being tortured to death in another room just down the corridor. The torture room was bricked up and inaccessible, but on the wall of this holding room were pictures that the Kuwaiti prisoners drew of their captors alongside messages to their loved ones; they knew they would be killed and they wanted to leave a record. Elsewhere on the base were photographs showing how the occupying Iraqi forces had thrown Kuwaitis into baths of acid. Mirage pilots had been shot in the squash courts. The station commander was badly beaten before being dragged by a rope behind a truck up and down the main road in AAS before finally being hanged from a lamppost. Similar atrocities were repeated across Kuwait. It was grim... Now confronted with this unpleasant evidence, my view became crystal clear. It was absolutely worth it. We all put our lives on the line; it was part of the deal... But we helped liberate Kuwait and in doing so made the world a better place. I'm very proud to have been a part of it.'

Jerry Witts (OC 31 Squadron), the Tornado detachment commander at Dhahran with the ground crew whose unstinting hard work had made the air campaign possible. (Simon Hadley)

5

1991-1995
The New Order

End of Hostilities

The RAF personnel at Tabuk, Dhahran and Bahrain were swiftly repatriated at the end of the war, as were most of the aircraft. Sqn Ldr Moule and Sq Ldr Coulls led the first four aircraft from Dhahran back to Brüggen, a flight which was, as Coulls recalls: 'an eight-and-a-half hour trip with four AAR brackets. At the western end of the Mediterranean, we were given a sharp reminder of the fact that we were now back in a different regime when we met a tanker that had been flown out from the UK by a crew that had not been involved in the operation. During Operation *Granby*, we had, of necessity, re-written many of the routine peacetime procedures, not least for AAR. Therefore, we joined the tanker in a tactical formation and radio silent, and promptly (and quite rightly) received a severe ticking off from the tanker captain, insisting that we use the published procedures. Back to normality.'

Six aircraft, crewed from Brüggen, were retained at Bahrain to maintain a presence in the region. Although, thankfully, there was no need for more operational flying, the crews at Bahrain were able to run a busy flying programme with hi-lo-hi profile sorties into Saudi Arabia for four-versus-one low-level simulated attack missions by day or four-ship parallel track auto-TF sorties by night. Most of these flights were supported by a Victor tanker, which was also based in Bahrain; the Tornados remained in Bahrain until May 1991.

After post-operational leave, most of the Tornado squadrons attempted to settle into a new post-Cold War, post-*Granby* routine. At Brüggen, Marham and Honington it was pretty much business as usual: the resident squadrons picked up the 'traditional' sequence of detachments to Goose Bay and Deci. The focus was very much on training and, in particular, the training of the new crews who had arrived over the previous six months and whose CR work-up had been interrupted by operations in the Middle East. Most of the Tornado squadrons took part

Operating from Bahrain in the aftermath of the Gulf War, a pair of Tornado GR1s covered with the grime of a hard-fought campaign; also the pollution caused by burning oilfields. (Mike Lumb)

A Tornado GR1 crewed by Steve Turner and Mike Lumb banks over the Arabian Desert. (Mike Lumb)

Painted in the 75th Anniversary livery of 45 Squadron, the Tornado display aircraft was flown by TWCU instructors Guy Riley and Steve Kinnaird. (Geoffrey Lee/ Plane Focus)

in Exercise *Mallet Blow* in July. Fortunately some credit was allowed for having fought a real war and the Taceval regime was relaxed slightly, so that the Tornado stations could expect their first post-war Taceval in 1993.

At Laarbruch, it was a different story: the *Options for Change* Defence White Paper had announced the closure of the RAFG stations at Wildenrath and Gutersloh and the disbandment of the three Tornado GR.1 strike/attack squadrons at Laarbruch. The Phantom FGR.2 squadrons at Wildenrath disbanded during the course of 1991 and the station closed in April 1992. The imminent closure of Gutersloh meant that the Harrier GR.5 squadrons there would be displaced to Laarbruch, so, despite their recent impressive performance on operations, XV and 16 Squadrons were disbanded in the autumn of 1991. Although 20 Squadron remained at Laarbruch until September 1992, it did so as the sole remaining Tornado squadron, as II Squadron had moved to Marham in December 1991.

Training in North America had resumed in the summer of 1991 with detachments to Goose Bay, and early 1992 saw participation in Exercise *Red Flag*. Unfortunately 14 Squadron's *Red Flag* was cursed by poor weather and crews flew only a handful of sorties. Two other major deployments in the first half of the year were when the whole of 13 Squadron deployed to Royal Norwegian Air Force (RNoAF) base at Evenes (Narvik) in northern Norway for a reconnaissance exercise in March, and 31 Squadron took part in Exercise *Magic Carpet* in Oman over April and May.

The major problem for RAFG squadrons was the lack of low-flying in Germany: now crews were faced with long transit times back to the UK in order to carry out their routine training. To some extent this inconvenience was tempered by the introduction of routine

The Tornado line at Goose Bay, Labrador, looking to the northeast into the distance Gosling Lake leads into Lake Melville. (Dougie Roxburgh)

The 'see-off' [dispatch] crew display the safety pins which have been removed from the weapon pylons. The aircraft have been returned to standard camouflage, but the tally of operational missions flown during the Gulf War has been retained under the cockpit, as can be seen on the aircraft in the background. (Dougie Roxburgh)

Ground crew carrying out maintenance on a Tornado GR1 parked on the line at Goose Bay. (Dougie Roxburgh)

AAR for the Germany-based squadrons and by the introduction of the larger 2,250-litre underwing fuel tanks: both of these measures served to increase the amount of low flying that could be achieved after the tedious transit from Germany to the UK had been completed. Another very practical innovation was the establishment of a Tornado Turnaround Facility (TTF) at Leuchars. Manned by ground crew from Brüggen, who were permanently seconded to Leuchars, the TTF enabled squadrons to plan for a hi-lo profile, turning and re-planning at Leuchars, before returning to Brüggen via a lo-hi sortie.

The time spent on medium-level transits was not entirely wasted. The introduction of medium-level tactics had expanded the portfolio of weapons profiles that needed to be practised: as well as the 'traditional' low-level delivery profiles, Tornado crews were now also required to keep up to speed with medium-level laydown and high-angle dive techniques. So transits now often included a simulated attack profile, or a medium-level range detail.

As both the Cold War and Gulf War receded into the past, the Tornado Force was left in something of a quandary as to what its role in the 'new world order' might be: it now seemed unlikely that the concrete bunkers and HAS of the Cold War era would ever be used for real and the future appeared to be in deployed operations beyond Europe. The permanent infrastructure of the Cold War began to be dismantled and, reflecting developments like the formation of the NATO Rapid Reaction Force, the emphasis moved towards mobility. The new tactical skills gained during the Gulf War also needed to be consolidated: at Brüggen it was decided that 14 and 17 Squadrons would become specialists in TIALD and LGB operations and that IX and 31 Squadrons would specialize in SEAD operations using ALARM.

A Tornado GR1 from 31 Squadron in formation with a VC10 tanker of 101 Squadron during the deployment to Thumrait, Oman in 1992. (31 Squadron)

A Tornado GR1A from 13 Squadron painted in arctic camouflage for a detachment to Evenes, Norway. (Kev Noble)

After the Gulf War, Tornado GR1 crews were expected to maintain their proficiency in medium-level operations as well as low-level tactics. Here a 14 Squadron aircraft drops a stick of four inert 1,000lb free-fall bombs from medium level. (Geordie Smith via Stu Reid)

The four squadrons which formed the Brüggen Wing were divided into ALARM or TIALD specializations. One of the ALARM specialist units was 31 Squadron. (Simon Hulme)

The other ALARM specialist squadron at Brüggen was IX Squadron. (Geoffrey Lee/ Plane Focus)

Operation *Jural*

However, before much thought could be put into such specializations, Iraq once more intervened to divert attention. During the Gulf War the Kurds in the north of the country and the Marsh Arabs in the south of the country had attempted to revolt against the Ba'athist regime and these uprisings had been crushed. In order to protect the Kurds from further violence at the hands of the Iraqi forces, a 'No Fly Zone' (NFZ), mandated by the United Nations, had been established in the north; the NFZ effectively prevented the Iraqi army and air force from operating any aircraft north of the 36th Parallel. RAF Jaguars had been deployed to the Turkish base at Incirlik as part of the British contribution to air operations (known as Operation *Warden*). By mid-1992 it was apparent that a similar arrangement was needed to protect the Shi'ite Arabs in southern Iraq from punitive operations by Iraqi government forces. Originally it was envisaged that the British contribution to this new NFZ would comprise a small number of Tornado GR1A reconnaissance aircraft, which would operate at low level in much the same way as they had done successfully in the Gulf War. They would be used to gather intelligence about, and to monitor, the Iraqi ground forces, while US and French fighter aircraft prevented the Iraqi Air Force from flying south of the 32nd Parallel.

Unfortunately for this plan, the US leadership of the coalition had already decreed that no aircraft were to operate below 10,000ft and since the TIRRS was specifically designed for low-level operations it was quickly apparent that the Tornado GR1A was the wrong platform to use. Instead, the two existing TIALD pods would be carried by Tornado GR1s to be used as 'mobile security cameras' to film activity on the ground below the NFZ. In fact this original and unorthodox use of targetting pods pre-dated the USAF concept of Non-Traditional Intelligence Surveillance and Reconnaissance (NTISR) by ten years. The US/coalition operation was known as Operation *Southern Watch*, and the British participation was

Tanker support for Operation Jural *was provided by a dedicated Victor K2 tanker from 55 Squadron which was based at Bahrain. A TIALD-equipped Tornado GR1 waits for the first pair of Tornados to refuel.*

Two TIALD pods used for Operation Jural *were known as 'Beckie' and 'Rachel'.*

given the name Operation *Jural*. Six Tornados deployed to Dhahran in August to commence operations. The detachment was led by 17 Squadron, although it included a number of TIALD specialists from other units, including Flt Lt Noble and Flt Lt Cass, who had done so much of the development work for the pods. A Victor tanker deployed to Bahrain to provide AAR support for the detachment.

By now the prototype TIALD pods used during the Gulf War had been replaced in service by two early production pods; these were dispatched to Dhahran, where they were known as Becky and Rachel. The daily *Jural* routine was to mount an operational fourship made up of two pairs, each in turn comprising TIALD-armed reconnaissance aircraft and a 'shooter' escort. All aircraft carried live guns and missiles. Once in Iraqi airspace, the fourship would split into its constituent pairs to cover the reconnaissance task. Each TIALD aircraft was allocated a number of 'points of interest' in Iraq to film as well as various line searches following roadways through the marsh area to the south of the Euphrates and to the east of the southern reaches of the Tigris. At medium level, with the navigator very much 'heads in' while monitoring the TIALD picture, the reconnaissance aircraft was vulnerable to attack either by fighter aircraft or SAMs, hence the need for the 'shooter' escort. In practice the four Tornados would make up only part of a much larger coalition package operating within the NFZ and there was an almost continuous presence of coalition air-defence aircraft such as F-15D Eagle and the Dassault Mirage 2000.

Aircraft that were not used for operational sorties could be used for training flights into Kuwait, which gave crews an opportunity to see at first hand the battlefields of the Gulf War. Each squadron was responsible for providing crews for a three-month period, but rather than the entire squadron deploying for the whole period a system of 'roulement' was introduced, whereby crews were cycled through Dhahran for a six-week tour. Staggered starting dates for each pair of crews meant that there would be a continuous presence of locally experienced crews. In November, 617 Squadron took over from 17 Squadron and then, in turn, handed over to 14 Squadron.

A Tornado GR1 in 14 Squadron markings on recovery to Dhahran after an operational sortie over Iraq. The aircraft carries 2,250-litre under-wing fuel tanks and is armed with AIM-9L missiles.

Although the daily reconnaissance task had become routine by mid–December, there were strong indications that the Iraqis intended to contest the NFZ. SAM systems were deployed below the NFZ and later in the month, Iraqi fighters began to make high–speed dashes into the NFZ. On 27 December, an Iraqi MiG–25 Foxbat was shot down by a USAF F-16 Fighting Falcon, tensions rose dramatically and the coalition began to prepare airstrikes to neutralize the threat to its aircraft operating in the NFZ.

The Operation Jural detachment at Dhahran on Christmas Day, 1992; most of the personnel were from 14 Squadron at Brüggen.

'Podge' Middleton fitting the steering vanes to a 1,000lb LGB loaded onto the shoulder pylon of a Tornado GR1 at Dhahran. The puddles on the ground are evidence of the heavy rainfall at Dhahran in early 1993. (Podge Middleton)

A Dhahran-based Tornado GR1 refuels from the port-wing hose of a Victor K2 during an Operation Jural sortie.

Operation *Ingleton*

The first airstrike was launched on the night of 13 January 1993. A package of some 100 aircraft, operating from a number of bases in Saudi Arabia and the USS *Kittyhawk*, attacked the nodal points of the command and control system of the Iraqi air-defence network. Known SAM-3 sites south of the 32nd Parallel were also targetted. The RAF contribution, codenamed Operation *Ingleton*, comprised four Tornados led by Sqn Ldr M.J.W. Napier and Fg Off C. Platt, which attacked the air-defence headquarters and the radar control bunker at Al Amarah.

After AAR from the Bahrain-based Victor, the Tornados crossed the border. Flt Lt C.D. Bearblock, the Number 3 pilot, described his experiences: 'the first bombs to go off will be the big American strike on Tallil as we pass to the east. Eyes left and five... four... three... two... one... FLASH... Wow... The whole night sky lights up right on zero hour with the flash of multiple bomb explosions. It's the most impressive sight I've ever seen. I discuss with Taff; "they know we're coming now, expect to see the RHWR light up." For the first time the flight ceases to be like all other training missions – this time they're really going to shoot us. Soon afterwards the upper winds are stronger than forecast and I start to fall behind the time line using maximum dry power. The only way to catch up is to use burner, but this will be visible to all those on the ground for miles around – the Iraqis won't need radar – they will be able to see us. We have no choice but to use it. Burner in for seven agonising seconds, all the time waiting for the RHWR to light up as the Iraqis lock onto me and Taff. Burners out; back on the timeline. Nothing happens... immense relief.

'Taff finds the IP on the radar and all is looking good. I hear Mike and Spiv making all the calls between spiker [designator] and bomber that tell me that all is running to plan for the front pair. Mike calls "bombs released" and shortly after another almighty flash lights the sky ahead of us... I hold the course steady and release our weapons in turn. I call "bombs released" and I can't turn away from the target fast enough. As I turn I see the flashes from my bombs

A Tornado GR1 taxies out for an Operation Ingleton *mission, with LGBs loaded under the fuselage.* (Podge Middleton)

Two Tornado GR1s, on an operational mission, formate on a Victor K2 from 55 Squadron before heading towards the Iraqi border. (Mal Craghill)

– great relief that they went off – I hope that they hit the target. I also see flashes of triple-A, but no guidance on the RHWR – they're firing blind into the night and all being well, we should be above it.'

From the rear cockpit of the Number 4 aircraft, Fg Off Craghill used his TIALD pod to mark the target. 'The thermal picture was good,' he recalls. 'The site was easy enough to find and we "captured" in good time. The bomber released and we started to lase. Cookie had been giving me a countdown but stopped at what should have been bomb impact. I called "keep talking" to which his reply was a thoroughly helpful "keep lasing" Then the bombs impacted, and it looked to me like they had gone short by maybe 100ft or so; but with all the dust kicked up by the impact it was difficult to get any clear picture of the damage... Sometime later, when a Bomb Damage Assessment (BDA) photograph of the target surfaced, it showed that while the first bomb did indeed go short by 100ft, the second was a direct hit and what had been a square building was now missing most of its eastern and southern walls.'

Five days later, the four Tornados flew a second mission, this time in daylight, against the radar control building at An Najaf. 'Our attack was planned from west to east, with the spiker actually running about two miles north of the NFZ on the run-in, as the target was so close to the line' recalled Fg Off Craghill. 'After release we would turn right, to be heading south, back inside the NFZ at bomb impact. We were spiker for the second pair again, the difference being that this time we would his time were sharing the same target, such was its importance. Again the target was easy enough to find within the site, once you had the road layout memorized from target study, but the difficulty lay in actually finding the site. Our maps did not show it very well, but the site was perched on the edge of a big ridge running north/south, forming a distinctive western boundary... as it was, on the run in to the target the lead spiker could not identify the target, so they peeled off south to set up for a re-attack…I eventually found the target area, which showed up much better with the TV sensor than IR – an advantage of the dual-capable TIALD pod. However as we approached the bomber's release point, I had broken out of the site, but not our actual target. As I had the site layout memorized, I was confident of being able to find it, so when the bomber crew called that they were approaching release point and Cookie enquired if I was "captured," I replied "no, but I will be." Cookie cleared the bomber to release: now the pressure was really on and I had to nail the target. I found the entrance to the compound, followed the main road from Baghdad into the site, turned south, and then back west and – bingo. There was the target. As Cookie counted down to impact time for me, I turned on the laser and waited for impact. I actually saw the bombs come into the TIALD picture from the bottom left and blow through the sand wall surrounding the target, straight into the bunker. With three direct hits I was confident of another kill, so I transmitted for the rest of my formation to hear "touchdown and the crowd goes wild" Unfortunately I keyed the wrong radio and the call went out on Strike Primary and was heard by every coalition aircraft airborne. The AWACS crew responded with a confused "uh, roger" and we headed for home.'

The crisis in southern Iraq was quickly resolved and Operation *Jural* continued its routine. By now 31 Squadron had taken over the reins at Dhahran and Wg Cdr I. Hall introduced the sensible requirement that all crews practised dummy attacks as well as their reconnaissance tasks while over Iraq, in order to make sure that they would be ready, if called upon again for offensive action. Since Operation *Jural* sorties lasted typically about 3hr and there were no other distractions at Dhahran, operationally deployed crews might achieve 50hr flying in a month, rather than the more typical 15 to 20hr they would have flown at home. However the operational hours flown at medium level were, in reality, of low quality in comparison to a hard workout in the UK low-flying system.

The Home Front

Throughout 1993 the operational commitment to *Jural* continued in parallel with the routine training regime at the main Tornado bases. The Taceval teams visited Brüggen and Marham in May and July respectively and Goose Bay and Deci both saw almost continuous detachments through the summer months. Further afield, II Squadron took part in Exercise *Dapex* from Torrejon, near Madrid and Exercise *Distant Thunder* from Akinci airbase northwest of Ankara and 13 Squadron participated in Exercise *Cope Thunder* from Eielson AFB near Fairbanks, Alaska. Apart from practising their reconnaissance role, these exercises also gave crews the opportunity to fly in the attack role in large packages of aircraft – much as coalition forces had operated during the Gulf War. According to Flt Lt S.H. Cockram, who had recently joined II Squadron after a seven-year tour at Brüggen, *Cope Thunder* was the 'best exercise ever with largest amount of airspace and most tactical flexibility, albeit with limited low-level options.'

However the increasingly large number of conflicting demands on front-line units was taking its toll. 'Overall,' thought Flt Lt Cockram, 'it was becoming increasingly incoherent to tie the exercise programme into the operational one. There were many efforts to do non-formed units on operations with the concomitant authorization issues across the Tornado Wings. Frequently first tourists were getting a total of 90hr for ten months of the year so we were always reporting on first tourists having less than thirty hours in three months

A 27 Squadron Tornado GR1 at low level over the sea: the unit was renumbered to become 12 Squadron when the Buccaneer squadron of that number was disbanded in autumn 1993. (Mal Craghill)

Two Tornado GR1As from 13 Squadron over the English countryside. The squadron also participated in Exercise Cope Thunder *in Alaska in 1993. (Rick Brewell)*

A Tornado GR1 of 31 Squadron flying over Germany: the end of the Cold War also marked the end of meaningful low flying in Germany and most of the flying from Brüggen followed a 'hi-lo-hi' profile to use the UK Low Flying System. (Simon Hadley)

Early in 1994, there was a complete re-shuffle of the UK-based Tornado GR1 squadrons with 13 Squadron moving from Honington to join II Squadron at Marham. (via Kev Noble)

Both 617 and 12 Squadrons were re-equipped with the Tornado GR1B version and moved to Lossiemouth to fill the maritime-attack role. (RAF Museum)

The TWCU, now renumbered as XV (Reserve) Squadron, also moved from Honington to Lossiemouth. (via Benny Bentham)

throughout that ten-month period. Then for their two months on ops they could get between a 100 and 200hr so command and group did not think there was a problem. To my mind, with TIALD, ALARM and Paveway III (PW III) on the cards, there were currency as well as recency issues – and we were finding it ever more difficult to stay on top of the jet. Although accident loss rates had dropped as we moved to medium level, we were asking first tourists to do much more than had been expected of the junior pilots and junior navigators in Cold War days.'

A New Role

When the Buccaneer maritime squadrons were disbanded in autumn 1993 and spring 1994, there was a major re-shuffle of the Tornado squadrons in the UK. In October 1993, 27 Squadron was re-numbered 12 Squadron before moving to Lossiemouth and six months later they were joined by 617 Squadron. Both squadrons re-equipped with the Tornado GR1B variant. Meanwhile, Honington had closed as a flying base and 13 Squadron had moved to Marham – arriving in a spectacular diamond-nine formation on 1 February – thus making Marham the base for two Tornado GR1A reconnaissance units. The other unit at Honington TWCU – now re-numbered to become XV (R) Squadron – moved to Lossiemouth in late 1993. Thus, in early 1994, the Tornado GR1 Force comprised four strike/attack squadrons at Brüggen, two reconnaissance squadrons at Marham and two maritime squadrons and an OCU at Lossiemouth.

The prime weapon of the Tornado GR1B was the BAe Sea Eagle anti-shipping missile. The weapon is loaded on Tornado of 617 Squadron. (Geoffrey Lee/ Plane Focus)

Maritime-attack tactics called for close coordination between the Tornado force and the Nimrod MR2 maritime patrol aircraft – here with a Tornado GR1B of 12 Squadron. (Darren Berris)

A Tornado GR1B of 617 Squadron, loaded with Sea Eagle missiles. (Geoffrey Lee/ Plane Focus)

The Tornado GR1B was modified to carry the BAe Sea Eagle anti-ship missile and the two Tornado squadrons adopted the maritime tactics that had been perfected by the Buccaneer force. 'In the mid-Nineties NATO was still heavily focused on the Russian threat,' explained Flt Lt Craghill, by now a QWI on 12 Squadron, 'and tactics were modelled against a Surface Action Group (SAG) of the Russian Navy often made up of an aircraft carrier, cruisers, destroyers, frigates and support/replenishment ships known collectively as "oilers." Russian surface combatants tended to be well-equipped with anti-air capabilities including long, medium and short-range SAMs, multi-barreled radar-guided guns and active countermeasures such as chaff dispensers to fool radar-guided missiles, all of which were treated with great respect by the attacking aircrew.

'A SAG would be usually be arranged with air-defence ships closest to the anticipated threat direction, protecting the High Value Unit (HVU) – usually the carrier or oilers. All of the ships had Electronic Surveillance Measures (ESM), which would allow them to search actively for air threats using radar, and search passively for the tell-tale radar and radio transmissions of surveillance and attack aircraft. Given that some of the SAMs had ranges upwards of ninety miles, and the maximum range of the sea-skimming Sea Eagle was around sixty miles, the two keys to a successful attack were deemed to be surprise (both in terms of timing and attack direction) and target saturation (having as many missiles simultaneously targeting the SAG as possible).'

The standard formation tasked against a Russian SAG would be six Tornado GR1Bs, each armed with two Sea Eagles. A successful attack on such a well-defended target depended on up-to-date intelligence supplied by Nimrod MR2 Maritime Patrol Aircraft (MPA). The Nimrod would transmit a continuously updated Surface Picture (SURPIC) by radio to the Tornado formation as it waited at readiness in the HAS. From this information the Tornado formation could plot the position of the SAG and also the relative positions within in it of the HVU. If necessary, attack directions could be amended to match the latest intelligence.

'Approaching the SAG at ultra-low level to avoid being detected by enemy radar, the formation would execute the attack template,' continued Craghill, 'with the six aircraft fanning out widely to create a series of different attack headings designed to make it difficult for the SAG to defend against all twelve Sea Eagle missiles. SURPIC updates would be used to feed a target position to the Sea Eagle's internal navigation system, with the Tornados accelerating to 540kt as they approached the firing point. Now well inside the engagement envelope for the SAG's long-range SAMs, remaining undetected was critical; however, if there was any doubt about the accuracy of the MPA's SURPIC, the Tornado's own radar could be used to confirm the SAG's disposition immediately prior to firing – although this would put the Tornados at immediate risk from the formidable air defences.

'At a pre-determined time all six Tornados would simultaneously launch their missiles at the SAG and immediately execute a turn away from the threat. From there on the Sea Eagle was autonomous, using its radar altimeter and inertial navigation system to sea-skim at 0.85Mach (M) towards the target. Approaching the SAG the missiles would fly a 'pop-up' manoeuvre to allow their active radar sensor to acquire the target. The missiles would then return to ultra-low level to hit their target just above the water line, where the 230kg warhead would cause maximum damage. Despite this attack profile, and the difficulty for the SAG's defences of hitting such fast, low-flying targets, it was assumed that not all of the Sea Eagles would make it to their target, and that they would not all target the HVU, hence the use of twelve missiles.'

Another view of a Sea Eagle-armed Tornado GR1B of 617 Squadron. (Rick Brewell)

The main exercise commitment for the maritime squadrons was the NATO Joint Maritime Course (JMC), which was a twice a year, two-week exercise conducted around the northern approaches of the UK. A typical JMC would include surface vessels, submarines and MPAs from assorted NATO navies. Whilst the surface element carried out anti-submarine operations, they would be subject to attack by maritime Tornados. In order to give the ships the best training value, after a simulated Sea Eagle launch, rather than breaking away as they would for real, the Tornados would assume the same flight path as the missiles and continue to towards the ships at low level and high speed: this gave the ships the opportunity to exercise their own close-in weapons systems as they attempted to engage the Tornados.

The conversion to the new role was not without its problems. One navigator on 12 Squadron commented that 'about half of the squadron had crossed over from 27 Squadron and it was a bit them and us. It was not a nice atmosphere and in my opinion not good for morale. I had never done the maritime role before and the conversion sorties were a little on the "I've done it before why can't you?" side. Not conducive to learning easily. Plus the software had not been updated to cope with a moving target so we were reduced to using Buccaneer techniques, which meant loads of heads-in for the navigator while he retyped about twelve new waypoints every time the target position was updated, sometimes only a few minutes before the release time for the Sea Eagle. I hated the maritime role: hours at 100ft over the sea followed by minutes of frantic typing concluding with more hours at 100ft over the sea.'

A Busy Year

By 1994 the Tornado Force seemed as if it had established a post-Cold War, post-Gulf War routine. The calendar for training in North America was a full one: the aircraft were at Nellis AFB in February for Exercise *Red Flags* by 13 and 14 Squadrons, before moving to Goose Bay for 12, 14, IX, 13 and II Squadrons to use for Exercise *Western Vortex* over the spring and early summer. In July they were at Eielson AFB so that IX and II Squadrons could take part in Exercise *Cope Thunder*, then back to Goose Bay for Exercise *Western Vortex*es involving 617 and 31 Squadrons; then on to Nellis once more in September and October for Exercise *Red Flag* flown by 12 and 617 Squadrons. Exercise *Red Flag* now included night and medium-level operations as well as the low-level flying of the original Cold War days. The training facilities at Goose Bay had also increased in scope, and it was not unusual for the visiting RAF, GAF and Royal Netherlands Air Force (RNLAF) units to put together a large COMAO (Combined Air Operation) of thirty-plus aircraft opposed by GAF F-4F Phantoms, CAF CF-18 Hornets and even RAF Tornado F3s. Throughout the year Deci was visited by each of the Tornado squadrons, although by now the detachments tended to once yearly, combining both APC and ACMI.

A Tornado GR1 of 31 Squadron on the ramp at Nellis AFB, ready for an Exercise Red Flag *sortie.*

A Tornado GR1 of 14 Squadron. (Geordie Smith via Stu Reid)

A Tornado GR1B of 12 Squadron. (Darren Berris)

Squadron exchanges were part of the annual calendar for a Tornado squadron. Here a 17 Squadron Tornado GR1 accompanies a Spanish Air Force F-18 Hornet on a joint sortie from Zaragoza. (Chris Stradling)

Back in the UK and Europe, routine exercises continued, including Exercises *Brilliant Invader* and *Brilliant Foil*, which were the successors to the *Mallet Blow* of Cold War days. Exercise *Brilliant Invader* took place in the spring and *Brilliant Foil* in the autumn, and both followed the general format of *Mallet Blow* (although they seemed to avoid the latter's association with poor weather), but they also included AAR, OLF and range slots at more unfamiliar ranges such as Luce Bay. Additionally the reconnaissance squadrons continued to mount short detachments including, in the spring, II Squadron deploying to Torrejon once more for Exercise *Dapex*, and to Bodø, Norway for Exercise *Strong Resolve* and 13 Squadron to Akinci for Exercise *Distant Thunder*. Of this latter exercise, Sqn Ldr Noble wrote 'we were hosted by a Turkish Air Force (TAF) F-16 Fighting Falcon–equipped squadron. The flying

A Tornado GR1B of 12 Squadron. (Darren Berris)

A Tornado GR1 of 31 Squadron at low-level in the UK. Many sorties flown from Brüggen took advantage of the Tornado Turnaround Facility (TTF) which had been set up at Leuchars, using ground crew on loan from Brüggen squadrons. (via Simon Hulme)

included low-level reconnaissance around Turkey and attacks against US Navy ships in the Mediterranean.'

The problem with all of the training activity in North America, Sardinia and operational activity in Saudi Arabia was that these three deployments took first priority for aircraft and equipment spares; the much-reduced spares stock in the aftermath of *Options for Change*, the result was a serious lack of serviceable aircraft at the home bases. For example, at Brüggen in 1994 it was not unusual to have only two or three aircraft serviceable on the entire Wing. This made non-exercise flying, such as CR training for new crews, formation leader work ups and supervisory checks very difficult to achieve. The workload for the engineers was increased dramatically, too, by the need to take parts from some aircraft in order to make

A Vinten Vicon reconnaissance pod loaded under a Tornado GR1. The pod enabled Tornado crews to obtain high-resolution photographs during operational reconnaissance sorties over northern and southern Iraq. (Larry Williams)

others serviceable. Spare engines were in particularly short supply and as C.Tech Spanswick pointed out 'the RB199 engine would last a matter of hours, so engine changes were pretty much the norm. Spares always seemed to be in short supply and were constantly seemed to be robbing… even engines with only five hours' life left in them.' From the aircrew perspective, Flt Lt M.J. Sharp, a pilot on 14 Squadron, recalled that 'my lasting memory of that time was no aircraft and, aside from detachments, a struggle to get minimum hours and even then mostly low quality.'

Operation *Driver*

Against this backdrop Operation *Jural* continued as the main focus for each squadron's activities. As units followed each other through Dhahran, it was not entirely surprising, given the diverse roles now filled by the Tornado Force, that each squadron would wish to change the routine to do things their own way. 'Dhahran was interesting in the early Nineties,' commented Spanswick, 'because for three months a UK Squadron would be in place followed by a Brüggen squadron for three months. What always used to amuse me was the rewriting of the Engineering Order book by squadron Senior Engineering Officers (SEngOs) to reflect current operating procedures at Lossiemouth, Marham or Brüggen.' Nevertheless the engineers retained their sense of humour and thanks to their efforts and a fully-equipped spares back up; the aircraft at Dhahran enjoyed a high serviceability rate. In August the operational capability of the detachment was further improved with the introduction of a new reconnaissance sensor: 14 Squadron was the first unit to use the Vinten Vicon pod, a 'traditional' reconnaissance pod carrying high-resolution cameras, enabling crews to cover points of interest more effectively than they could with the TIALD video. Aircraft still flew in pairs, but now one carried the Vicon pod, while the other carried the TIALD pod.

In October, political and military tension in the Gulf region increased once more when Iraqi armour was detected moving towards the Kuwaiti border. The response was Operation *Driver*, which involved the immediate dispatch of six aircraft from 14 Squadron to reinforce the detachment at Dhahran. The aircraft flew out from Brüggen on 11 October and started flying operations over Iraq two days later. The crisis quickly resolved itself, but for a nearly month until the aircraft returned to Brüggen on 9 November, six-ship formations were dispatched into the NFZ to carry out simulated attacks against military targets. Once again, Operation *Jural* slipped back into its routine.

Operation *Warden*

The Tornado Force also assumed responsibility for Operation *Warden* from the RAF Jaguars and Harriers when those aircraft were required for operations over the Balkans in April 1995. Flying operations for Operation *Warden* took place from the Turkish Air Force base at Incirlik, just outside Adana in the central south of the country. Without the strict Islamic laws of Saudi Arabia, and with a rather more favourable climate, Incirlik proved to be a more pleasant location than Dhahran. The first unit to deploy to there was 617 Squadron and over the next year the UK-based squadrons took on Operation *Warden*, while Brüggen squadrons assumed full responsibility Operation *Jural*. One unfortunate effect of doubling the number of operations was to stretch the supply chain even further; another was that rather than covering a two-month period of operations, each unit now had to cover a four-month stint.

The northern NFZ was much smaller than its southern counterpart, covering the area of Iraq north of the 36th Parallel; it included the city of Mosul and the Zagros Mountains, which marked the borders with Turkey and Iran. The sorties over the northern NFZ followed a similar pattern to missions over southern Iraq, but there were some notable differences. Firstly, reaching

A TIALD-equipped Tornado GR1 flown by a II Squadron crew over Iraq during an Operation Jural *sortie.* (II Squadron)

A Tornado GR1A from II Squadron painted in temporary arctic camouflage ready for Exercise Strong Resolve *at Stavanger, Norway.* (II Squadron)

A Tornado GR1A of II Squadron flies over the Norwegian mountains during Exercise Strong Resolve *in spring 1995.* (II Squadron)

A Tornado GR1B from 12 Squadron flying through the Lake District at low-level in August 1995. (Adrian Walker)

the crossing point into Iraq involved a transit of nearly 500 miles eastwards along the border between Turkey and Syria, or almost twice the distance from Dhahran to the Iraqi border in the south. Secondly, the terrain was markedly different: under the southern NFZ the ground was virtually all at sea level, but under the northern NFZ the mountains rose to 13,000ft; Mosul itself sat at their foot, on the headwaters of the Tigris. However, one benefit of operations in the northern NFZ was that the Iraqi forces were much less active in the area.

Despite the increased transit times, the smaller area of the northern NFZ meant that the typical duration of an Operation *Warden* sortie was about the same as those on Operation *Jural* – between two-and-a-half and three-and-a-half hours. Tanker support was provided by a VC10, which was also based at Incirlik, and the Tornados carried out reconnaissance with both the TIALD pod and the Vicon pod over various Points of Interest (PoI). The flying was somewhat tedious but at least the mountain scenery added some interest. 'There was no lead-in training with the pod,' recalled Flt Lt Grout 'all the training was done in theatre shadowing the in-theatre guys. It was a steep learning curve, but we cracked it.'

Other Activities

Despite the busy operational schedule and the continued lack of spares at the main bases, there was no let-up in the exercise schedule. For example, in the first half of 1995, II Squadron took part in Exercise *Crimson Falcon* (a reconnaissance exercise) at Rheims and Exercise *Strong Resolve* in Norway and 12 Squadron took part in Exercises *Atlas Dawn* in Morocco and Exercise *Linked Seas* (a maritime exercise) from Gibraltar. This latter exercise was run under the auspices of the NATO Iberian Atlantic Area Command (COMBERLANT) and involved UK, Spanish and Portuguese forces. Flt Lt Grout remembered that 'the Spanish took great

A Tornado GR1 flown by a 14 Squadron crew operating from Marine Corps Air Station (MCAS) Yuma, Arizona during Exercise Arid Thunder. (Darren Legg)

pains to jam our radio frequencies with music even when we were on their side: they hated us being in Gibraltar. We whizzed all over parts of the Atlantic Ocean hanging on and trying to keep up with the moving target.' This year it was the turn of 14 Squadron to deploy to Akinci to take part in Exercise *Distant Thunder*.

Another major commitment during the summer was the deployment of twenty-four Tornados from Brüggen to Leeming, in order to mount a flypast by sixteen aircraft over Buckingham Palace on 17 June as part of the Queen's Official Birthday celebrations. The formation was led by Gp Capt G.L. Torpy, the station commander at Brüggen, with Sqn Ldr Klein.

Exercise *Arid Thunder*

'Exercise *Arid Thunder* was born in a men's toilet after a dinner in London,' recalled Sqn Ldr S. Kinnaird. 'The MoD needed to de-engineer a large number of time-expired BL755 Cluster Bombs Units (CBUs) and it was going to cost around £500 pound per bomb.' On overhearing a conversation, Kinnaird, who had recently returned from an exchange tour with the US Navy, suggested that it might be more cost-effective – and offer much better training value – to drop the weapons instead. Unfortunately there were no ranges in Europe that would allow live cluster bombs to be dropped, but Kinnaird knew that it was possible to drop them at the Chocolate Mountain complex in Nevada. 'Anyway I contacted my friends at the US Marine Corps,' continued Kinnaird, 'and an exercise was born.'

The first unit to deploy for Exercise *Arid Thunder* was 13 Squadron, which started flying from the USMC air station at Yuma on 3 November. They were followed consecutively

Exercise Scorpion Wind: *two USMC Grumman EA-6B Prowler EW aircraft refuel from a VC10 tanker of 101 Squadron, accompanied by three Tornado GR1s.* (Tom Boyle)

by 14 and 617 Squadrons, and each two-week detachment dropped around 140 CBUs. The range sorties lasted around 90min, dropping sticks of four CBUs on an array of vehicle hulks at the end of a narrow canyon. For the aircrew the experience of dropping live CBUs provided number of other good lessons: 'the major issue was the smoke when there was no wind. We aimed for minimum spacing over the target, but you couldn't see anything,' remembered Flt Lt I. Walton, a QWI on 14 Squadron. 'The targets were in a dust bowl and the smoke from CBUs was amazing: it still obscured the targets some two minutes later... overall it was a really eye opening detachment weapons wise and great experience.' Sqn Ldr J.B. Klein agreed, adding that: 'the detachment overall was excellent fun but probably of limited tactical value due to range and airspace constraints... but highly revealing in that some crews missed the target even with a long stick of four CBUs. A good lesson for all'

For 14 Squadron it was a two-part detachment: the first half was spent dropping CBUs on the range and in the second half the squadron took part in the USMC Exercise *Scorpion Wind*. Unfortunately the airspace around Yuma proved to be quite restricted and the Tornados were limited to low-level link routes between various weapons ranges, working with USMC F-18 Hornets.

Meanwhile, 31 Squadron had deployed to Dhahran for Operation *Jural* and 12 Squadron to Incirlik for Operation *Warden*. Of the three Tornado main operating bases, only Marham had a full complement of squadrons at the end of the year: both of the Lossiemouth squadrons were deployed away and at Brüggen only IX and 17 Squadrons were at home.

6

1996-2001

Operational to the Finish

Mid-Life Update

Planning for a 'Mid-Life Update' (MLU) for Tornado GR1 had started in the 1980s. With the Cold War in full swing at that time, the original concept was to improve the aircraft's low-level deep strike capability by making it more 'stealthy.' The TFR was to be replaced by a Terrain Reference Navigation (TRN) system, similar to that used at the time by cruise missiles, which would use a new covert radar altimeter. Crews would also be able to use Forward Looking Infra-Red (FLIR) sensors and their cockpits would be fully compatible with Night-Vision Goggle (NVG). Modifications were also proposed to reduce the radar cross-section of the aircraft by using radar-absorbent material in the engine intakes and introducing a modified canopy. The project was originally planned to start the early 1990s, but the inevitable budgetary pressures led to the inevitable slippage in the time line. Then the end of the Cold War, along with lessons learnt from the Gulf conflict, intervened leading to a revised, delayed (and much reduced) solution.

The MLU configuration was eventually finalized in 1994 with funding for an initial eighty aircraft to start the modification programme from 1996. These aircraft would be re-designated as Tornado GR4 and the modifications would now include the FLIR system, an integrated GPS navigation system and a 1553 digital databus, which would enable full integration of laser-designator pods and GPS-enabled weapons with the aircraft's stores management and weapons-aiming systems. One of the two 27mm Mauser cannon would be removed to make space for the FLIR equipment. Improvements to the data loading and recording systems were also incorporated.

In early 1996, the RAF began to return Tornado GR1s to British Aerospace for updating; however, the aircraft first had to be de-modified from the current operational standard (for

A pair of Tornado GR1s begin their take-off roll at the start of an Operation Warden *sortie over northern Iraq.* (Darren Berris)

A Vicon-equipped Tornado GR1 closes on the port-wing hose of a VC10 tanker of 101 Squadron during an Operation Warden *sortie.* (Carl Wilson)

A Tornado GR1 of IX Squadron, loaded with ALARM missiles. (Geoffrey Lee/ Plane Focus)

A Tornado GR1A of 13 Squadron refuelling during the deployment to the Far East in March 1997. (Simon Hadley)

A Tornado GR1A from 13 Squadron about to overfly the strafe panel at Song Song range at low level. (Simon Hadley)

A Tornado GR1B of 12 Squadron in the new all-grey colour scheme carries its war load of two Sea Eagle missiles. (BAe Heritage)

example to be able to operate TIALD, or ALARM) to return them to the same state that they had been in when first delivered to the RAF. This process caused a great amount of work for engineers, who were already stretched trying to support operational and exercise commitments with a reduced stock of spares.

The beginning of 1996 saw 31 Squadron mounting Operation *Jural* from Dhahran and 12 Squadron at Incirlik for Operation *Warden*. In the USA, the North America training aircraft were at Nellis AFB ready for Exercise *Red Flag* by IX Squadron. These aircraft would later move back to Yuma for Exercise *Arid Thunder* CBU-dropping by 17 Squadron, which took place in February. Another exercise in the USA was Exercise *Purple Star*, a large-scale Combined Joint Task Force (CJTF) exercise for which 617 Squadron deployed to NAS *Oceana*, Virginia in April. The UK's participation to *Purple Star* comprised some 12,000 personnel and included with a Royal Navy carrier task force comprising thirty vessels as well as the 5th Airborne Brigade from the British Army.

Perhaps the most significant event of 1996 from the Tornado crews' perspective was the bombing of the domestic accommodation site at Dhahran on 25 June. The truck-bomb attack,

TWCU crews periodically took part in major exercises: here a XV (R) Squadron Tornado GR1 flies low over the sea during the NATO Air Meet at Ørland, Norway. (Chris Stradling)

which killed a number of US personnel at the Khobar Towers complex, was carried out by Hezbollah. Thankfully there were no British casualties, but Operation *Jural* in its entirety was moved to the RSAF Prince Sultan Air Base (PSAB) at Al Kharj, some seventy miles to the southeast of Riyadh. Here summer daytime temperatures reached over 50°C, so the working day had to start at 02:30hrs local time in order to use cooler periods. This move represented a massive reduction in the quality of life for the RAF personnel on detachment in Saudi Arabia. Firstly accommodation was in tents, which, although air conditioned, provided little respite from either the heat of the Arabian summer or the noise of aircraft moving on a busy airfield; secondly there was no opportunity, as there had been at Dhahran, for short 'rest and recuperation' breaks in the more liberal and cosmopolitan atmosphere of Bahrain. As a result, morale suffered amongst all RAF personnel.

The operational flying task continued and the sortie profile for a typical Operation *Jural* mission remained largely unchanged. Some squadrons introduced a six-day working cycle for aircrews which consisted of planning on Day 1 followed by leading the formation on Day 2, flying as Number 4 on Day 3, as Number 3 on Day 4, as Number 2 on Day 5 and then having a day off from flying on the sixth day. However, political tension increased in the region over the summer when Iraqi forces were deployed into northern Iraq to fight Kurdish militias. In response, the US launched two cruise missile attacks on military targets in Iraq and from August the southern NFZ was extended up to the 33rd Parallel, thus increasing the size of the area to be patrolled by Coalition aircraft.

Far East Deployment

The operational commitments over Iraq continued, but spring 1997 also saw two exercise deployments to the Far East. The Five Powers Defence Arrangements (FPDA) for the defence of Singapore and Malaysia had been agreed by Singapore, Malaysia, Australia, New Zealand and the UK in 1971. The following years had seen a number of small-scale exercises, but in 1997 it was decided to hold an air exercise named Exercise *Elang Osprey* followed by Exercise *Flying Fish*, a large joint maritime exercise. The UK participation to these exercises, which was intended to demonstrate the ability to deploy armed forces globally, would include six Tornado GR1s, along with a naval task force.

The first Tornado unit to deploy to Malaysia was 13 Squadron, who trailed the aircraft via Akrotiri, Seeb and Columbo to Royal Malaysian Air Force (RMAF) Butterworth in early March. Over the next four weeks, Exercise *Elang Osprey* included low-level flying, fighter evasion, weaponry at Song-Song range and air-combat training. 'I recall that the ECS [Environmental Control System] struggled to cope with the humidity,' wrote Flt Lt S.C. Hadley. 'As a consequence, there were lots of sorties where there would be a muffled bang and then lots of water would flood out of the air ducts onto the IN, reconnaisance kit et cetera. We then had to turn the heat up to maximum to clear out the water, which was clearly marvellous... Flying over the jungle was fantastic... the sort of scenery that you might see in the latest *Star Wars* movie. There were birds all over the place, big ones, and that led to a few bird strikes. As a result we always diverted as pairs in case of an ejection. The trees were enormous, and despite having a 100-ft tree escape piece of kit [lanyard] to get us down from a tall rainforest tree, given that these trees were around 300ft tall and there was no proven capability for the emergency radios to penetrate the jungle canopy, we thought it best to play safe.'

From mid-April it was the turn of 12 Squadron, to take part in Exercise *Flying Fish*, during which they operated in the anti-shipping role. The squadron returned the aircraft to the UK in the first week of May, in time for another maritime exercise, *Linked Seas*, for which they joined elements of 617 Squadron at Rota, Spain. Fg Off A. Robbins, newly arrived on 12 Squadron, recalled 'regular sixships carrying out 100ft low-level ASUW attacks on NATO and USN ships off the Spanish coast, a British pastime inherited from Nelson's time. Continuing that fine tradition, our USN exchange dude Sammy rather naughtily bounced a load of live flares across the deck of the *Principe Asturias* the Spanish flagship.' Another maritime deployment followed in

RAF ground crew of 14 Squadron at Ali Al Salem (AAS) air base, Kuwait, during Operation Bolton. In the background is a battle-damaged HAS. (Martin Spanswick)

A Tornado GR1 equipped with a TIALD pod extends its airbrakes during an Operation Bolton sortie. (Carl Wilson)

September for 617 Squadron, this time to Sigonella, Sicily. This did not go well and, in the words of Wg Cdr Dugmore, OC 617 Squadron, 'it was a goat from start to finish. The aircraft got a soaking from a thunderstorm on day one and never recovered. Plus, Italian ATC could not cope with us wanting to launch several aircraft in quick succession.'

Meanwhile the summer months had seen IX, 14 and 31 Squadrons training in Alaska in Exercise *Cope Thunder* and 12 and 31 Squadrons firing AIM-9L missiles from RAF Valley.

Operation *Bolton*

Since the end of the Gulf War the UN had been monitoring Iraq's compliance with UN directives on biological and chemical warfare. The work of a team of inspectors established by the UN Special Commission (UNSCOM) had largely been unnoticed by the media, but they were thrown into the limelight during late 1997 when the Iraqis stopped co-operating with UNSCOM. As part of the diplomatic response to Iraq, the UK initiated Operation *Bolton* in October to reinforce British presence in the region. The Saudis were unwilling to allow offensive operations to be carried out from their territory, so initially Operation *Bolton* comprised the deployment of HMS Invincible, augmented by the Harrier GR.7s of 1 Squadron, to the Persian Gulf. They arrived in theatre in late January. However, in the meantime the Kuwaitis had expressed a willingness to host combat aircraft and on Friday 6 February, just three months after completing their previous operational tour, 14 Squadron at Brüggen was given 48hrs notice to return to the Middle East. Crews were immediately recalled from leave and detachments. 'I was skiing in Val d'Isere,' recalls Flt Lt S.E. Reeves, 'when I got a call saying "come on back" so I had to hire a car and drive back to Brüggen.' The squadron also had crews taking part in the night Tactical Leadership Training (TLT) exercise at Leuchars: 'the TLT staff came and instructed the two 14 Squadron crews to return to Brüggen immediately' recalled Flt Lt K.R. Rumens. 'At the time we had absolutely no idea why. The next day back at Brüggen the Boss briefed all of the 14 Squadron aircrew and engineers and informed us that first

A Tornado GR1 from 17 Squadron leads a Tornado GR1B of 12 Squadron over the Canadian countryside near Cold Lake during Exercise Maple Flag. (Carl Wilson)

thing Monday morning we would be taking nine Tornado GR1s out to a base in Kuwait. We were to get ready for war immediately.'

An advance party of engineers was despatched to get the airfield ready for operations. As he disembarked from the aircraft, Ch Tech Spanswick was reminded of the disparaging comments he had made a few months beforehand when he had first seen Al Kharj. 'We arrived at Ali Al Salem at about 04:00hrs with thunderstorms all round, and in the darkness we could just make out collapsed tents and rivers of mud and waterlogged sand everywhere. I said "Finchy, do you remember what I said when we arrived in Al Kharj… well it just has got worse" In my opinion Ali Al Salem was a unique deployment: to my knowledge it was the first time an RAF Tornado squadron had deployed, completely on its own (with no support from any other squadron and certainly no help form the Americans) to a bare-based operating location, especially being so close to the Iraqi border. It was quite scary, as we had no idea what was going to happen, no idea how long it was going to last, nor when we would get home. All we knew was that we had twenty-four hours to get the place up and running to accept thirteen Tornados being deployed from UK and Brüggen. A couple of years earlier I had driven past Ali Al Salem when going to a Kuwait bombing range and saw the devastation of the base with bombed out HASs and building et cetera. However, it was all extremely exciting in a very nervous way and we pulled together as a complete squadron. Twenty-four hours later, the runway was clear and we had sorted out the aprons in front of the HASs to accept the aircraft. It was quite an awesome sight to see thirteen Tornados taxi in, in pitch-black conditions at a bombed out airfield in the middle of the Kuwait desert. And on top of that it was only a few hours later the jets were ready for their first mission over Iraq. And so on a diet of boiled rice and boiled chicken our adventures began… again.'

Back at Brüggen the whole station worked over the weekend to get the aircraft ready and on 9 February 1998, nine Tornados left Brüggen heading for Kuwait. A further four aircraft deployed directly from the UK. Ali Al Salem Air Base, which lay some twenty-five miles to the west of Kuwait City, had been re-occupied by the Kuwaiti Air Force (KAF) after the Gulf War, but details about the airfield were scant. 'As squadron QFI,' continued Flt Lt Rumens, 'I was tasked with briefing the squadron with what facilities the airfield had. The brief was pretty lean. We had no charts/plates, no information on radar services or approach aids. I had worked out from satellite imagery the approximate runway direction and length and it looked like concrete. In fact the only thing we knew was phoned through to us from Tom Boyle, our former Boss, who was already in theatre. Tom informed us that Kuwait City International Airport would see us into the area on their radar and then chop us to Ali Al Salem Tower for which a frequency was provided.' After a 7½hr flight, the Tornados reached Kuwait in darkness. The runway lighting showed up well, but on taxying off the runway Flt Lt Rumens discovered that 'there were no lights anywhere else on the airfield so we were waved off of the runway by a few engineers who had torches and we shut down and chocked nine Tornados in a tight "gaggle" on a bit of concrete just off the end of the runway. The next day in the light the engineers had to tow aircraft to the parking places.' The airfield was still in the semi-destroyed state in which it had been left after the Gulf War.

Over the next two days, the squadron established a dispersed operating base in one of the HAS sites. Each of the large HAS had an enormous hole in the roof, thanks to the attention of Coalition aircraft during the Gulf War. Despite the holes, the shelters provided ideal storage space for engineering equipment. In one HAS the operations and engineering facilities were set up inside long tents, each of which was protected with sandbags. Initially the aircraft were parked in the open outside the shelters but later on, as the temperatures rose, light-weight canopies were constructed to protect airframes, engineers and aircrew from the sun. Weapons were delivered to Ali Al Salem and the TIALD pods being used by 17 Squadron for Operation *Jural* were flown in from Al Kharj. Forty-eight hours after arriving in Kuwait, 14 Squadron declared itself ready for operations.

In the end, the Tornados were not required for attack operations. Diplomatic initiatives had quickly defused the crisis and a new agreement between Iraq and UNSCOM was signed on 17 February. However the squadron remained in Ali Al Salem for the next three months to fly *Jural*-type sorties in the southern NFZ. Within each pair of aircraft, the leader would be TIALD-equipped and also be loaded with two Paveway II LGBs; his wingmen would carry the Vicon pod. Flying continued around the clock and most crews flew a mixture of day and night missions. When compared to Dhahran or Al Kharj, Ali Al Salem was much close to Iraq, resulting in much reduced transit times to Iraqi airspace: sortie times were therefore shorter than on previous detachments, typically being around 2hr. As previously, Coalition aircraft took the opportunity of being in Iraqi airspace to carry out practice attacks on military installations and on occasions the Tornados were partnered with Harrier GR.7 aircraft from 1 Squadron which were now operating ashore from Ahmed Al Jabbar south of Kuwait City.

Between the operational sorties there was an opportunity for some training, low-flying in Kuwait and using the ranges at Al Abraq and Udari. There were also Air-Combat Training sorties as well as fighter affiliation training with KAF F-18 Hornets and more combined training sorties with the Harriers.

Operation *Bolton* had replaced Operation *Jural* and now included all RAF operations in the southern NFZ. Thus when 12 Squadron took over responsibility for the Kuwait detachment in early May, the Tornado GR1 force was supporting three simultaneous operational detachments: six aircraft remained at Incirlik for Operation *Warden*, and six more were at Al Kharj with a further twelve at Ali Al Salem for Operation *Bolton*. With a full calendar of training exercises and the MLU programme in full swing, the Tornado squadrons would be stretched to cover all the commitments; however responsibility for Operation *Warden* was returned to the Jaguar force at the end of September.

Over the summer months 617, 17 and 14 Squadrons took part in Exercise *Maple Flag* from CAF Cold Lake base. The exercise included aircraft from Germany, UK, New Zealand and the US as well as the Canadian hosts. Domestic exercises included a station exercise at Lossiemouth, during which aircraft were sent to Kinloss in a simulated chemical threat environment, to practise the ability to deploy at short notice.

Strategic Developments

The Strategic Defence Review (SDR), published by the British Government in July included some far-reaching developments for the Tornado GR1 force. The WE177 nuclear weapon had already been withdrawn earlier in the year, so the strike role, once the primary role of the Tornado GR1 in Cold War days, had been given up completely. The SDR also signalled the end of the maritime role for the Tornado GR1B, although 617 Squadron would complete one last JMC exercise in October. In this latter exercise the squadron took part in large anti-shipping packages, flying against ships from Germany, France, Netherland and the Royal Navy as they sailed around the northern coast of Scotland. The exercise alternated daily between blue water and coastal operations and the squadron mounted two daily waves each of four or five aircraft simulating Sea Eagle tactics.

The final fallout from SDR was the confirmation that RAF Brüggen would close in 2000 and that 17 Squadron would be disbanded in early 1999. 'I had been tipped off by a mate at High Wycombe (and sworn to secrecy) that the squadron was going to go while we were at Goose Bay,' recalled Wg Cdr Coulls, OC 17 Squadron, 'so I was the only one who knew it was coming, although rumours had been flying for a couple of months. Jock Stirrup, at the time AOC 1 Group, came down about halfway through to tell us formally. The leadership challenge was an interesting one… we had been away from home for five of the previous six months and still had a month left in Kuwait and now a massive dose of uncertainty had been introduced. However, we got away with it and left with a good reputation.'

In September 1998, 14 Squadron resumed Operation *Bolton* from Ali Al Salem (AAS) Air Base. The operational pattern was much as it had been earlier in the year, except that political tension was mounting once more, after Iraq declared in August that it would not, after all, cooperate with UNSCOM. Following further diplomatic activity, on 31 October Iraq announced that it would cease all forms of interaction with UNSCOM. Even so there was very little activity below the NFZ over the next two months, making the flying over Iraq pretty dull. Apart from 'counting flies by the thousand, interspersed with particularly uninspiring (and very definitely alcohol free) evening meals at the Kuwait Officers' Mess,' Flt Lt D.W. Hales thought that the 'operational highlights were forty-five degree dive with [inert] PW II at Udairi range and a few opportunities for HE strafe at Al Abraq.' The squadron also carried out some air-combat training and some affiliation training with the KAF F-18 Hornets. At the beginning of November, 14 Squadron handed over to 12 Squadron.

This Tornado GR1 of XV(R) Squadron has been repainted in the new all-grey finish. (XV Squadron)

After more diplomatic manoeuvring at the UN, the Iraqis reneged on an agreement to cooperate with UNSCOM and as a result it withdrew all its personnel from Iraq on 11 November 1998. The following day, the US and the UK warned Iraq that it would face a substantial military strike if it did not return to full compliance with UN Resolutions. On 14 November, the US and the UK authorized the launch of an initial wave of strike aircraft. The Tornado crews in Kuwait had planned and briefed their mission and were just about to walk for the sortie when they were cancelled. At the last minute, Iraq had agreed to 'unconditional resumption of cooperation' with UNSCOM, so the planned air strikes were called off. However, Iraqi cooperation was short-lived and only a month later the political tension had escalated once more

In early November, Wg Cdr S.G. Barnes, OC 12 Squadron, had taken over as detachment commander at AAS and had ensured that a number of contingency plans were in place in case the squadron was called upon again for operations. 'As things progressed, and the op looked more likely,' recalled Wg Cdr Barnes, 'the formation leaders were co-opted into the plan. Throughout, the squadron engineers were tremendous and produced the aircraft we needed for each wave. They moved equipment and weapons to satisfy the requirement for four aircraft per wave with TIALD pods (we had only four) were they could.'

Desert Fox – Night One

The deadline for Iraqi compliance with the UN resolutions passed on 16 December and US and UK forces were authorized to fly airstrikes, which the US military named Operation *Desert Fox*. The detachment at AAS flew three operational waves early that evening. As there were just four TIALD pods available for all of the operational waves, only the leader and Number 3 within each fourship carried TIALD pods: thus within each pair one aircraft self-designated before cooperatively designating for the wingman. The first fourship was led by Wg Cdr Barnes with Flt Lt J.E. Linter with each aircraft armed with two PW II. They were tasked against the SAM-3 site near Basra (with each pair attacking a different radar system within the site) and then bombing a radio-relay site just to the north. The attack was planned so that SAM site and relay station were far enough apart for each TIALD aircraft to mark two different targets. As they neared the target area, the Tornados met with light anti-aircraft fire, but no missiles were fired at them. The lead aircraft attacked the SAM-3 site successfully, but the TIALD pod on Number 3 aircraft did not work, leaving Flt Lt Linter to use the only serviceable pod to mark both of the Desired Points of Impact (DPIs) at the radio-relay station.

Sqn Ldrs M. Royce and L. Fisher led the second wave against targets on Tallil airfield and a radio-relay station just to the north at An Nasiriyah. 'The lead pair dropped [destroyed] a large hangar on the northern side of the airfield with three PW IIs and the back pair removed a pair of HAS on the southern side of the runway,' wrote Flt Lt Royce later. 'One HAS exploded quite spectacularly turning night into day for about twenty seconds; such was the force of the residual explosion.' In the Number 4 aircraft, Fg Off A. Robins recalled that: 'all targets were hit, including a massive secondary explosion on the HAS... a very large mushroom cloud came up to meet us... we thought we'd hit a nuke... someone said "OOH that's gotta hurt" (a *Fast Show* quote) and we all sped off hurriedly in batwing and burner. I remember that nobody landed with any extra fuel that night... USN had thoughtfully loosed off some HARMs at a SAM-6 site, and there was loads of triple-A as they put up a lot of stuff against us.' It later transpired that the hangar at Tallil had contained the 'Drones of Death' – Czech-built L-29 *Delfin* (Dolphin) training aircraft, which were being modified as remotely-piloted vehicles to carry biological weapons and the HAS had been an ammunition store. 'Satellite imagery the following day showed scorched land and no sign of there ever having been a HAS.' reported Flt Lt Royce.

The third fourship, led by Flt Lt J.P. Griggs and Sqn Ldr T.N. Harris, took off shortly after the first one. They were to attack a Republican Guard barracks at Al Kut and once again all aircraft were armed with two PW IIs, with only lead and Number 3 carrying TIALD pods. 'We decided we would do a "double run" guiding our own bombs then, as soon as they impacted, switching to the target for Number 4's bombs which were already in the air,' reported Sqn Ldr D. Armstrong, who was flying the Number 3 aircraft. 'In the event, this was a bad idea... not enough time to get fixed on the second target and too much pressure on our own target run knowing the bombs were already flying.' The sortie also ended with some excitement. 'Our leader got Roland launch warnings linked with a flash on the desert floor as we approached the Kuwaiti border on the way home,' continued Sqn Ldr Armstrong. 'He immediately went into his evasive manoeuvre and banged the wing tanks off. Jez said it was the longest two seconds of his life after he hit the jettison button' As it turned out, the flash on the desert floor was caused by US Navy aircraft dropping their weapons on a 'dump' target, of which the RAF detachment was unaware because of communications difficulties with the USN ships; it transpired that the simultaneous Roland warning was also spurious, caused by microwave links in the desert. 'The engineers gave Jez the bill for the tanks,' added Armstrong.

In the meantime, six crews from 617 deployed to AAS on 17 December to support the operations. 'We arrived just after the first trip had taken off and we awoke the next morning to the participants mooching about having faced the reality of combat' remembered Sqn Ldr A.K.F. Pease. 'They had had a couple of close calls with Roland launches... Jez Griggs had jettisoned tanks and taken evasive action. Those of us who deployed from 617 Squadron were not used in anger. We did some training flights in Kuwait and having deployed thinking we would be away for a couple of months we actually got home in time for Christmas which was a bonus.'

Desert Fox – Night Two

On the second night of the operation, 18 December, the Tornado waves were launched with enough time spacing between them for all aircraft could carry a TIALD pod and self-designate their own targets; in turn, this allowed a much more compressed attack. Wg Cdr Barnes led his formation against the SAM-3 site at Tallil, attacking the Low Blow and Perfect Patch radars and two HQ buildings within the complex. Once again the attackers were met with very light triple-A, but no SAMs were fired. As Wg Cdr Barnes later summarized the sortie 'the plan "ran on rails" and all DPIs were hit successfully.'

'Night two saw us doing a coordinated bombing run on the Republican Guard Barracks at Al Kut,' recalled Sqn Ldr Royce, 'with a whole bunch of US bombers and the standard SEAD and fighter escorts. The enemy sent up quite a fierce triple-A defence but no missiles (though I'm sure the EW assets had neutralized whatever they may have had to hand; I had never seen so many HARMs fired at one sitting).' Once again, however, the difficulty in coordinating with the US Navy was illustrated when their formation ahead of the Tornados slipped back on their ToT. 'We later calculated that their bombs were within 10sec of dropping through our formation/canopies and hitting the lead aircraft,' reported Fg Off Robins.

The third wave carried out their attack in the early hours of 19 December. This successful mission, led by Flt Lt Griggs and Sqn Ldr Harris, was also tasked against targets in the Al Kut area.

Desert Fox – Night Three

On the third night of operations the Tornados were armed with the new PW III 2,000lb weapon. 'DPIs were running out and I had argued (forcibly) with HQ that some of the targets were not worth risking lives over,' recalled Wg Cdr Barnes. 'I had proposed sending a twoship only, but we were re-allocated more sensible targets. The target area was Al Kut, close to the 32nd Parallel, and the targets were Low Blow, Perfect Patch and two HQ buildings (*déjà vu*). There were real problems with coordination as we couldn't contact the ship… we didn't get the correct detail and we ended up doing our own thing de-conflicted by height and time, but running in a clockwise direction with the rest of the package going the opposite way. There was a lot of triple-A en-route and particularly in the target area. SEAD reported some missiles fired at the package… but I did not see any. Three DPIs were hit, and Number 3 guided his weapon safely into open desert having misidentified the target. I think this was the first operational use of PW III and at the very least validated tactics and procedures with this weapon. The ground crew piped me into the shelter on return (a piper standing on top of the cab of one of the tractors) leading the aircraft to the shelter, which was very emotional.'

A second wave, led by Sqn Ldr Royce took off shortly after the first wave. This formation, tasked against bunkers and another radio-relay station just outside Basra, was also loaded with PW IIIs. However, the mission was cancelled while the formation was flying a holding pattern before they crossed the border into Iraq, and the aircraft returned to AAS with their weapons.

'In all 12(B) Squadron dropped forty-eight PW II and four PW III accurately,' concluded Fg Off Robins. 'Notable moments were the US Navy trying to kill us… and a fine young navigator, Jonny Meadows, dragging a bomb off the DMPI into the desert because he wasn't

A pair of Tornado GR1s in front of a damaged HAS at AAS airbase. (Graham Pitchfork)

(correctly) happy with his TIALD picture. The poor navigators had to "stir the porridge" on some dreadful pre-acquisition pictures in the early-ish days of TIALD: often pictures would not bloom until very late, very tricky in the increasingly legal world of targeting.'

Iraq and NFZs

After a slightly delay, 12 Squadron handed over to II Squadron in Kuwait in early January. Operation *Desert Fox* had been the first time that RAF aircraft had dropped bombs on targets in Iraq since the Operation *Ingleton* missions in early 1993 and it marked a massive change in policy by the Iraqi government. For while they had been prepared to tolerate the southern NFZ in the post-*Ingleton* years, after *Desert Fox* they declared that they would no longer recognize the NFZ and they would engage aircraft flying over their territory. From then on attacks on Coalition aircraft became commonplace over southern Iraq, with both anti-aircraft guns and SAMs being fired. 'Triple-A was a big threat and prevalent; there were numerous occasions when you'd suddenly notice a new cloud formation appear near to you… then realized that it was 120mm-odd calibre triple-A airburst,' reported Flt Lt L.P. Williams, a navigator on II Squadron. The Rules of Engagement (RoE) for British Forces were changed and a series of Response Options (RO) were introduced, permitting limited offensive action over Iraq. These ranged from RO1, which was an attack flown in direct response to an Iraqi act of aggression, to RO5 which was a pre-planned strike against an Iraqi installation or weapon system.

On 31 January, II Squadron aircraft led by Sqn Ldr G.R. Wells attacked targets at Tallil with PW II and the same team followed up with two more attacks against Tallil on 10 and 21 February. The following day the detachment carried out a PW III attack on a bunker at Ar Rumaylah. The tasking came in at short notice and required the fourship to be at the runway threshold ready for an immediate launch. As the day's operational wave was already airborne on a standard reconnaissance sortie, Sqn Ldr M.C. Alton and Flt Lt Williams were called in on their 'day off' to lead the mission. 'I had never even seen a PW III properly, let alone dropped one and certainly had no clue about planning considerations,' commented Flt Lt Williams. Nevertheless, the crew put together an effective plan and led the formation out to the runway to wait for the word. 'After about twenty minutes at the end of the runway the operations desk transmitted the code word and we were off, to shatter the peace and quiet of Iraq as some departing USAF A-10s had been shot at,' continued Williams. 'One big factor was the wind. We had already planned to use the tailwind (PW III likes wind from behind), but it turned out to be easily 100kt (rather more than we anticipated), so we had to adjust our pickle point on the target run by about two miles.' Subsequent reconnaissance showed that the DPI had been hit accurately.

By now it was clear that the demands of the MLU programme were making it almost impossible for the Tornado GR1 force to maintain six aircraft at Al Kharj as well as twelve aircraft in Kuwait. In February 1999, responsibility for the Al Kharj detachment was passed to the Tornado F3 force; in many ways the F3 was a much more suitable aircraft for enforcing a NFZ than was the Tornado GR1. In the north, Operation *Warden* was taken over by the Jaguar force.

Operation *Engadine*

However any thoughts that the Tornado GR1 force might enjoy a respite from operations proved to be premature. Throughout the 1990s, the Former Republic of Yugoslavia was riven by savage civil wars and during the decade British military aircraft became increasingly involved in UN and NATO operations over the Balkans. In the mid-1990s, RAF Jaguars, Harriers and Tornado F3s, as well as Fleet Air Arm (FAA) Sea Harriers, had intervened in the war in Bosnia-Herzogovina. Then, in late 1998 another war erupted in nearby Kosovo. In March 1999, after attempts to resolve the conflict through diplomacy had failed, NATO commenced air operations against Serbia. The RAF fixed-wing contribution to NATO forces comprised initially a detachment of Harriers based at Gioia del Colle, near Venice. The Harriers flew the first offensive sorties of Operation *Engadine* over Kosovo on 24 March 1999.

Both the VC10 tanker from 101 Squadron and the Tornado GR1A of II Squadron are in the all-grey colour scheme being applied to all tactical aircraft in RAF service. The Tornado is armed with live 1,000lb bombs. (Rick Brewell)

Just four days later Parliament decided to increase the number of RAF aircraft available for Operation *Engadine* and on Sunday 28 March, Tornados from Brüggen were earmarked for this commitment.

Unfortunately 17 Squadron had been disbanded in the week before the operation. 'We had been nominated as a "centre of excellence" for TIALD and Paveway III early in 1998 and were the lead squadron at Brüggen,' remembered Wg Cdr Coulls, 'with 14 Squadron nominated as next in line. My QWIs had become genuine experts and had actually rescued a PW III trial in the UK that was going bad. Kosovo kicked off as we were disbanding and PW III was about to be used for the first time in anger... and Brüggen's experts (I still had about six crews that were TIALD/PW III Combat Ready) were sitting around partying. Needless to say, persuading the hierarchy to see sense and let us do the operation was not possible (I tried my hardest), so 14 Squadron got to do it with a bunch of people that were not trained. The crews were doing the TIALD workup during the transits to the Balkans.'

As the remaining specialist TIALD/LGB squadron, 14 Squadron, commanded by Wg Cdr T.M. Anderson, was earmarked as the lead unit and it provided twelve crews. Under the command of Wg Cdr R.A.C. Low, 31 Squadron were in the final stages of their work-up for deployment for Operation *Bolton* and were able to provide another six crews, with the final balance of crews from IX Squadron commanded by Wg Cdr G.J. Bagwell. However with few TIALD pods available for training outside operations in the Gulf, none of the crews at Brüggen were particularly current in TIALD/LGB operations.

A further complication was the instruction by the ATOC that Tornado operations were to be flown as sixships, made up of two pairs of bombers each escorted by a 'spotter' to warn of SAM launches. This tactic had been adopted by the Harrier force in operations over the Balkans and while it may have been a sensible precaution for single-seat aircraft, it was of doubtful relevance to twin-seat aircraft carrying out long-range operations with laser systems. The instruction seems to have been an example of micro-management by staff officers with little tactical appreciation; and it would have serious consequences later both in terms of tactics and of weapons accuracy.

However one initiative that did work particularly well was the arrival at Brüggen during the next few days of three VC10 tankers from 101 Squadron. A very close relationship quickly developed between tanker crews and the Tornado crews, enabling them to operate together very effectively.

After a few days of frenetic activity at Brüggen, which included some 'engineering miracles,' ten Tornado GR1s and six TIALD pods were ready for action. Apart from preparing crews, aircraft and weapons ready, there was another problem to be overcome in the few days available. Although Brüggen had spent the Cold War decades at a high state of readiness for wartime operations, all of that expertise had been lost; much of the infrastructure had also been dismantled during the 1990s, as the emphasis shifted to deployed operations. For example, secure communications, which had been removed from the squadron operations building over the previous 10 years, had to be reinstalled.

The operational crews were divided amongst three teams: a 'green team' and a 'red team' in which the bomber crews were provided by 14 Squadron and a further team crewed by 31 Squadron crews; the 'spotter' crews for each team were provided by IX Squadron.

The first operational mission from Brüggen was led by Sqn Ldr J.K. Hogg and Sqn Ldr S.P. Rochelle on the night of 4/5 April. Six Tornados, crewed by 14 Squadron's 'green team,' were

A pair of 31 Squadron Tornado GR1s armed with ALARM missiles. (Rick Brewell)

tasked against targets on the periphery of Kosovo. The first three aircraft took off from Brüggen at 21:30hrs following their VC10 tanker with the second wave, comprising three more Tornados and another VC10, getting airborne 5min behind them. No diplomatic clearance had yet been received for the operation, so instead the tankers filed a flight plan for a routine training flight to Aviano, Italy. The two formations flew south through eastern France to the Mediterranean coast, then routed via Corsica east across Italy. There were thick clouds across France, so the Tornado pilots had to work hard to keep station with their tankers. The transit also included two refuelling brackets, which again were carried out in challenging conditions. This procedure was somewhat over-complicated by the presence of three, rather than the more usual two, Tornados with each tanker. The aircraft broke out of the cloud as they reached the Adriatic, but the crews discovered that the whole of the airspace was already filled with other NATO tankers and strike aircraft: the Brüggen crews had not received the airspace coordination instructions detailing the positions of these tanker tracks. However, after being cast off by their VC10s, the Tornados worked their way through the mêlée and rendezvoused with pre-strike tankers to the south of Macedonia. 'This was actually a pair of TriStar tankers, operating in formation for the first time,' Wg Cdr Anderson later described. 'The AAR was a nightmare; the Tornados were heavily laden and draggy with their weapons on board; the tankers were at the top of the Tornados' effective operating altitude; and the tankers, which had much more excess thrust than the Tornados, had apparently forgotten about the need to make gentle power corrections. I have never before or since experienced such a difficult and heart-stopping AAR event; the Tornados were in and out of combat power just trying to get engaged and then to stay in, all in the inky black and as the clock ran rapidly down to "push time". In the event, Rocky [Sqn Ldr Rochelle] made one of the ballsiest calls I have witnessed and [delayed] the whole night mission of goodness knows how many aircraft for 10min to enable the Tornados to tank.'

After refuelling, the Tornados crossed the border into Serbia and headed towards their targets, where they were greeted with heavy anti-aircraft fire. The first pair attacked the highway bridge

A Tornado GR1A of II Squadron at low-level over the UK. (Rick Brewell)

at Jezgrovice (along the shores of Lake Gazivoda 40 miles northwest of Pristina) with PW IIs, while the second pair delivered PW IIIs onto the rail tunnel near Mure (some 50 miles north of Pristina) on the boundary between Kosovo and Serbia. The NVG-equipped spotters were able to act as pathfinders for the bomber crews: 'for example,' explained Sqn Ldr Legg, 'cloud structure and gaps are clearly seen miles ahead on goggles in the dark… this allowed the spotter crews (from IX Squadron) to give direction for best attack to the bomber crews with TIALD.' Each bomber dropped its weapons, using the TIALD pod to self designate. All NATO aircraft shared the same planned weapon impact time with the objective of achieving a simultaneous cut of all road and rail links into Kosovo. 'As our weapons impacted,' recalled Sqn Ldr Rochelle, 'the whole of Kosovo lit up. There must have been 150 major explosions around Kosovo.' After completing their attacks, the aircraft returned home via the same route, having first rendezvoused again with the TriStar tankers for post-strike AAR. The Tornados landed back at Brüggen in daylight after a 7½hr flight.

The following night Flt Lt S.J. Hulme and Sqn Ldr A.S. Frost led a team from 31 Squadron against hardened storage bunkers at Pristina airfield. 'The sortie didn't start well, with the obligatory crew-out at formation check in.' remembered Flt Lt Hulme. 'Fifteen minutes later, after a rather rapid start and with Adrian Frost still having barely regained composure after a bit of sprint across the 14 Sqadron HAS site, we taxied out to chase the two VC10s and five Tornados that were already heading south towards the Mediterranean and the first tanker bracket off the coast of Nice. About halfway across France, I caught up with my formation, the weather was fantastic and it made for a great sight; however, it was not long before I was cursing having three Tornados on each tanker as we hit the forecast poor weather off the French coast. Close formation in thick cloud, at night on a tanker is not fun at the best of times but we were to get plenty of practice that first night. Kudos to the VC10 guys as it can't have been much fun for them especially as we all re-joined post strike over the Adriatic with the VC10 still plugged into the back of a Tristar… and only intermittently visible as they bounced in and out of cloud. The

The 'Green Team' (made up from 14 and IX Squadrons) in the 14 Squadron crew room at Brüggen after the first mission over Kosovo. Standing: John Hogg, Dave Galie, Timo Anderson (OC 14 Squadron), Rich Howell, Kev Gambold, Grant Page; seated: Euan Fraser, Paul Lenihan, Dave Wood, Kev Jones, Pete Rochelle, Darren Legg. (Keven Gambold)

mission went well with good weather once we hit the "box" and target runs that went smoothly and with only very light triple-A.'

However, the remaining crews encountered problems as the unfamiliarity with laser-guided weaponry in general – and the PW III in particular – began to tell. 'This attack was unsuccessful as the wrong codes were given to the LGB (my first LGB sortie),' reported Flt Lt R.L. Hawkins, who was flying with Flt Lt T. Burke. 'At that time LGB operations were only conducted by a select few who did not wish others to know about the magic, so very few briefings were given. I typed in the correct code but did not "enter" so the bomb remained on the basic training setting. It missed.'

In the Number 2 aircraft, Flt Lt S. Oakes and Sqn Ldr J.G. Niven fared little better. 'My first-night nerves proved to be unnecessary,' declared Sqn Ldr Niven, 'as we encountered no resistance whatsoever, no triple-A, no SAMs, no fighters… nothing. However, the mission was almost a complete failure, with no weapons on target from our drops. The first lesson was unfolding, with the Wing's other missions producing the same result. Disappointed and relieved in equal measure, and six or so hours after taking off, we eased our way down through the dawn sky to be met by an anxious station commander. Apart from the all-important attack, all had gone like clockwork.'

Flt Lts S. Reeves and I.D. Hendy led their 'red team' against Pristina Barracks on 6 February; each bomber was armed with two PW IIs. 'Probably the most challenging aspect of the whole thing was the tanking on the way down during the early part,' recalled Flt Lt I.J. Cosens. 'Pretty much the whole period was stormy across southern Europe… and at our levels you spent a lot of time on the transit [in cloud] on a tanker getting bumped all over the place. It was a relief at the Adriatic to get dropped by them and go on your own.' After leaving the tankers the Tornados crossed into Serbia. 'There was a lot more triple-A [than over Iraq],' continued Cosens, 'especially as you crossed the border… it was like fireworks night with the tracer rounds going up much higher than I expected.'

Although NATO was operating over Kosovo virtually round-the-clock, typically mounting about 600 sorties each day, the rate of flying for Tornado crews was relatively low. With tasking for six aircraft each day, but crewing for three or four constituted six-ship formations, they might expect to fly once every three to four days. Theoretically the operational crews worked on a four-day cycle, commencing on the evening of Day 1 with the main mission planning, which began at 23:00hrs after the issue of the Air Tasking Order (ATO) for the following night. During the night the plan would be revised as the intelligence from the previous day's operations was fed back. That evening (Day 2) the crews would report for a meteorology and intelligence brief at around 21:30hrs, followed by sight of up-to-date target imagery and any final alterations to the plan, before a formation briefing at 22:05hrs. After a final weather update the crews would go out to the aeroplanes just after 23:00hrs to be ready for the formation check-in at midnight, with the first take offs some 10 minutes later in the early hours of Day 3. After the mission they would stand down for a day and then start the process again on the evening of Day 4. In practice, however, the flying rate was less regular as the weather over the Balkans affected tasking. Laser-guided weapons needed a clear line of sight between designator and target, and bomb and target, so any substantial cloud in the target area would preclude Tornado operations.

On 12 April, the 'green team' attacked the ammunition storage facility at Cacak and targets on the nearby airfield at Obvra some 70 miles south of Belgrade. Two nights later it was the turn of the 'red team,' which bombed Nis airfield. Although some hits were scored on both of these attacks, neither mission was entirely successful, a reflection both of the lack of practice because of the shortage of TIALD pods at Brüggen in the previous years and of the practical difficulties of laser-guided operations in cloudy skies.

On 17 April, another mission against a military communications site Ivanjila by the formation from 31 Squadron illustrated the challenges facing the Tornado crews. After refuelling in cloud and turbulence that Sqn Ldr Niven described as 'easily the worst conditions I had ever flown in,' the formation crossed the Adriatic. 'Thankfully, the weather cleared over the Adriatic,' continued Niven, 'so we reformed into our two three-ship trail and headed off into 'badlands'. We made ready for the attack: weapon package selected (two PWII); TIALD uncaged… let's find that target and get the job done. But nothing happened. Reselect… a few flashes on the screen, but still nothing… Not a single TIALD operational, no weapons released. Three-and-a-half-hours flying through the worst weather most of us had ever experienced, only to be denied by a system that was never designed to be flown at altitude, never mind in icing conditions.' The TIALD pods had been designed for 3- to 4-hour operations in clear weather: the designers could never have foreseen that they might instead be used for numerous consecutive missions of twice that length, flown through almost continuous rainstorms. The same was true of the LGBs, which were also designed to be carried one way and then be dropped; those loaded onto the (superfluous) spotters were flying up to 8-hr return flights through cloud, ice and rain before being re-loaded for use on another day. Wg Cdr Low recalled carrying out pre-flight checks on his weapons and finding that all three seeker heads were full of water and therefore unlikely to guide.

Over the next 14 days the weather over the Balkans deteriorated further and Tornado missions were cancelled. 'Poor weather is to be expected in Balkans during the spring and it was to be a feature of the campaign for me,' wrote Flt Lt Hulme, 'with a number of weather scrubs pre-launch, one cancellation before we had even made it out of the Brüggen control zone and two no-drops due to weather in the target area. The lack of GPS-guided munitions, the poor performance of those early generation TIALD pods and some tricky atmospheric conditions made for extremely challenging sorties… far harder than the conditions most were used to in the Middle East from the *Warden* and *Jural* deployments where most of the crews at Brüggen had earned their spurs patrolling Iraq.'

In late April, there was talk of a land invasion of Kosovo and 14 Squadron crews were stood down from medium-level operations, tasked instead with becoming current at Operational Low Flying (OLF) to support ground forces. The plan was for IX Squadron to lead a forward deployment to Solenzara, Corsica at the end of May to continue the medium-level air campaign with 31 Squadron while 14 Squadron prepared to support the ground war. The crews on 14 Squadron flew a number of training sorties in the UKLFS, before the plan was changed again and they resumed laser operations over Serbia. On 28 April, the 'green team' attacked the airfield at Podgorica, Montenegro, just a short distance inland from the Adriatic coast.

Meanwhile, the formation from 31 Squadron had endured more frustration thanks to the continuing bad weather over Serbia and Kosovo. Their sortie on 25 April was cancelled shortly after take off, but four nights later it seemed that the run of bad luck had ended. The weather cleared sufficiently and the formation carried out a completely successful attack against the ammunition storage site at Valjevo, aroundt 40 miles southwest of Belgrade. The following night the 'red team' attacked the Petroleum/Oil/Lubricants (POL) storage facility at Vitanovac, a few miles southeast of Obvra.

The Kosovo war was probably the first time since the Second World War that RAF bomber crews had flown offensive operations from their home base. Previous operations over the Falklands, the Middle East and the Balkans had all been flown from detached bases, which were on a war footing. For most squadron personnel, both air and ground crew, it seemed bizarre that they were fighting a war, while the rest of the station continued as normal with the peacetime routine. This was also true of family life, and while some aircrew found living at home while flying on operations to be comforting, others found it difficult. Also some of the wives found the situation very stressful. Much of the campaign was flown over the school Easter holidays and Sqn Ldr Niven remarked that 'it was quite odd to plan and fly a combat mission, then set off with the family to a theme park, or cycle round the station on our way to the pool or bowling alley.'

One aspect of operations from Brüggen, which Wg Cdr Low found to be very moving, was the way that many of the personnel at Brüggen would congregate on the road around the airfield to watch the aircraft depart, as a show of solidarity. Also, local families would wait around the perimeter fence outside the airfield to see the aircraft off.

At the end of April, authorization was granted for a more direct route to Serbia through the Czech Republic, Slovakia, Hungary and Croatia. This routing reduced sortie times to around 5hr and required just one pre- and one post-strike AAR bracket. On 2 May, the new route was used for the first time for an attack on the airfield at Obvra. Although the name Obvra was marked on the NATO map, the airfield was more properly Ladeveci Air Base, home to a wing of Soko J-22 Orao (Eagle) ground-attack aircraft and Gazelle attack helicopters. For this mission, all four bombers, led by Sqn Ldr D.W. Gallie and Flt Lt E. Fraser, were armed with two PW II LGBs: the first two were tasked against a hangar and the control tower, while the second pair were to bomb aircraft parked on hard-standings at the south-east end of the airfield. The attack 'package' also

A Tornado GR1 of 31 Squadron, armed with ALARM missiles.
(Rick Brewell)

included four F-16CJ Wild Weasels and a pair of EA-6B Prowlers to provide defence suppression for this target, which was defended by at least three SAM sites known to be in the area. After overflying Croatia and Bosnia towards Sarajevo the formation turned onto an easterly heading for the attack. The Tornados met with heavy anti-aircraft fire as they approached the target area and then, just after the first weapons impacted, two SAM-3s were launched against them. The missiles were aimed at Number 2 of the lead pair, forcing Wg Cdr Anderson into a hard defensive manoeuvre to escape them. The Wild Weasels responded to the SAM launch by firing a HARM missile at the Low Blow radar, but in the next few seconds three more SAM-3s left the launchers. Eight miles behind the first pair of bombers, the leader of the rear pair saw what was happening ahead: 'I could see the missiles going for the leader' recalled Sqn Ldr Rochelle. 'We continued to prosecute our attack and you see on my TIALD video this SAM-3 screeching across the screen.' At this stage, missile guidance radar for a SAM-3 locked onto the Spotter aircraft flown by Flt Lt Wood, who was forced to jettison his tanks and run out to the north. The rear pair was also on the receiving end of the SAM site: 'as we were coming off the target there were missiles coming up behind us,' continued Sqn Ldr Rochelle 'and as we started to defend against those, one exploded not far behind our jet… so it was a pretty hair-raising.'

Meanwhile the crew of the fourth bomber found themselves in the midst of the action. Five SAM-3 and two HARMs had already been fired during their target run. 'I saw one missile come after us and then explode below,' recalled Flt Lt Gambold. 'I assumed we would just ditch the bombs and go home, but I heard Otis [Flt Lt Page] say "right then, let's go drop 'em" and I thought, alright then, why not.' After completing his attack, the aircraft was engaged by two more SAM-3s, forcing Flt Lt Gambold to manoeuvre and break the radar lock. He lost a lot of altitude in the process, but he still found time to comment 'busy tonight' over the radio, to the amusement of the other crews. However the excitement was not quite over: yet another SAM-3 was launched from a second site and to escape it he had to jettison his fuel tanks and perform a last-ditch break, before running out from the target area at low level. According to Wg Cdr Anderson: 'the Wild Weasel crews later reported that they had never seen their HARM targeting system scopes simultaneously light up with so many radar emitters and target-tracking radars.' Once clear of the Missile Engagement Zone (MEZ) the six Tornados gathered back together and made their rendezvous with the tanker in Hungarian airspace. On the recovery to Brüggen, instead of the usual instrument approach to land, Sqn Ldr Gallie led the six Tornados for a low-level break into the visual circuit, to announce to the world that they were back from what had been the most difficult sortie thus far. Battle Damage Assessment (BDA) later showed that all four bombers had achieved direct hits on their aiming points.

After another break caused by the weather, operations resumed on 10 May with a mission flown by the green team against storage units in the barracks at Leskovac, some 45 miles northeast of Pristina. The following night the 31 Squadron team attacked the Barë road bridge at Mitrovica and on 14 May the red team flew one of the last missions to use the longer southerly route to Serbia, in order to attack the POL storage facility at Sjenica airfield. This mission was not entirely successful, as low cloud interrupted the guidance of some weapons during the last few seconds of the attack, but it was notable because the station commander, Air Cdre I.W. McNicholl, joined the formation.

On 19 May, the formation from 31 Squadron was tasked against a militia depot approximately 10 miles west of Belgrade. Unfortunately, no one in the tasking organization thought to inform the bomber crews that their target was almost next door to the local air defence operations centre and that it might therefore be keenly defended. 'The target was a small complex only a couple of hundred feet across and with four separate DPIs,' recalled Flt Lt Hulme, who led the sortie. 'The combination of still wind conditions and lots of built-up areas meant I split my sixship into two and planned 15min between attacks. It was a bit unusual but I did not see many other options. Everything went well with the a direct hit on target and then as a made a hard ninety degree left turn to avoid flying over Belgrade the sky suddenly filled with triple-A that appeared to be bursting around my ears. I kept the weave going as we headed back to the west but a few seconds later as I banked to the right and caught site of a bright flash at ground level and then two bright orbs of light snaking upwards. My RHWR was clear but I was taking no chances and manoeuvred aggressively until it was clear they were not tracking me. It wasn't until the debrief and we had listened to all the time synchronized TIALD videos that we worked out I had seen a salvo of SAM-3s fired at my Number 3 who had a pretty close shave having not reacted to his RHWR indications until a little too late for comfort. Composure regained and having ascertained that we had hit the first two DPIs, I made the decision to abort the second half

Aircrew on 14 Squadron after the Kosovo campaign. (Dave Hales)

of the formation... needless to say there were no complaints as they had seen the chaos unfold in the distance.'

In the Number 2 aircraft, Sqn Ldr Niven commented that: 'it's fair to say that my one sortie in the vicinity of Belgrade exposed me to the most spectacular firework display I will ever witness, with triple-A tracer everywhere. SAMs as well, possibly, but so far I didn't see any too close to us. We lined up in trail, the target a storage site. Soon, our leader was calling "chaff, flare," the action call for defensive measures to be deployed... then "tanks". Again an action call for the 'man-in-back' to jettison the almost-full fuel tanks and bomb load in response to a severe and imminent threat, thus shedding a great deal of weight and permitting greater manoeuvre. They were only a few minutes ahead of us, but were getting all the attention; to be honest, I was quite happy with that. You could hear the tension in Gilbert's voice as he made the calls. A good look out around us before going heads-in for our attack. We did have Number 3 behind us, whose job was to watch our tail. It was more of a psychological boost, as quite how they would spot a missile heading our way in the gloom is anyone's guess. So we pressed on. Again I had a very good mark on the target, followed by weapon release and there was an almighty explosion, and a fireball that blanked my screen for a time, then a pall of smoke and flame rising rapidly into the air... job done.'

Over the next week it was the turn of the IX and 31 Squadron crews to stand down from operations, as they set up the forward operating base at Solenzara. However, the 14 Squadron crews kept up the pressure: on 24 May the Batanjnica Petrol Storage was attacked, as was the ammunition storage at Ralja, thirty miles southeast of Belgrade on 26 May. On 27 May, the Belgrade SAM support facility was bombed and the following day the ammunition storage sites at Boljevac around 100 miles southeast of Belgrade and Sremska Kamenica, near Novi Sad, were also bombed.

'Strangely enough, the further into Serbia you went, the less intense the air defence,' reported Flt Lt Cosens. 'Maybe there wasn't much left of it after those early days. The first time we were

Aircrew of 31 Squadron at Solenzara, Corsica at the end of the Kosovo campaign. The Tornado GR1 is armed with an ALARM on the outer stub-pylon and an AIM-9L on the inner. (Simon Hulme)

given a target in Belgrade area surrounded by a fully- integrated air-defence system we were all a little surprised by the fact it was probably the quietest night we had.' However this was not true of Ralja, which was particularly heavily defended: apart from heavy anti-aircraft artillery fire, Wg Cdr Anderson recorded that three SAM-6s were launched during his attack.

The Boljevac/Sremska Kamenica mission on 28 May marked the end of direct operations from Brüggen. By then the Solenzara detachment was fully operational and the remaining Tornado operations over Serbia were mounted from there. On 4 June, Flt Lt Hulme led his formation against a radio-relay site at Rudnik, but was unable to drop any weapons because of the weather; the next day a formation from IX Squadron was also thwarted by weather and their mission was cancelled as they waited in the AAR tracks. The final Tornado mission of the air campaign over Kosovo, flown on 7 June by a formation from 31 Squadron, was also the first daylight sortie carried out by RAF Tornados. Led by Flt Lt Hulme and Wg Cdr Low the formation carried out an ALARM missile attack on a SAM-6 battery near Sjenica. Unlike the ALARM missions flown nine years previously during the Gulf War when the missiles were loaded on the shoulder pylons under the fuselage, on this sortie each aircraft carried the missiles on stub pylons above the underwing fuel tanks. The mission was successful and NATO air operations formally ceased three days later. The Solenzara detachment stayed in theatre for another few weeks, before they were recalled, returning to Brüggen on 23 June.

Tornado GR4

On 11 May 1998, the first of the post-MLU modified aircraft, known as Tornado GR4, was delivered to IX Squadron at Brüggen. Other squadrons began to have 'previews' of the new aircraft from early in 1999. In the UK, 13 Squadron became the lead unit for introduction of the GR4. Externally the only noticeable difference between the GR1 and GR4 aircraft was that the latter mounted a FLIR turret under the nose, alongside the LRMTS fairing. However, the avionic fit

A Tornado GR1 from TTTE at low-level through the Lake District; TTTE disbanded in 1999, leaving each nation to take full responsibility for its own Tornado training. (Adrian Walker)

Goose Bay continued to be a major training detachment for Tornado squadrons: the typical weather conditions are well illustrated in this photograph. (Darren Berris)

On the disbandment of TTTE, the TWCU became the Tornado Operational Conversion Unit (TOCU). This atmospheric image shows the clean-wing Tornado GR1 of TOCU. (Chris Stradling)

Another view of the clean wing Tornado GR1 used by TOCU for air displays.
(Chris Stradling)

inside the aircraft was markedly different from the older variant: in particular a new data-bus in the weapons system allowed for more complex weapons to be used. Amongst these, thanks to the lessons learnt over the Balkans, would be the Enhanced Paveway II, which incorporated a GPS-guidance system to back up the laser-guidance. On the Tornado GR4 individual weapons could be programmed by the navigator and dropped accurately without laser-guidance if necessary. For the first time the RAF had an all-weather Precision-Guided Munitions (PGM) capability from medium level, so that clouds would no longer limit operations as they had over Serbia. As more aircraft emerged from the MLU programme, the squadrons started to operate a mixture of GR1s and GR4s.

One bone of contention which Tornado crews had with the GR4 was that it lacked many of the in-service modifications and clearances which were necessary for operations over Iraq, so, for the first few years, the Tornado GR4 proved to be less operationally capable than the GR1. For this reason a number of GR1 aircraft were kept for operational flying from Kuwait and for training in North America.

In 1999, the TTTE was disbanded and each nation provided its own conversion training to the Tornado. In the case of the UK, the RAF part of TTTE was amalgamated with the TWCU to form the new national Tornado Operational Conversion Unit (TOCU) at Lossiemouth. In a departure from previous practice, where all the Tornado training had been carried out in

Ground crew from II Squadron prepare a Tornado GR1 for an Operation Bolton *sortie over southern Iraq. The aircraft is loaded with a TIALD pod and two 1,000lb LGBs.* (Larry Williams)

The tradition of using a girl's name for the TIALD pods continued from the Gulf War. (Larry Williams)

Many of the HAS on Iraqi airfields were too damaged to house RAF aircraft, a number of light-weight shelters were assembled to provide the Tornados with some protection from the elements. (Larry Williams)

A Tornado GR1 from IX Squadron in the Labrador Low-Level Training Area (LLTA) near Goose Bay. (Chris Stradling)

the UK, the TOCU was amongst the units that detached to Goose Bay over the late summer. With the closure of Deci, Cyprus became the destination of choice for squadrons wishing to carry out Air Combat Training, and both 12 and 14 Squadrons ran ACT detachments at Akrotiri in the autumn of 1999. In the case of 14 Squadron, four Tornados detached to Akrotiri on 12 November for a week-long weaponry and air-combat camp. Each day waves of aircraft would get airborne in pairs, loaded with eight practice bombs and go straight into the range pattern at Episkopi. After dropping their bombs they would then climb up for air-combat manoeuvring until they had used their fuel and then recover to Akrotiri after a short but very intense sortie.

Operation *Resinate*

Throughout the rest of 1999 and the beginning of 2000, Iraqi forces in southern Iraq had actively sought to engage Coalition aircraft operating in the NFZ. In response Tornados from AAS were frequently called upon to attack Iraqi air-defence elements. By August 1999, there had been over 200 violations of the NFZ and 300 SAM launches against coalition aircraft in the previous eight months and in that time Tornados had carried out airstrikes against twenty-three targets. The pace of operations continued through the autumn and winter and examples of so-called 'kinetic' sorties included a six-ship attack on targets at Al Kut by IX Squadron crews on 11 October and strikes by 14 Squadron against S-60 anti-aircraft gun batteries at Al Turbak on 19 February and at Tallil on 11 March.

Over the period from the end of Operation *Desert Fox* until May 2000 the Tornados dropped the equivalent of 78 tons of ordnance over southern Iraq. This period of operations was eloquently summarized by Wg Cdr J.B. Klein as: 'fairly frequent bombing various relatively

A Tornado GR1 captured in its element at low-level. (Chris Stradling)

cheap triple-A pieces with a very expensive bomb, usually under SAM and triple-A fire.' During the 2000, Operations *Bolton* and *Warden* were amalgamated under the aegis of Operation *Resinate*. The detachment of twelve Tornado GR1s was also reduced to eight aircraft.

Meanwhile RAF Brüggen was winding down towards closure and IX, 14 and 31 Squadrons prepared to move to home. Although Brüggen and Laarbruch had survived the first phase of cuts that were enacted immediately after the Gulf War, it was clear that the RAF's presence in Germany would end sooner rather than later. Laarbruch had closed in 1999 and the final drawdown came two years later with the closure of Brüggen. The two ALARM-specialist units, IX and 31 Squadrons joined the two reconnaissance squadrons at Marham, thus – in theory at least – forming a reconnaissance/SEAD wing, while the last unit to leave Brüggen, 14 Squadron, moved to Lossiemouth in December 2000, where it joined 12 and 617 Squadrons and the TOCU.

Although most of the squadrons had given up their last Tornado GR1s in late 2000, a handful of Tornado GR1s continued to be used for Operation *Resinate* through 2000 and 2001. The tempo of bombing sorties continued and, for example, during IX Squadron's operational deployment in the autumn of 2000 the squadron carried out an RO3 attack on a SAM-3 site at Al Kut on 9 October and an RO1 attack on a S-60 anti-aircraft battery at Basra on 2 November.

The last operational sortie flown by a Tornado GR1 from AAS was in mid-2001, by which time a sufficient number of Tornado GR4s had been modified to meet the operational requirements in theatre. Although this last sortie might be seen as the end of an era, it was in reality merely the end of the first part of the Tornado GR story: and the continuation of that story had already started two years beforehand with the introduction of the Tornado GR4.

APPENDIX 1
Squadron Markings

Tornado GR1s were sprayed in a 'wrap-around' green/grey disruptive camouflage from when the aircraft entered service in 1982 until around 1998. The national markings carried on the aircraft comprised roundels on the wing upper and lower surfaces, a tail flash on the fin and a roundel on either side of the forward fuselage or on the engine intakes. Each unit painted its unique squadron markings on its aircraft, including an individual aircraft identification letter (or in the case of the early days of 27 Squadron, a number).

The aircraft identification letters were preceded by a squadron identification letter from 1985 onwards as follows: Brüggen Wing: A – IX Squadron, B – 14 Squadron, C – 17 Squadron, and D – 31 Squadron. Laarbruch Wing: E – XV Squadron, F – 16 Squadron (later used by 12 Squadron at Lossiemouth), and G – 20 Squadron. Marham Wing: J – 27 Squadron, and AJ – 617 Squadron. The reconnaissance squadrons and the conversion units were not included in this system.

During the Gulf War, the aircraft in theatre were sprayed in a 'Desert Pink' scheme – with no national markings. As the conflict progressed the ground crew painted mission markers under the cockpit and this practice quickly expanded to include unofficial nose art. After the Gulf War the aircraft were returned to standard camouflage, but many retained the mission markers painted below the cockpit.

From 1998, as the aircraft underwent major servicing they were re-spayed an all-over light grey scheme. The squadron markings were modified so that they fitted on to panels that could be exchanged (thus saving re-painting if aircraft were re-allocated to another unit). The panels were: the main battery access panel on the lower front fuselage, an access panel on the fin and the di-electric cap on the fin.

Individual squadron markings were as follows:

II Squadron
Laarbruch 1988–1991; Marham 1991–2001
Nose: White disc containing black Staffordshire knot; flanked by black bar with white triangles.
Tail: aircraft letter in black within a white triangle outlined in black.

IX Squadron
Honington 1982–1986; Brüggen 1986–2001; Marham 2001
Nose: Roundel; flanked by dark green arrowhead with yellow outline.
Tail: Dark green bat insignia; aircraft letters black with white outline.

12 Squadron
Marham 1993–1994; Lossiemouth 1994–2001
Nose: Roundel; flanked by green arrowhead, outlined in white.
Tail: Black/white/green stripe superimposed with white disc containing red/brown
fox's mask; aircraft letters in black white outline.

13 Squadron
Honington 1990-1994; Marham 1994-2001
Nose: Roundel; flanked by blue (bottom) & green (top) striped bars with yellow zigzag.
Tail: Blue stripe with yellow outline, superimposed with white shield containing black lynx head and grey sword: aircraft letter black with yellow outline.

14 Squadron
Brüggen 1985-2001; Lossiemouth 2001
Nose: Winged crusader emblem; flanked by white bar, outlined in blue, containing blue diamonds.
Tail: Line of nine blue diamonds, later changed to seven with white leading edges; aircraft letters black with white outline.

XV Squadron
Laarbruch 1983-1991; as XV(R) Sqn Honington 1992-1993; Lossiemouth 1993-2001
Nose: roundel.
Tail: White XV; aircraft letters black.

16 Squadron
Laarbruch 1984–1991
Nose: Roundel; flanked by black bar with yellow outline.
Tail: Black stripe, outlined in yellow, superimposed with black disc containing "saint" insignia; aircraft letters black with yellow outline.

17 Squadron
Brüggen 1985–1999
Nose: Roundel; flanked by white arrowhead containing black zigzags.
Tail: Shield, diagonally halved in black (upper left) and white (lower right) containing red gauntlet; aircraft letters black with white outline.

20 Squadron
Laarbruch 1984–1992
Nose: White disc containing eagle carrying sword in front of yellow sunrise; flanked by light blue bars with red (upper) white (middle) green (lower) stripes.
Tail: Nil; aircraft letters black with light blue outline.

27 Squadron
Marham 1983-1993
Nose: Roundel; flanked by light green arrowhead outlined in yellow.
Tail: Red stripe, superimposed with yellow disc outlined in green, containing green elephant; aircraft letters green with yellow outline.

31 Squadron
Brüggen 1984-2001; Marham 2001
Nose: Roundel; flanked by yellow (top half) and green (bottom half) arrowhead.
Tail:Yellow/gold Star of India; aircraft letters black with white outline.

617 Squadron
Marham 1983-1994;
Lossiemouth 1994-2001
Nose: Roundel; flanked by black bar with red outline, containing red lightning flash.
Tail: Black fin tip with red lightning flash; aircraft letters in black with red outline.

Tornado GR1 of the Bahrain Wing 1991, armed with JP233.

Tornado GR1 of the Dhahran Wing 1991,
armed with 1,000lb high explosive (HE) bombs.

Tornado GR1 of the Tabuk Wing 1991,
armed with 1,000lb Laser-Guided Bombs (LGB).

APPENDIX 2
Tornado
Aircraft List

TTTE – Tri-National Training Establishment
TWCU – Tornado Weapons Conversion Unit
TOEU – Tornado Operational Evaluation Unit
BAe – British Aerospace
MoD (PE) – Ministry of Defence (Procurement Executive).
Versions: s – strike: t – trainer: a – reconnaissance: b – Sea Eagle

Serial	Unit	Code	Remarks
ZA319 t	TTTE	B-11	Preserved, gate guard at MoD, Bicester
ZA320 t	TTTE	B-01	Instructional airframe, RAF Cosford
ZA321 s	TTTE	B-58	Scrapped
ZA322 s	TTTE	B-50	Scrapped
ZA323 t	TTTE	B-14	Instructional airframe, RAF Cosford
ZA324 t	TTTE	B-02	Scrapped
ZA325 t	TTTE	B-03	Preserved, Manston museum
ZA326 t	MoD (PE)		Preserved, Bruntingthorpe museum
ZA327 s	TTTE	B-51	
	617 Sqn	O	Spares airframe, BAe Warton
ZA328 s	BAe Warton		Spares airframe, BAe Warton
ZA329 s	TTTE	B-52	Mid-air collision at low-level night near Appleby, Cumbria, 9 August 1988 with ZA593 – Flt Lt J.N.S. Watts, Lt U. Sayer GAF killed

Serial	Unit	Code	Remarks
ZA330 t	TTTE	B-08	Mid-air collision with light aircraft near Nottingham, 21 January 1999 – Lt M. Di Carlo ItAF; Flt Lt G.J. Hurst killed
ZA352 t	TTTE	B-04	Scrapped
ZA353 s	TTTE	B-53	Preserved – private ownership
ZA354 s	MoD (PE)		Preserved, Elvington museum
ZA355 s	TTTE	B-54	Preserved – private ownership
ZA356 t	TTTE	B-07	Scrapped
ZA357 t	TTTE	B-05	Instructional airframe, RAF Cosford
	13 Sqn	T	
ZA358 t	TTTE	B-06	Scrapped
	TWCU		
ZA359 s	TTTE	B-55	Preserved – private ownership
ZA360 s	TTTE	B-56	Scrapped
	TWCU		
ZA361 s	TTTE	B-57	Instructional airframe, RAF Cosford
ZA362 t	TTTE	B-09	
	TWCU		Preserved, Inverness museum
ZA365 t	27 Sqn		
	20 Sqn	GZ	
	617 Sqn	AT	
	27 Sqn		
	12 Sqn	JT	Converted to GR4
ZA366 t	TWCU		Rear fuselage fire, 3 June 1987 – Wg Cdr N.R. Irving Wg Cdr A.V.B. Hawker ejected
ZA367 t	TWCU		
	II Sqn	Z	Converted to GR4
ZA368 t	IX Sqn	Y	
	TWCU		
	617 Sqn	AJ-P	Rear fuselage fire Moray Firth, 19 July 1994 – *Hauptman* A. Stumpf GAF, Flt Lt S.T. Pretherick both ejected
ZA369 s	TTTE	BR-61	
	TWCU		Converted to GR4
a	II Sqn	II	
ZA370 s	TWCU		
a	II Sqn	A	Gulf War, Dhahran. Converted to GR4
ZA371 s	TWCU		
	20 Sqn	GF	
a	II Sqn	C	Gulf War, Dhahran. Converted to GR4

Serial	Unit	Code	Remarks
ZA372 s	TWCU		Converted to GR4
a	II Sqn	E	Gulf War, Dhahran – *Sally T*
ZA373 s	TTTE		
a	II Sqn	H	Gulf War, Dhahran. Converted to GR4
ZA374 s	TWCU		
	17 Sqn	CN	Gulf War, Dhahran – *Miss Behavin'*
	617 Sqn	AL	Preserved, Wright–Patterson museum, USA
ZA375 s	TWCU		
	14 Sqn	BN	
b	617 Sqn	AW, AJ-W	
ZA376 s	TOEU	E	
	27 Sqn	JL	Gulf War, Dhahran – *Mrs Miggins*
	20 Sqn		Departed while manoeuvring during bounce, near Lubberstadt, Germany, 10 May 1991 – Sqn Ldr P. Mason, Flt Lt R. Woods ejected
ZA392 s	XV Sqn	EK	Gulf War, Bahrain Hit ground during JP233 attack Shaibah, Iraq, 17 January 1991 – Wg Cdr T.N.C. Elsdon, Flt Lt R.M. Collier killed
ZA393 s	TWCU		
	17 Sqn	CQ	Gulf War, Tabuk – TIALD – *Sir Galahad*
	14 Sqn	BE	Converted to GR4
ZA394 s	20 Sqn	GP	
a	II Sqn	I	Mid-air collision with Jaguar near Hexham, 9 January 1990 – Flt Lt I.J. McLean, Flt Lt N. Johnston ejected
ZA395 s	27 Sqn		
	16 Sqn	FP	
a	II Sqn	N	Converted to GR4
ZA396	20 Sqn	GE	Gulf War Bahrain. Shot down by SAM Tallil, Iraq, 19 January 1991 – Flt Lt D.J. Waddington Flt Lt R.J. Steward, ejected PoW
ZA397 s	TWCU		
	XV Sqn	EN	
	31 Sqn	DM	
a	II Sqn	O	Gulf War, Dhahran Mid-air collision with a Tornado during tanker trail near Grand Rivière, Canada, 1 August 1994 – Flt Lt I. Knott, Sqn Ldr D.H. Macleod ejected
ZA398 s	TWCU		
	31 Sqn	DN	
a	II Sqn	S	Converted to GR4

Serial	Unit	Code	Remarks
ZA399 s	20 Sqn	GA	Gulf War, Bahrain – *Hello Kuwait, G'bye Iraq (Granny)*
	617 Sqn	AC	
b	617 Sqn	AJ-C	
ZA400 s	TWCU		
	9 Sqn		
a	II Sqn	T	Gulf War, Dhahran. Converted to GR4
ZA401 s	20 Sqn	GJ	
a	II Sqn	R	Converted to GR4
ZA402 s	BAe/MoD (PE)		
ZA403 s	17 Sqn	CO	Gulf War, Dhahran
			Damaged by own VT fused bombs, Ar Rumaylah, Iraq, 24 January 1991 – Flt Lt S.J. Burgess, Sqn Ldr R. Ankerson ejected PoW
ZA404 s	TWCU		
a	II Sqn	W	Converted to GR4
ZA405 s	TTTE	BR-62	
a	II Sqn	Y	Converted to GR4
ZA406 s	TWCU		
	31 Sqn	DN	Gulf War, Tabuk – TIALD
	17 Sqn	CI	Converted to GR4
ZA407 s	TWCU		
b	617 Sqn	AJ-G	Gate guard, RAF Marham
ZA408 s	TWCU		Mid-air collision with Jaguar two miles west of Sheringham, Norfolk, 15 August 1985 – Sqn Ldr A.E. Boxall-Hunt, Flt Lt T.S. Cave ejected
ZA409 t	XV Sqn	W/EW	
	TWCU		
b	12 Sqn	FQ	
ZA410 t	XV Sqn	EX	Converted to GR4
	20 Sqn	GX	
	12 Sqn	FZ	
ZA411 t	XV Sqn	Y	
	16 Sqn		
	TWCU		
	20 Sqn	GY	
	617 Sqn	AS	
b	617 Sqn	AJ-S	
ZA412 t	16 Sqn	FZ, FX	
	20 Sqn	GT	Converted to GR4

Serial	Unit	Code	Remarks
ZA446 s	XV Sqn	F, EF	Gulf War, Tabuk – *MacRobert's Reply*
	17 Sqn	CJ	
b	617 Sqn	AJ-H	
	SAOEU		Converted to GR4
ZA447 s	XV Sqn	EA	Gulf War, Tabuk – *MiG Eater*
b	12 Sqn	FA	Converted to GR4
ZA448 s	XV Sqn	EB	lost control during evasive manoeuvre Nellis ranges Exercise *Green Flag*, 30 March 1988 – Flt Lt T.D. Robinson, Flt Lt S.P. Townsend ejected
ZA449 s	BAe/MoD (PE)		
ZA450 s	XV Sqn	EC	
b	12 Sqn	FB	Converted to GR4
ZA451 s	XV Sqn	ED	Lightning strike – UWT caught fire near Jever, 6 February 1984 – Sqn Ldr I. Travers-Smith, Flt Lt F.P. Smith ejected
ZA452 s	20 Sqn	GK	Gulf War, Tabuk – *Gulf Killer*
	14 Sqn	BP	
b	12 Sqn	FC	Converted to GR4
ZA453 s	XV Sqn	EG	
	17 Sqn	CG	
	617 Sqn	AM	
b	12 Sqn	FD	Converted to GR4
ZA454 s	XV Sqn	EH	Engine failure; rear fuselage fire northeast of Goose Bay, Canada, 30 April 1990 – Flt Lt P.K. Simpson, Flt Lt S.K. Barnfield (IX Sqn crew) ejected
ZA455 s	XV Sqn	EJ	Gulf War, Bahrain – *Triffid Airways*
	16 Sqn	FE	
	31 Sqn	DP	
b	12 Sqn	FE	
ZA456 s	20 Sqn	GB	Converted to GR4
	Bahrain	M	Gulf War, Bahrain – *Hello Kuwait, G'bye Iraq (Mel)*
	617 Sqn	AQ, AJ-Q	
ZA457 s	TOEU	O	
	IX Sqn	AJ	
	17 Sqn	CE	Gulf War, Dhahran – *Bob*
	617 Sqn	AJ	
b	617 Sqn	AJ-J	Preserved, RAF Museum, Hendon
ZA458 s	16 Sqn	FB	
	17 Sqn	CE	Converted to GR4
ZA459 s	XV Sqn	EL	Gulf War, Bahrain

Serial	Unit	Code	Remarks
	617 Sqn	AB	
b	617 Sqn	AJ-B	Converted to GR4
ZA460 s	16 Sqn	FD	Gulf War, Tabuk – *Fire Dancer*
	617 Sqn	AA, AJ-A	
			Scrapped
ZA461 s	IX Sqn	AM	
	20 Sqn	GA	
	31 Sqn	DK	Gulf War, Dhahran
	617 Sqn	AM, AJ-M	
	12 Sqn	FD	Converted to GR4
ZA462 s	XV Sqn	EM	
	17 Sqn	CG	Converted to GR4
ZA463 s	20 Sqn	GL	
	Bahrain	Q	Gulf War, Bahrain – *Flying High*
1	7 Sqn	CR	Converted to GR4
ZA464 s	XV Sqn		
	20 Sqn	GM	Mid-air collision with ZA545 near Spurn Head, 14 August 1990 – Wg Cdr J. Buckler ejected, Sqn Ldr G.C. Graham killed
ZA465 s	16 Sqn	FK	Gulf War, Tabuk – *Foxy Killer*
	XV Sqn		
	17 Sqn	CD	
	617 Sqn	AF	
b	617 Sqn	AJ-F	
	12 Sqn	FF	Preserved Imperial War Museum, Duxford
ZA466 s	16 Sqn	FH	Caught raised barrier at Tabuk, 18 October 1990 – Sqn Ldr I.B. Walker, Sqn Ldr R. Anderson ejected
ZA467 s	16 Sqn	FF	Gulf War, Tabuk. Crashed during loft recovery Ar Rutbah, 22 January 1991, Iraq – Sqn Ldr G.K.S. Lennox, Sqn Ldr K.P. Weeks killed
ZA468 s	16 Sqn	FN	
	XV Sqn	EN	St Athan crew lost control after nose-wheel red after take-off from Laarbruch, 20 July 1989 – Flt Lt I. Hartley and navigator ejected
ZA469 s	20 Sqn	GD	
	Bahrain	I	Gulf War, Bahrain
	617 Sqn	AO, AJ-O	Converted to GR4
ZA470 s	16 Sqn	FL	
	14 Sqn	BQ	Converted to GR4

Serial	Unit	Code	Remarks
ZA471 s	16 Sqn	FJ	
	XV Sqn	ER, E	Gulf War, Bahrain – *Snoopy Airways (Emma)*
	617 Sqn	AK	
b	617 Sqn	AJ-K	
ZA472 s	XV Sqn	EE	Gulf War, Bahrain
	17 Sqn	CT	Converted to GR4
ZA473 s	16 Sqn	FM	Gulf War, Tabuk – *Foxy Mama*
b	12 Sqn	FG	Converted to GR4
ZA474 s	16 Sqn	FG	
b	12 Sqn	FF	
ZA475 s	16 Sqn	FC	
	Bahrain	P	Gulf War, Bahrain – *Triffid Airways*
	12 Sqn	FH	Gate guard, RAF Lossiemouth
ZA490 s	20 Sqn	GG	Gulf War, Dhahran – *Gigi*
	14 Sqn	BR	
b	12 Sqn	FJ	
ZA491 s	20 Sqn	GC	
	Bahrain	N	Gulf War, Bahrain – *Snoopy Airways (Nikki)*
b	12 Sqn	FK	Converted to GR4
ZA492 s	16 Sqn	FE	Gulf War, Tabuk and Bahrain
	31 Sqn	DJ	
b	12 Sqn	FL	Converted to GR4
ZA493 s	20 Sqn	GH	Mid-air collision with Jaguar near Keswick, 17 June 1987 – Flt Lt N.J. Campion, Flt Lt J.S. Head ejected
ZA494 s	27 Sqn	15, M	Loss of control after flap failure on approach Goose Bay, 18 July 1984 – Wg Cdr J.B. Grogan, Flt Lt J.V. Plumb ejected
ZA540 t	TTTE		
	27 Sqn	06	
	617 Sqn	JQ	Rear fuselage fire over Bristol Channel, 12 September 1991 – Flt Lt A. Edwards, Wg Cdr J. Ball ejected
ZA541 t	617 Sqn	S	
	16 Sqn		Converted to GR4
ZA542 s	27 Sqn	04/JA	Converted to GR4
ZA543 t	IX Sqn		
	TWCU	TO?	Converted to GR4
ZA544 t	14 Sqn	BX	
	TWCU	TP	Converted to GR4

Serial	Unit	Code	Remarks
ZA545 s	TWCU		Mid-air collision with ZA464 off Spurn Head, 14 August 1990 – Major D. Wise USAF, Flt Lt J.F. Bowles killed
ZA546 s	27 Sqn	05,JB	
	617 Sqn	AJ-C	Converted to GR4
ZA547 s	27 Sqn	03/JC	Converted to GR4
ZA548 t	TWCU	TQ	Converted to GR4
ZA549 t	27 Sqn	08	
	XV Sqn		
	TWCU	TR	Converted to GR4
ZA550 s	27 Sqn	JD	Converted to GR4
ZA551 t	617 Sqn	T	
	TWCU		Converted to GR4
ZA552 t	16 Sqn	FZ	
	TWCU	TS	
	II Sqn	X	Converted to GR4
ZA553 s	27 Sqn	01/JE	Converted to GR4
ZA554 s	617 Sqn		
	27 Sqn	11	
	31 Sqn	DM	Converted to GR4
ZA555 t	TWCU		Rear fuselage fire, 12 July 1984 – Flt Lt J. Magowan, Sqn Ldr E.J. Wyer ejected
ZA556 s	TWCU	TA	Converted to GR4
ZA557 s	27 Sqn	12	Converted to GR4
	TWCU		
ZA558 s	617 Sqn	F	Pilot incapacitated, crashed ten miles northwest of Cromer, 28 October 1983 – Flt Lt I.C. Dixon killed, Sqn Ldr G. Thurston ejected
ZA559 s	IX Sqn	U	
	617 Sqn		
	TWCU	F	Converted to GR4
ZA560 s	27 Sqn		
	617 Sqn	C	
	TTTE	B-59	Converted to GR4
ZA561 s	27 Sqn	02/JH	Hit sea during loft recovery manoeuvre, 16 August 1990 – Gp Capt W.L. Green, Sqn Ldr N. Anderson killed
ZA562 t	27 Sqn	JT	
	TTTE	B-15	
	TWCU	TT	Converted to GR4

Serial	Unit	Code	Remarks
ZA563 s	27 Sqn	10	
	XV Sqn	EP	
	TWCU	TC	Converted to GR4
ZA564 s	IX Sqn	S	
	27 Sqn	14/JK	Converted to GR4
ZA585 s	617 Sqn	G	Converted to GR4
ZA586 s	IX Sqn	A	Total electrical failure at night six miles northwest of Kings Lynn, 27 September 1983 – Sqn Ldr M.D. Stephens killed, Flt Lt N.F. Nickles ejected
ZA587 s	IX Sqn	B	
	20 Sqn	GN	
	TWCU	TD/TF	Converted to GR4
ZA588 s	IX Sqn	C	
	TWCU		
	17 Sqn	CP	
	TTTE	B-52	
	TWCU	TM	Converted to GR4
ZA589 s	IX Sqn	D	
	TWCU		
	31 Sqn	DC	
	TWCU	TE/TZ	Converted to GR4
ZA590 s	IX Sqn	E	
	TWCU		Scrapped
ZA591 s	IX Sqn	F	
	TWCU		
	16 Sqn	FN	Converted to GR4
ZA592 s	IX Sqn	G	
	617 Sqn	B, MB	Converted to GR4
ZA593 s	IX Sqn	H	
	617 Sqn	M/F	Mid-air collision with ZA329 at low-level night near Appleby, Cumbria, 9 August 1988 – Flt Lt C.D. Oliver, Flt Lt A.D. Cook killed
ZA594 t	TWCU		
	XV Sqn	EY	
	TWCU	TU	Converted to GR4
ZA595 t	IX Sqn	K	
	TWCU	TV	Converted to GR4
ZA596 s	IX Sqn	L	
	TWCU		Converted to GR4

Serial	Unit	Code	Remarks
ZA597 s	IX Sqn	M	
	TWCU	TA	Converted to GR4
ZA598 s	IX Sqn	N	
	TWCU		
	617 Sqn	S	Converted to GR4
ZA599 t	IX Sqn	Z	
	TTTE	B-16	
	TWCU	TX	Converted to GR4
ZA600 s	27 Sqn	07	
	17 Sqn	CM	
	TWCU	TH	Converted to GR4
ZA601 s	XV Sqn		
	617 Sqn	M	
	31 Sqn	DP	
	TWCU	TI	Converted to GR4
ZA602 t	IX Sqn	P, AZ	
	TTTE	B-13/B-17	
	TWCU	TX	Converted to GR4
ZA603 s	27 Sqn	08	Navigator command ejected crew near Schweinfurt, Germany (near miss with USAF Fairchild A-10), 8 November 1984 – Flt Lt E.D. Smith, Sqn Ldr G. Williams
ZA604 t	TWCU		Converted to GR4
	TWCU	TY	
ZA605 s	617 Sqn	G	Mid-air collision; hit by No 2 during night join up near Marham, 10 December 1986 – Flt Lt R.P. Lewis, Flt Lt A.M. Randle ejected
ZA606 s	27 Sqn	09	Converted to GR4
	TWCU		
ZA607 s	617 Sqn	P	Converted to GR4
	17 Sqn	CG	
	IX Sqn	AN	
	TWCU	TJ	
ZA608 s	617 Sqn	Z, A	Converted to GR4
	TWCU	TK	
ZA609 s	617 Sqn	J	Converted to GR4
ZA610 s	27 Sqn		
	617 Sqn	B	Flew into the sea thirty miles east of Flamborough Head during RV with Buccaneer tanker, 12 December 1985 – Flt Lt M. Barnard, Flt Lt J. Sheen killed

Serial	Unit	Code	Remarks
ZA611s	617 Sqn TWCU	A TG	Converted to GR4
ZA612 t	17 Sqn TWCU	CX TZ	Converted to GR4
ZA613 s	617 Sqn TWCU	N TL	Converted to GR4
ZA614 s	617 Sqn TWCU	E TB	Converted to GR4
ZD707 s	14 Sqn	BK	Gulf War, Dhahran. Converted to GR4
ZD708 s	BAe		Converted to GR4
ZD709 s	IX Sqn 20 Sqn 14 Sqn	AH GJ BR	Converted to GR4
ZD710 s	14 Sqn	BJ	Multiple bird strike on take-off at RAF Abingdon, 14 September 1989 – Wg Cdr R.A. Wright, Sqn Ldr M. Lawton, ejected [IX Sqn crew]
ZD711 t	31 Sqn	DY	Converted to GR4
ZD712 t	14 Sqn	BY	Converted to GR4
ZD713 t	31 Sqn 14 Sqn TWCU	DX BY TW	Converted to GR4
ZD714 s	14 Sqn IX Sqn	BE AP	Converted to GR4
ZD715 s	20 Sqn 31 Sqn	GF DB	Converted to GR4 Gulf War, Dhahran – *Luscious Lizzie*
ZD716 s	TOEU	O	Converted to GR4
ZD717 s	17 Sqn	CD	Gulf War, Bahrain – *Hello Kuwait, G'bye Iraq* Shot down by SAM near Fallujah, Iraq, 14 February 1991 – Flt Lt R.J.S.G. Clark ejected PoW, Flt Lt S.M. Hicks killed [XV Sqn crew]
ZD718 s	20 Sqn 14 Sqn	GE BH	 Flew into ground during OLF training, Oman, 13 January 1991 - Flt Lt K.J. Duffy, Flt Lt N.T. Dent killed
ZD719 s	IX Sqn	AD	Gulf War, Dhahran and Tabuk – ALARM – *Check Six.* Converted to GR4
ZD720 s	17 Sqn IX Sqn	CK AG	 Converted to GR4

Serial	Unit	Code	Remarks
ZD738 s	31 Sqn	DD	Hydraulic failure near Pickering, 27 July 1987 – Flt Lt I.B. Walker, Flt Lt S.J. Lloyd ejected
ZD739 s	IX Sqn	AC	Gulf War, Tabuk – *Armoured Charger*, Converted to GR4
ZD740 s	31 Sqn	DA	Gulf War, Dhahran – *Dhahran Annie*, Converted to GR4
ZD741 t	IX Sqn 20 Sqn 31 Sqn	AY GT DZ	Converted to GR4
ZD742 t	17 Sqn	CY/CZ	Converted to GR4
ZD743 t	17 Sqn TWCU	CZ/CX	Converted to GR4
ZD744 s	14 Sqn	BD	Gulf War, Bahrain and Tabuk – *Buddha*, Converted to GR4
ZD745 s	IX Sqn 14 Sqn	AB BM	Gulf War, Dhahran – *Black Magic*, Converted to GR4
ZD746 s	31 Sqn IX Sqn	DJ AB	Gulf War, Tabuk – ALARM – *Alarm Bell*, Converted to GR4
ZD747 s	31 Sqn IX Sqn	DK AL	Gulf War, Tabuk – ALARM – *Anna Louise*, Converted to GR4
ZD748 s	31 Sqn IX Sqn	DG AK	Gulf War, Tabuk – ALARM – *Anola Kay*, Converted to GR4
ZD749 s	TOEU	U	Converted to GR4
ZD788 s	17 Sqn	CB	Converted to GR4
ZD789 s	17 Sqn IX Sqn	CE AM	Rear fuselage fire; burnt out on landing at RAF Brüggen, 23 February 1996 – Flt Lt S.E Reeves
ZD790 s	XV Sqn 31 Sqn	D, ED DL	Gulf War, Bahrain – *Snoopy Airways (Debbie)* Converted to GR4
ZD791 s	14 Sqn	BG	Gulf War, Bahrain Shot down by SAM, Ar Rumaylah, Iraq 17 January 1991 – Flt Lt J. Peters, Flt Lt J. Nichol [XV Sqn crew] ejected PoW
ZD792 s	17 Sqn	CF	Gulf War, Dhahran, Bahrain – *Nursie*, Converted to GR4
ZD793 s	17 Sqn	CA	Converted to GR4
ZD808 s	17 Sqn	CJ	Flew into ground after bounce near Munster, Germany, 10 May 1988 – Flt Lt S.M. Wright, Flt Lt J.P. O'Shea killed

Serial	Unit	Code	Remarks
ZD809 s	IX Sqn	AA	
	14 Sqn	BA	Gulf War, Bahrain – *Hello Kuwait, G'bye Iraq* *(Awesome Annie)*
	TWCU		Flew into ground during weather abort near Kirkeaton, Northumbria, 14 October 1999 – Flt Lt R.A. Wright, Flt Lt S.P. Casabayo killed
ZD810 s	17 Sqn	CG	
	IX Sqn	AA	Gulf War, Tabuk – ALARM, Converted to GR4
ZD811 s	31 Sqn	DF	Converted to GR4
ZD812 t	16 Sqn	FV	
	14 Sqn	BW	Converted to GR4
ZD842 t	14 Sqn	BZ	
	17 Sqn	CY	
	TWCU		Converted to GR4
ZD843 s	31 Sqn	DH	Gulf War, Dhahran, Converted to GR4
ZD844 s	31 Sqn	DE	Gulf War, Tabuk – TIALD – *Donna Ewin*, Converted to GR4
ZD845 s	14 Sqn	BA	
	IX Sqn	AF	Gulf War, Tabuk – ALARM – *Angel Face* Engine failure and rear fuselage fire near Laarbruch, 26 February 1996 – Sqn Ldr N.L. Risdale DFC, Wg Cdr S.W. Peach ejected
ZD846 s	14 Sqn	BL	Departed during high AoA manoeuvring southwest of Munster, 11 January 1996 – Capt Spinelli ItAF, Sqn Ldr C.J. Donovan ejected
ZD847 s	17 Sqn	CH	Gulf War, Dhahran – *Where Do You Want It?*, Converted to GR4
ZD848 s	14 Sqn	BC	Gulf War, Tabuk – TIALD
	31 Sqn	DM	Converted to GR4
ZD849 s	17 Sqn	CC	Converted to GR4
	14 Sqn	BT	
ZD850 s	17 Sqn	CL	Gulf War, Tabuk – ALARM – *Cherry Lips*, Converted to GR4
ZD851 s	31 Sqn	DC	Converted to GR4
	IX Sqn	AJ	Gulf War, Tabuk – ALARM – *Amanda Jane*
ZD890 s	Bahrain	O	Gulf War, Bahrain – *Hello Kuwait, G'bye Iraq (Reclining Nude)*, Converted to GR4
	IX Sqn	AE	

Serial	Unit	Code	Remarks
ZD891 s	14 Sqn	BB	Mid-air collision with a GAF Alphajet, near Wiesmoor, Germany, 13 January 1989 – Flt Lt M.P. Smith, Flt Lt A.G. Grieve killed
ZD892 s	IX Sqn	AF	
	?	H	*Snoopy Airways (Helen)*
	14 Sqn	BJ	Converted to GR4
ZD893 s	20 Sqn	GF	
	IX Sqn	AG	Gulf War Tabuk - ALARM Crashed Tabuk, Saudi Arabia after control restriction, 20 January 1991 – Sqn Ldr P.K. Batson, Wg Cdr M.C. Heath ejected
ZD894 s	14 Sqn	BE	Control restriction crashed near Wesel, Germany, 30 June 1987 – Flt Lt J.P. Moloney, Flt Lt J.A. Hill ejected
ZD895 s	14 Sqn	BF	Gulf War, Dhahran, Converted to GR4
ZD996 a	IX Sqn	AK	
	II Sqn	I	Converted to GR4
ZE116 a	IX Sqn	AL	
	31 Sqn	DG	
	II Sqn	K	Converted to GR4
ZG705 a	13 Sqn	A	Converted to GR4
ZG706 a	TOEU	E	Converted to GR4
ZG707 a	13 Sqn	B	Converted to GR4
ZG708 a	13 Sqn	C	Flew into ground at Gen Ogle, Scotland, 1 September 1994 – Flt Lt P.J.M. Moseley, Flt Lt P.P. Harrison killed
ZG709 a	13 Sqn	I	Converted to GR4
ZG710 a	13 Sqn	D	Converted to GR4
ZG711 a	13 Sqn	E	Converted to GR4
ZG712 a	13 Sqn	F	Converted to GR4
ZG713 a	13 Sqn	G	Converted to GR4
ZG714 a	13 Sqn	H	Aquaplaned on landing and left runway Goose Bay, Canada, 14 September 1995 – Capt J. Semmeling RNLAF, Flt Lt M. Looseley ejected
ZG725 a	13 Sqn	J	Engine fire crashed in sea off Sardinia, 19 September 1994 – Flt Lt Ring, Flt Lt E. P. Moriarty ejected
ZG726 a	13 Sqn	K	Converted to GR4
ZG727 a	13 Sqn	L	Converted to GR4

ZG729 a	13 Sqn	M	Converted to GR4
ZG750 t	13 Sqn	Y	Converted to GR4
ZG752 t	13 Sqn	Z	Converted to GR4
ZG754 t	IX Sqn	AW	Converted to GR4
ZG756 t	IX Sqn	AX	Converted to GR4
ZG769 t	IX Sqn	AY	Converted to GR4
ZG771 t	31 Sqn	DW	Converted to GR4
ZG773 s	BAe		GR4 prototype
ZG775 s	17 Sqn	CC	Converted to GR4
ZG777 s	31 Sqn	DP	Converted to GR4
ZG779 s	31 Sqn	DK	Converted to GR4
ZG791 s	31 Sqn	DC	Converted to GR4
ZG792 s	31 Sqn	DD	Converted to GR4
ZG794 s	31 Sqn	DJ	Converted to GR4

Index